Social Welfare in Canada

SOCIAL

WELFARE

IN CANADA

IDEALS, REALITIES, AND

FUTURE PATHS

Second Edition

ANDREW ARMITAGE

Canadian Cataloguing in Publication Data

Armitage, Andrew
    Social welfare in Canada

2nd ed.
Bibliography: p.
Includes index.
ISBN 0-7710-0792-2

1. Public welfare – Canada. 2. Charities – Canada.
3. Social service – Canada. I. Title.

HV105.A75 1988 361'.971 C88-093746-7

Printed and bound in Canada

McClelland and Stewart
The Canadian Publishers
481 University Avenue
Toronto, Ontario
M5G 2E9

CONTENTS

ACKNOWLEDGEMENTS

The opportunity to produce this revised edition was provided by the School of Social Work at the University of Victoria, which in 1987 again gave me the opportunity to teach and write following an absence of ten years from the university. A special thanks to Dean Brian Wharf, Professor Marilyn Callahan, and Dr. Michael Prince for specific help with sources and the opportunity to share ideas. I also again received advice from Dr. Dick Splane.

McClelland and Stewart have been exemplary as publishers, keeping the first edition in print and encouraging me to make this revision on several occasions.

Molly, Mark, Paul, and Timothy remain my loving companions.

FOREWORD TO THE
SECOND EDITION

The first edition of *Social Welfare in Canada* was written in 1973–74 following a decade of working and teaching in the social services in Canada. This second edition is written following a second decade, 1976–86, working as a social administrator. The years since 1974 have been a period of major change in Canadian society with significant impact on the Canadian welfare state that had been institutionalized by the early 1970s. There has been a full range of public attitudes – from commitment, to doubt and uncertainty, to retrenchment and re-examination. Resources were initially expanded, then cut back, and today they remain restrained. Periodic interest in reform has often faded rather than culminated in change, leaving unanswered questions for some future policy agenda.

The major programs and institutions of the welfare state have remained intact from the early 1970s. Thus, much that was written then remains a useful account of the ideals and realities of Canadian social welfare. Those changes that have taken place have not always brought us closer to the objectives that were then highest in our social priorities. Despite this (or perhaps because of it), change to our welfare institutions is required because of change in other major features of the social order. The vision of those who thought that we could plan our social future and achieve those plans through our social policies now seems more distant than it did in the 1970s. The following are some of the changes having a cumulative impact on social welfare, requiring recognition in this second edition.

1. *Demographic.* The maturing "baby boomers" of the 1946–66 period have been a major factor affecting all social institutions. The impact of the boom on housing has been largely absorbed with the result that there are now fewer housing construction issues to be dealt with, and housing policy is primarily concerned with the housing of disadvantaged minorities. The impact on child rearing, education, and child welfare is evident in a rising number of young children needing services – "the echo boom" – at the same time as the number of teenagers and young adults is falling proportionate to the total population. The impact on employment has been to fill all the middle-level and professional positions with a surfeit of qualified and experienced candidates, thus exercising substantial pressure on older workers to leave, triggering intense competition for advancement, and blocking entry to those in their early twenties. For the future, beyond the year 2000 or earlier, there are the issues of retirement incomes, housing, and health care for this group.

The second major demographic factor has been continued immigration (and the changing character of immigration). Immigration remains a significant issue in social policy. The total number of immigrants has declined from 200,000 per year in the later 1960s to approximately 85,000 per year and is now dominated by immigration through family sponsorship and refugee entry. Greater affluence in Western Europe has meant that fewer immigrants come from countries with Caucasian populations and that most immigrants are joining established minority groups. In addition, there have been admissions or entry of persons with less than full citizenship status, e.g., work permits, "pending refugee" status, and illegal immigrants, who live in Canada but who can be outside the eligibility requirements of welfare institutions.

2. *Economic.* The assumptions of steadily rising affluence have been replaced by a sense that the summit of collective prosperity may have been achieved and that change, adaptation to change,

and continued competitiveness are essential to maintain present standards of living.

Economic change has been cyclical, with a recession/survival/ adaptation cycle being followed by the community as a whole. For some individuals the results have been severe, particularly as unemployment rates have continued with what appears to be a long-term upward trend, rising during periods of recession and then stabilizing during periods of recovery. Welfare institutions are now faced with rising numbers of long-term unemployed and by the cost of sustaining them in minimal decency, an issue not foreseen when the present programs of social security were designed, nor foreseen when a guaranteed income through negative taxation (or similar means) was being discussed in the 1970s.

For the social services it has to be recognized that the debate about whether to expand or contract welfare resources is now less a debate about how to direct rising collective wealth and more a debate about how to divide existing wealth. After the 1981–82 recession, growth was slower and unevenly distributed within Canada. This has required critical examination of spending to find ways to reduce service costs. Unit cost reduction, whether by technological change, reduced labour costs, privatization, or increased efficiency, has been seen as a strategy to expand service and also a strategy to absorb funding reductions.

The fiscal context of government actions has changed radically. Instead of rising revenues and projections of a continued rise, revenues have been stable. Because spending was already extending beyond revenues in the 1970s, the 1980s have seen three negative effects: revenues were not available for new programs; revenues were not there for existing programs; the debt incurred by past programs had to be serviced.

The social services have been eroded and, in some cases, cut to answer this dilemma, a dilemma sharpened for the federal government by debt and rising levels of military expenditure, and by a continuing political agenda at the federal and provincial levels to "enhance" economic recovery through major symbolic capital projects. With these "priority" issues on the agenda, government has often failed to consider changing social expenditure requirements. There has also been change in personal attitudes. Competitiveness as an individual quality is more approved and is viewed as necessary to the enjoyment of affluence. Politically, this has contributed to the ascendancy of an individualistic and conservative ideology.

3. *Political.* The election of conservative governments in the United Kingdom and the United States indicates that we are not dealing with a Canadian phenomenon but rather the return of individualistic emphasis as a cultural phenomenon. Indeed, Canada appears to have resisted this trend in Western society more than most, particularly at the federal level.

Nevertheless, support has weakened for new redistributive measures and for collective action generally. Some of the constituencies that have supported welfare objectives, such as trade unions, have themselves been weakened by the same broad trends, while newer constituencies that provide a focus for some welfare issues, such as women and native peoples, have to this point lacked the breadth of support required for a full recognition of the issues that concern them. In addition, although the senior civil service has retained substantial influence, the power of experts with depth of knowledge of the welfare sector has been reduced by general policies that emphasize rotation between ministries and "management" rather than sectoral expertise. Faced with weakened support and at times radical cutbacks and program withdrawals, there has been division, too, within the ranks of welfare state advocates between those who favour a defensive incrementalism and have become skilled in mobilizing to resist change and those who are prepared to take the risks of radical re-examination with a view to change, so that the relevance of welfare state benefits is assured in the 1980s and beyond.

4. *Social service effectiveness.* The issue of public support for the social services has not been one of simply shifting ideology and asserting individualistic cultural values. Claims of social service effectiveness, in some instances, have been exaggerated, and the "nothing works" conclusion of some studies of services aimed at criminal recidivism have influenced public and professional views.

We have become more aware of major personal dilemmas and trauma faced by children and women in our society, particularly in relation to sexual exploitation and abuse, but we have become sceptical as to whether the social expenditures of government can ever obtain the welfare ideals that were thought of as being their rationale – relief of social problems, full employment, greater equality, lower crime rates, greater freedom. The decade of the seventies, a time of experimentation in the social services, generated enough criticism and scepticism to contaminate those areas where real accomplishments were made. Although not all initiatives "worked," this did not mean that none worked, but the pendulum of public opinion reversed and the objectives of minimizing government cost and "interference" took over from the objectives of providing help. Short-term intervention aimed at reducing damage to the abused child, for example, replaced a commitment to provide the consistent support to families that could have prevented abuse.

In the ever-changing field of technology, attention has shifted from interest in person-to-person relationships as a focus for intervention to an interest in institution-to-client relationships and the technology that supports them – record systems, data transmission, inter-agency co-ordination. In this field there have been true technological advances, with a major process of conversion occurring from manual/paper systems of records and analysis to electronic direct-entry systems. The future vision for these systems includes the opportunity for greater individualism, knowledge, and professional support, but their initial introduction has been often characterized by an increase in centralized control and an emphasis on processing and on the application to social control.

5. *Social service organizations.* New understanding of the social services and their full effect on society has also developed from examination of the behaviour of "human service organizations." The existing institutions of welfare have been found to have a life of their own, with significant effects on the community.

Management knowledge has grown, but so has the complexity of the management task. Concern with internal program objectives, such as contracting practices, professional relationships, and organizational values, has become essential. Broad public policy principles, such as restraint and privatization, have been adopted by many governments. Social service organizations have been required to apply these principles within their work without having had the opportunity to judge them on their merits. Sometimes the results have been a loss of service, but more often the social service enterprise has been modified in ways that permit it to continue to provide services, and sometimes these principles have permitted an increase in both responsiveness and effectiveness.

6. *De-institutionalization.* A specific trend of major significance – de-institutionalization – has combined features of both long-term welfare service concerns and current funding exigencies. At last, the social service enterprise appears to be ridding itself of the heritage of major institutional concentrations of mentally handicapped, disabled, and mentally ill people in favour of community placement and support. Arguments based on humanity and professional knowledge have been allied with arguments based on cost. Reinvestment in buildings and institutional approaches, now over fifty years old, has been challenged. New patterns of service based on community placement and support services have been developed. Doing this well now requires a recognition of community costs and a commitment to sustained support for the future.

7. *Professional diversification.* The professional enterprise has also become more diverse. The dominance of social work has been modified at all levels. At the senior levels there is now a broader range of professional disciplines whose contribution to the total enterprise is established and the ascendancy of management expertise is confirmed. At the direct service level the development of child care as a professional endeavour distinct from, but allied with, social work receives increasing recognition.

Within social work the distinction between the case management of major services on behalf of the society and the provision of advice and guidance on a consensual basis has remained a continuing tension. At the community level there is a similar tension between, on the one side, social criticism and advocacy for change and, on the other, the provision of services. These are productive and important tensions in the continued development of the profession.

This second edition has been revised chapter by chapter to reflect these issues, to bring facts up to date, and to incorporate scholarly contributions and research. On this last point there has been much change. When the first edition was written Canadian texts on social welfare did not exist and the student had to reply on American and British materials, supplemented by Canadian government documents and articles. Today, students have the advantage of a thorough historical account in Dennis Guest's *Social Security in Canada*; two good readers contain a wide selection of authors and articles: Shankar Yelaja (ed.), *Canadian Social Policy*, and Joanne and Francis Turner (eds.), *Canadian Social Welfare*; and important texts on specific welfare issues and service sectors are to be found in such works as Ken Levitt and B. Wharf, *The Challenge of Child Welfare*, and Lars Osberg, *Economic Inequality in Canada*. These are supplemented by a much richer research and article literature.

Basic values that were recognized in the Foreword to the first edition remain. Foremost is that the pursuit of a just, tolerant, and humane Canadian society is a worthy objective and that social welfare measures have a major role in what has been achieved and what will be needed for the future. At that time I looked for a major increase in resources. A major increase remains possible. Canada's social expenditure at 21.7 per cent of Gross Domestic Product is far behind most Western European countries, where expenditures in the 30 per cent plus range are typical. The reasons why social policy objectives, for example in relation to poverty, have not been accomplished, and why even modest accomplishments are under attack, are political, not economic. In the field of income security we have to be concerned to protect from further deterioration the standards of living that have been achieved by low-income Canadians. In some provinces we are further from the objective of raising living standards above the poverty line than we were in 1974. In the field of personal social services we have to be concerned with the best use of limited professional and financial resources. In both fields effectiveness and efficiency are major concerns.

The reservations I expressed concerning the tendency of welfare institutions to bureaucratic and professional parochialism have been reinforced by my own administrative experience. The high ideals of the welfare state remain beyond the grasp of the welfare institutions that have been developed; and this can lead to defensiveness rather than re-examination, defensiveness to which self-interest and career security also contribute.

In my view the greater contribution to the ideals of a welfare state is being made by both critics and advocates of welfare institutions who identify unsatisfactory conclusions, know their facts, and continue to press for a process of purging, re-examination, and reform based on a vision of what can be achieved in the 1990s. This is a continuing process in which each generation makes choices as to how it will live and how it will treat others.

In this edition I have looked toward the 1990s, projecting major trends and tensions to assist in framing the choices we can make. Three major possibilities are discussed. The first is based on both a continued concern to restrict social expenditures and a laissez-faire attitude toward the institutions and programs that have been developed in Canada since the Second World War. This scenario represents current trends – the conventional wisdom that social expenditure is too high – and the vested interest of major human service organizations. The second is also concerned with restricting social expenditures but offers an active approach to existing institutions and programs. It is based on the premise that social welfare could be made more effective and efficient by a process of reform and rationalization. This scenario requires that governments address problems and contradictions in Canadian social welfare. It requires that detailed criticism, including conservative criticism, be treated seriously. It requires that the vested interests of major human service organizations be challenged. The third scenario is based on the second and adds to it a willingness to incur higher levels of social expenditure in order to build a society for the next century that will incorporate as fully as possibly the ideals of social welfare.

The choice is ours to make.

Chapter 1

INTRODUCTION

Social welfare is an institution of the countries of the Western industrialized world. Canada is one of those countries and its social welfare institutions have many similar features to those of the welfare institutions of the United States, Britain, Germany, etc. In all these countries, social welfare shares a common societal context that includes such prominent features as industrialism, affluence, a "free market" economic ideology, and democracy based on a universal adult franchise.

The role of social welfare in relation to these major institutions of society is complex, has varied between countries and between historical periods, and is the subject of a variety of differing interpretations. For example, social welfare can be viewed as a means to obtain social control in a society of inequalities; it can be viewed as the most efficient means of providing certain types of service, such as health care or education; it can also be viewed as an organized attempt to put humanistic values of the society into effect. These values include concern for the individual, faith in man, faith in democracy, equality and equity, social justice, and community.

In this book, this fundamentally moral view of the nature of social welfare is given primary importance. The reasons for this view are twofold:

(1) Such a view appears to the author to be most in keeping with the tone and substance of major statements of post-war Canadian social policy.

(2) Such a view is the motive behind the aspirations and commitments of the majority of professionals in social welfare institutions.

Evidence in support of these statements appears throughout this book. However, the adoption of this point of view is a matter of judgement.

This introductory chapter presents the author's view of the interactions among the state, the economy, the humanistic value base, and social welfare. Attention is given to the general form of such institutions in Western countries, with more particular attention being given to distinct features of Canadian institutions.

The National Context

The state is the fundamental political unit of society. The political affairs of mankind are fundamentally organized at the national level, international issues being negotiated between national units. Social welfare is a part of the internal affairs of national states. The state's actions may range from inactivity through support to such institutions as churches, philanthropic groups, the family, to the active conduct of programs of state provision. Throughout this range of activity the principal issues that may become the subjects of international dispute and settlement are financial or population issues.

The financial issues arise where the independence of particular states is eroded, either by the receipt of conditional aid or by issues of international insolvency. In either case, some of the conditions of a state's receipt of international support may influence the state's internal social welfare policies. Thus the conditions of aid to an underdeveloped country may either deliberately encourage certain types of social expenditure, for example, the training of doctors or teachers, or discourage such expenditures. Similarly, when a Western industrialized country's balance of payments is such that a considerable international debt occurs, the country may be required to adopt policies of financial restraint that influence social welfare expenditures through such effects as creating unemployment and limiting the government revenues available to finance programs.

The typical international social welfare agency or assembly is basically concerned with fraternal comparison, consultation, and support. The separate states exercise autonomy in the establishment of social welfare policies. Canada's social welfare policies are independent. Their scope has been neither widened nor delimited by the power of other nations. International welfare organizations serve to place Canada in context, within which Canada has been a follower rather than a leader.

Affluence

Canada is one of the relatively affluent states of the industrialized world, and the industrialized world is exceedingly affluent as compared to most of the "developing" world. The difference in the affluence of different states has been ascribed to such features as the extent of their natural resources, the industry of their peoples, terms of international trade, and differences in international power. Depending on one's point of view, the affluence of the Western industrialized countries can be ascribed to their good fortune and the industry of their peoples, or to their military expropriation of an undue portion of the globe for their use and their imperial exploitation of others.

The permanency of the world order within which the welfare state developed should be questioned. Major changes in the comparative affluence and strength of nations are occurring, and with these changes goes the need to adapt and change their welfare institutions, not only because they consume resources but because they contribute both positively and negatively to the character of a society and to the motivation of its members.

The modern Western welfare state is not only the creation of enlightened social policy. It is also sustained within an international order characterized by vast inequalities. It is for this reason that the Swedish social policy analyst Gunnar Myrdal writes: "We will never be able to come to grips with the international problems

of today and tomorrow if we do not squarely face the fact that
the democratic Welfare State in the rich countries of the Western
world is protectionistic and nationalistic."[1] Unless some measure
is taken of the issues of international development and unless the
welfare state is prepared to seriously engage these issues, it can
be judged as being both selfish and parochial by its own values.
This is not a book on international development, but it is important
to recognize that social welfare policies are found in fully developed form only in societies that have achieved a relatively high
degree of affluence, often involving a transfer of wealth from
societies less fortunately endowed with natural resources, less developed, or less powerful.

The Industrial Context

The establishment of modern industry led to one of the most
fundamental social revolutions in the history of mankind. Within
the space of the last two hundred years revolutionary changes in
the condition of mankind have taken place. The effects of industrialization on where and how people live have been profound.
On the one hand, standards of physical comfort, access to learning
and culture, ability to travel, and so on, all of which were un-
imaginable to the kings and princes of earlier eras, are now at-
tained. On the other, there have been the steady dislocation of
relationships between people, the breakdown of patterns of culture and independence formed through millennia of development,
and the creation of the instruments of deliberate or inadvertent
destruction of life on the globe.

The process of industrialism has been uneven between nations
and within nations. Canada's industrial development has several
distinct features. Primary industry has been unusually large (as
compared to other Western countries), and many of its products
– lumber, mineral ores, petroleum, hydroelectricity – have been
exported rather than being used in the process of manufacturing
products in Canada. It was customary to suppose that Canada's
strong resource base would result in the eventual development of
considerable manufacturing industry and a large population. However, this future now seems unlikely. Canada's proportion of the

American population north of the Mexican border has grown (1901: 6.5 per cent; 1921: 7.5 per cent; 1951: 8.3 per cent; 1971: 9.4 per cent), but when changes in the composition of the labour force are studied (Table 1), it is found that a decreasing proportion of persons are employed in primary industry as this sector has become more capital-intensive and less labour-intensive. Matching this shift in the labour force are increases in the proportions involved in white-collar and service occupations. The proportion engaged in blue-collar, manufacturing occupations has begun to decline.

A nation characterized by the lumberman, the miner, and the construction worker has become a nation characterized by the civil servant, the office worker, and the service industry worker – a large manufacturing sector does not appear to be developing. Nor has change ended. The industrial revolution's characteristic forms of work and production are in retreat, not only in Canada but throughout the leading nations of the developed world. The rapid increase in information-processing technologies and their application to all parts of our society, from word-processing to medicine to taxation, are causing major changes in work and hence in the relationship between workers and society.

The considerable and continuing social changes that have taken place have not been without social costs. Economic growth has been aided by government policies but has not been planned with

TABLE 1: *Distribution of the Labour Force, 15 years and Over, by Occupation Division, 1931–1981* (numerical distribution by 000's)

Occupation Sector	1931		1941		1961		1981	
	No.	%	No.	%	No.	%	No.	%
All	3,908	100	4,183	100	6,458	100	12,267	100
White-collar	957	24.5	1,058	25.3	2,446	37.9	3,465	28.2
Blue-collar	1,076	27.5	1,134	27.1	1,716	26.6	2,972	24.2
Primary	1,265	32.4	1,275	30.5	830	12.8	929	7.5
Transport	245	6.3	266	6.4	496	7.7	939	7.6
Service	362	9.3	438	10.5	800	12.4	3,399	27.7

SOURCE: *Census of Canada*, various years. A different system of occupational classification was used in the 1981 census; this has particularly affected the distribution between white-collar and service categories.

a continuing view as to its social effects. The social costs of social change have been allowed to lie where they fell. Thus, it was a novel idea that the James Bay Indians should be compensated for lost lands due to hydro development; that a workman dispossessed of usable skills by technological change should be compensated by the society; or that an elderly renter, whose neighbourhood is to be destroyed for new construction, should be rehoused. Formerly, these consequences of industrialism and economic growth were simply left unattended.

Many of our social welfare policies can be viewed as the secondary consequence of this inattention. Based on a varying mixture of human sympathy for the unfortunate and fear that they might seek radical social change, social welfare measures have been developed. The large field of income security policies can be viewed as a response to the problems of social dislocation caused by unplanned changes in demand for different types of labour. The large field of personal and community social services can be viewed as a response to the dislocation of community and family life caused by urbanization. Moreover, social welfare should not be identified exclusively with the problems of industrial society. Social welfare is also a product of the positive achievements of industrial society – people live longer and hence need more care; people live more by their brains and hence need more sophisticated education and training.

The Economic Context

The distinct form of the social welfare institution is a product, too, of economic ideology. The socialist countries of Eastern Europe are industrialized but their economic ideology involves central planning and control, and an institutional commitment to certain types of social expenditure, such as for day-care centres, medical care, and housing. It is not assumed that the individual should and can provide for himself. In contrast, the Western industrial countries hold a view of economic life that gives primary attention to the freedom of individual decision-making. The individual is expected to provide for himself. Social welfare provision is closely related to this Western view of economic freedom and responsibility.

The pages of Canadian government statements of social policy are filled with obeisance to the goals of economic growth, and with exhortations as to the values of economic self-reliance and independence. Further, these values have been increasingly emphasized as insecurity about the future of Western society has grown. The society's rhetoric entrusts its future to the private initiative of individuals rather than to institutions – whether unions, governments, or corporations. These deeply held values effectively place social welfare as a secondary aim of the society.

Social welfare expenditures are not always identified as contributing substantially to the quality of life. Instead, they are frequently identified as a burden, an item of unproductive expense the economy has to sustain. This view competes with the scarcely less negative view that social welfare expenditures are necessary to secure social stability. The funds serve to reduce deviancy and protect economic and social stability.[2] Today, one of the arguments for decreased social expenditure is that stability is not wanted in a society where the major challenge is one of change.

These views are shared by the Marxist critics of Western societies who view social welfare institutions as being "a central element in the framework of repression under which men live in market-dominated societies."[3] The welfare state is "a historical freak between organized capitalism and socialism, servitude and freedom, totalitarianism and happiness."[4] This Marxist view is worthy of careful study, as it provides unique insights into welfare institutions and their implicit functions.[5] The strength of the analysis is that welfare institutions are related directly to the economic functioning of capitalist society and to the maintenance of power by elites. Nevertheless, the analysis is less than fully satisfying: it fails to see the role of values as contributing to where a specific balance is struck between coercive social control (as in Chile) and control through relief and accommodation (as in welfare states).

The negative views of the role of social welfare expenditure are not held equally among the Western countries. However, there has been a trend to a wider acceptance of these views, as shown by the increasingly conservative thrust of governments in Britain, Canada, and the United States, all of which have recognized a limit to their commitment to support welfare institutions, shown a concern to prevent general expansion, and, in some cases, sought to reduce the relative level of expenditures. Reduction, though, has proved difficult. "Regarding the reform of the welfare state Thatcher, like Reagan, is mostly bark. And even without much bite she has created a consensus but against her. Thatcher has not seriously attacked either the theory or practice of the welfare state because her most important goal – the restructuring of the economy – causes dislocation that makes a safety net especially necessary."[6] A similar argument in support of welfare measures was used by the Macdonald Commission in Canada.

There are major variations in the percentage of various countries' economies that are devoted to social expenditure. Social expenditure is defined to include public expenditures on pensions, unemployment insurance, education, health care, and families (including family allowances).

TABLE 2: *Social Expenditures by Country, 1960 and 1981, as a % of Gross Domestic Product*

	1960	1981
Belgium	17.0	38.0
Netherlands	16.3	36.1
Sweden	14.5	33.5
Germany	20.5	31.5
Italy	16.5	29.1
Denmark	10.2	29.0
Austria	17.9	27.9
Ireland	11.7	27.1
Norway	11.7	27.1
U.K.	13.9	24.9
France	13.4	23.8
Canada	12.1	21.7
U.S.	10.9	21.0
New Zealand	13.0	19.6
Australia	10.2	18.6
Japan	8.0	17.5

SOURCE: *OECD Bulletin*, No. 146 (January, 1984).

These variations can only be partly accounted for by such variations as difference in the number of beneficiaries and the age structure of the population. They also represent differences in the priority given to social welfare, value choices made through democratic electoral processes. Clearly, Canada could allocate more of its gross domestic product to public social expenditures — if that is what is wanted by Canadians. The present total level of expenditure is modest in comparison to most Western European countries.

The Political Context

The universal adult franchise and the representative assemblies of the Western industrial countries provide the primary political context for social welfare. From time to time proposals for the reform of social welfare policies have appeared to be major factors affecting the electorate's voting patterns. The British election of a Labour government in 1945 provided a dramatic example of their importance. In Canada, the choice of Liberal governments in 1962 and 1965 would appear to have been influenced by the election pledge to introduce the Canada Pension Plan and Medicare. In a negative way, the Liberal losses in the 1972 federal election can be related to what was perceived to be an ill-designed reform of the unemployment insurance program. More recently this negative political influence has been strongly felt, with governments at all levels looking for ways to restrain and reduce rather than to increase welfare expenditures.

The existence in Canada of elected governments with social welfare powers at both federal and provincial levels of government is one of the major features that distinguishes Canadian social welfare provision from provision in other Western countries. The effects of this division of powers are examined in Chapter Four.

The Shared Values

Finally, social welfare provision in the Western industrialized countries is based on shared values. The fundamentally moral nature of social welfare objectives distinguishes social policy most sharply from economic policy. The moral transactions with which social welfare deals have the following values: (1) concern for the individual; (2) faith in man; (3) faith in democracy; (4) equality and equity; (5) social justice; and (6) community. These values are not exclusive to social welfare but social welfare represents a substantial organized attempt to obtain their fulfilment.

1. *Concern for the individual.* There is a central and continuing concern in the ideals and goals of the institution of social welfare with the individual. Wilensky and Lebeaux[7] find one such distinguishing characteristic in its "direct concern with human consumption needs." By this is meant that if government activities are placed on a continuum from activities directed to maintenance of the social system as a whole, such as national defence, monetary policy, and the administration of justice, to activities directed to providing benefit to individuals, for example, schools, recreational facilities, and health services, then social welfare must be classified among those activities organized primarily with respect to the needs of the individual.

In the profession of social work, the concern with the individual finds expression in both the casework principle of individualization and in the code of ethics. This concern is expressed, too, in the attachment of the institutions and professions of social welfare to a "humanistic" philosophy. It also finds negative recognition in the charge that social workers are "do-gooders" or "bleeding hearts," persons, that is to say, whose concern for human suffering and desire to help others exceeds what a rational person could expect to accomplish.

The United Nations Universal Declaration of Human Rights expresses the concern thus:

> Article 22. Everyone, as a member of society, has the right to social security, and is entitled to realization through national effort and international co-operation, and in accordance with the organization and resources of each State, of the economic, social and cultural rights indispensable for his dignity and the free development of his personality.[8]

2. *Faith in man.* Concern for the individual is matched by a high degree of faith in the individual. This faith finds expression in social welfare programs and social work activities directed toward both change in institutions and change in individuals. In the former case, the basic thesis is that man is restricted and prevented

from the fulfilment of his potential by ignorance and by ill-designed and inhumane social institutions. If these factors are changed, then man will achieve not only greater happiness and greater realization of his own potential but will be able to contribute to and receive more from his peers. When change in individuals is considered, the same basic thrust emerges. People can be helped to liberate themselves from their self-constructed prisons of ignorance, fear, and anger and thereby obtain greater personal fulfilment. The Senate Committee on Poverty expressed the value thus:

> A recent development in Canadian social philosophy is the emergence of the more positive human resource development approach. This philosophy recognizes the inherent value of the literate, educated and trained population. . . . Development of human resources to their greatest potential is regarded as a desirable objective in itself. . . .

The value is expressed, too, in the rejection of the basically suspicious thrust of normative economic theory. The idea that man is basically lazy, that productivity will only be produced when rewards are sufficient to overcome his laziness, is an offence to social welfare writers. David Woodsworth attacks incentive policies that are based on the assumption "that man is by nature greedy, lazy, etc.; that money incentives are required to make him work; and that it is perhaps an unfortunate necessity for industry to have a pool of unemployed and therefore miserable people from which to draw the energy (manpower) to work the machines, or to do the 'dirty work' of a society. . . . Not only is the 'market mentality' seen as corrosive of human dignity and identity, it is increasingly seen as inefficient, even in its own terms, for society as a whole."[9]

Thus it would appear that a high degree of faith is held in man's perfectability. Failure to obtain such perfection is interpreted as representing failure in institutions, socialization patterns, or opportunities. Such failures can be prevented or corrected. Failure to obtain perfection should not be considered typical of mankind; rather it should be treated as an unfortunate and correctable aberration.

3. *Faith in democracy.* Faith in democracy is an extension of faith in man from the individual to the collective. The value is applied to mean, in ideal terms, the participation of all affected parties in processes of decision-making on a basis of equity of influence. The ultimate resolution of difference is to be on the basis of rational argument and/or compromise, not on the basis of power.

Realistically it must be conceded that such is not the real state of Canadian political affairs. Hence, concern is frequently expressed as to the causes and effects of such inequality, together with admonition to change. However, a basic commitment to democracy, and more specifically to the typical form of democracy in Western industrialized societies generally and in Canada in particular (a universal adult electorate, a choice of political parties, periodic elections), remains.

The accepted instruments of change are thus persuasion, argument, protest, publicity, organization, interest group politics, alliances, etc. On the other hand, intimidation, violence, personal attack, not to mention revolution, are considered unsuitable and unethical means to the ends of social welfare.

4. *Equality and equity.* A strong egalitarian thrust is a central feature of social welfare values. The value finds expression in two related concerns: concern with poverty and concern with the extent of inequalities. A concern with poverty directs attention to the minimum standards of living that are to be tolerated in the society, regardless of the individual poor person's financial contribution to the society. A concern with the extent of inequalities directs attention to the relative standards of living of different groups of persons. In both cases, there is a clear rejection of the idea that the income distribution that is the result of inheritance, property, productivity, bargaining, and the like, should be allowed to stand.

Welfare economists have tried to formulate a general principle that expresses this thrust toward greater equality. The principle is based on the interdependence of persons within a society. The welfare of any individual cannot be maximized without consideration of the effects of his choices on others; thus, a theoretical rich man can increase his welfare by giving to a theoretical poor man. The benefit can take many forms: the poor man will be politically more amenable to the rich man keeping his wealth when he is not so desperately poor; the poor man will be better housed, clothed, and fed and hence, healthier; his health makes him a better potential worker and a less likely carrier of disease; the poor man will be a better consumer, increasing financial stability and thus preserving, too, the rich man's consumption. Because there is a real benefit conveyed to the rich man, he can be expected voluntarily to choose a greater degree of equality. Indeed, in the Pareto-optimal approach to income redistribution, "the test of a socially beneficial redistribution is that it should be voluntarily undertaken."[10] The "voluntarism" referred to is that of the theoretical rich man who seeks his own greatest welfare. The poor man's only influences lie in the way in which his life impinges on the rich man's.

Thus, while welfare economics provides a basis for understanding why redistribution takes place, it does not raise or answer the moral question as to whether the extent of poverty and/or inequality is just. This moral question is clearly expressed by the social policy analyst Runciman, who approaches the subject of inequalities from a point of departure which assumes that equality between persons is the beginning point from which discussion of difference should proceed.

> Starting, therefore, from the assumption that all social inequalities require to be justified it can, as a minimum, be shown that rational persons in a state of nature would agree on three broad criteria, or principles, in the light of which, subsequent inequalities of reward could be claimed to be just.[11]

These three principles are need, merit, and contribution to the common good. Of the three, "need" is regarded as the most basic. A man who is sick needs additional resources to obtain the most basic type of equality with his fellows. "Merit" is accepted as a criterion only to the extent that it equates with the willingness of individuals to do things that are difficult to do, involving demonstrable hardship and sacrifice to the doer. "Contribution to the common good" is accepted because everyone stands to benefit.

In Runciman's approach to inequality and equity the test of justice is acceptability to those who are least well off. Thus, whereas the Pareto-optimal view of inequality and poverty concentrates on the contract the rich should make with the poor, Runciman's social justice approach focuses on the contract the poor should require of the rich.

5. *Social justice.* The discussion of equality and equity leads to a discussion of social justice. Social justice includes concern not only with economic phenomena but also with other types of interpersonal transactions. Examples of such transactions include the relationship of a child to his or her parents; the relationships between men and women; the relationship between a person who is physically strong and one who is weak; the relationship between ethnic groups, etc. Rawls has suggested two principles of justice that are sufficiently broad to provide a beginning point for discussion of this wide range of social phenomena:

> First: each person is to have an equal right to the most extensive basic liberty compatible with a similar liberty for others. Second: social and economic inequalities are to be arranged so that they are both (a) reasonably expected to be to everyone's advantage, and (b) attached to positions and offices open to all.[12]

Applying these principles to the relationship between a child and his or her parents permits some inequality of status and freedom between parent and child, but only to the extent that such inequality can be reasonably expected to be to everyone's advantage. Thus a parent has no right to mistreat, exploit, or neglect a child while still holding to the right to parent. A moral basis thus exists for a social welfare function that aims to protect the welfare of children.

However, it should not be supposed that the principles of social justice are easily applied. Between parents and children the words "reasonably expected to be to everyone's advantage" require interpretation, and frequently interpretations differ between parent, child, and social welfare authorities. Thus a case of incest could be consensual between parent and child but not acceptable to the social welfare authority. A teenager who smokes pot or who is promiscuous may hold that his liberty in no way infringes on the liberty of others and should thus be allowed, but the parents and the child welfare authority may not agree. Finally, a parent

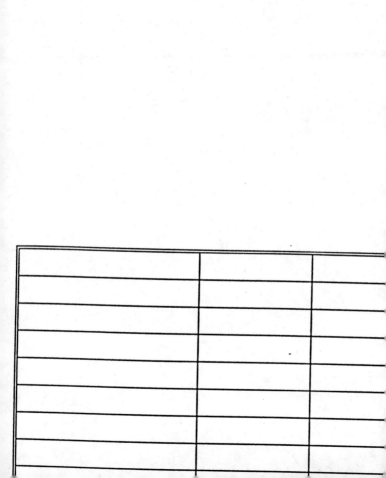

may consider that he is rightly chastising a child while the social welfare authority and the child consider the parent's actions to be abusive.

Difficulty in applying the principles of social justice can also be seen through reference to collective types of social transaction. Let us grant that the inequality between persons of native origin and others cannot reasonably be expected to be to everyone's advantage. Nevertheless, we can disagree as to whether the route to a more just society should be equated with the preservation and fulfilment of treaty and aboriginal rights or with a removal of these barriers to the integration of native peoples.

In practical terms, the resolution to these and other dilemmas of social justice lies within the boundaries of the political process. Hence, the importance of the attachment to, and confidence in, democracy.

6. *Community*. Finally, there are important values in the concept of community. These take the form of assertions that people should have the opportunity to fulfil themselves through their relationships with others. Part of the meaning of this is to be found in the discussion of democracy. Community provides (or should provide) the means for democratic expression and adjustment. Conversely, alienation and a strong sense of class separation are to be viewed as indications of dysfunction and social problems.

The value of community also finds expression in more immediate personal terms than is suggested by democratic participation. For example, the central objectives of such services as family life education, day care, homemaking, and mental health contain the ideal of improved relationships among people, including improved relationships between children and adults.

Ideally, people should live in a community from which they draw satisfying social relationships, which will provide adequate developmental opportunities for their children and in which participation, in deciding how the collective welfare is to be obtained, is open to all.

Values in the Societal Context

When these values are related to the societal context there are many obvious sources of conflict. The values of equality and equity conflict with the propensity of Western societies to create and maintain inequality through such mechanisms as inheritance, private ownership, and the resolution of scarcity through competitive bidding. The values of community conflict with the propensity to disrupt communities as part of the cost of industrial development and urbanization. The values of concern for the individual and faith in man conflict with the well-established tendency of modern industrial society to reduce man to a component in a machine

Eric Trist suggests that the conflict between welfare values and economic development processes has three phrases: "The relationship of welfare and development takes three principal forms: when development is a function of welfare; when welfare is a function of development; when welfare and development are interdependent functions."[13] The first of these represents the circumstances of pre-industrial society, in which welfare is conserved by such traditional structures as the family, stable social classes, religion, community, etc. In such societies, "development" is commonly perceived to be a threat to welfare. The second, where economic growth (development) takes precedence over welfare, typifies industrial society. Economic growth is the major focus of attention, and welfare (i.e., social welfare) is identified with those special situations that require attention because of unmet human needs. These "special situations" lead first to what Wilensky and Lebeaux define as a "residual" conception of social welfare: "The first (the residual view) holds that social welfare institutions should come into play only when the normal structures of supply, the family and the market, break down."[14] As society's understanding of the endemic nature of its needs has grown, so has the depth and continuity of commitment to social security measures.

Wilensky and Lebeaux use the term "institutional" to refer to this second concept of social welfare,

> . . . (which) implies no stigma, no emergency, no abnormalcy. Social welfare becomes accepted as a proper, legitimate function of modern industrial society in helping individuals achieve self-fulfillment. The complexity of modern life is recognized. The inability of the individual to provide fully for himself, or to meet all his needs in family and work settings

is considered a "normal" condition; and the helping agencies achieve "regular" institutional status.[15]

In the writings of Alfred Kahn these ideas are identified with the "social planning phase of the welfare state,"[16] and in the works of Romanshyn such ideas are linked with the concept of "social development":

> Social welfare as social development recognizes the dynamic quality of urban industrial society and the consequent need to adapt to change and to new aspirations for human fulfilment. It goes beyond the welfare state to a continuing renewal of its institutions to promote the fullest development of man.[17]

These ideas begin to approach a third concept of the relationship of welfare to development, where both are planned for together. However, this third concept appears to represent the aspirations of planners rather than the aspirations of the people of Western society, who continue to prefer to pursue individualistic paths and who resist a pre-planned destiny, though not unaided by a society where technological change continues to redefine social life and in which economic development is also not the subject of planning.

The practical consequence of the predominance of the second of those states referred to above is that social welfare values have to be advanced as a secondary response to change, with the purpose of dealing with contentious issues that conflict with established cultural values. The effects of this contention are seen in the way the welfare debates concerning the redistribution of income and the integrity of community are conducted. These two debates have a pervasive influence on the form of welfare provision. In the next two chapters the ideological form of these debates will be considered. Later, in Chapters Six and Seven, the influence on specific programs of income security and personal social services will be apparent.

Notes

1. Gunnar Mydral, *Beyond the Welfare State* (London: Duckworth, 1958), p. 119.
2. For an expanded discussion of views of the purpose of social welfare

expenditures, see Martin Rein, *Social Policy: Issues of Choice and Change* (New York: Random House, 1970), pp. 25–27.

3. Robert Pinker, *Social Theory and Social Policy* (London: Heinemann, 1971), p. 116.

4. Herbert Marcuse, *One Dimensional Man* (Boston: Beacon Press, 1966), p. 52

5. See, for example, Jeffry Galper, *The Politics of Social Services* (Englewood Cliffs, N.J.: Prentice Hall, 1975); Steven Wineman, *The Politics of Human Services: Radical Alternatives to the Welfare State* (Montreal: Black Rose Books, 1984); A.W. Djao, *Inequality and Social Policy* (Toronto: John Wiley, 1983).

6. George Will, in *Newsweek*, 22 June 1978.

7. H.L. Wilensky and C. Lebeaux, *Industrial Society and Social Welfare* (New York: Free Press, 1965), p. 145.

8. United Nations, *Universal Declaration of Human Rights* (New York, 1948), Article 31.

9. David Woodsworth, *Social Policies for Tomorrow* (Ottawa: Canadian Council on Social Development, 1971), pp. 7–8.

10. A.J. Culyer, *The Economics of Social Policy* (London: Martin Robertson, 1973), p. 74. Culyer's text is recommended to students interested in a discussion of Pareto optimality in social policy, and more generally as an introduction to welfare economics.

11. W.G. Runciman, *Relative Deprivation and Social Justice* (London: Pelican Books, 1972), p. 310.

12. John Rawls, *A Theory of Justice* (London: Oxford University Press, 1972), p. 60.

13. Eric Trist, "The Relation of Welfare and Development in the Transition to Post-Industrialism" (Ottawa: Canadian Centre for Community Studies, 1967, unpublished), p. 12.

14. Wilensky and Lebeaux, *Industrial Society and Social Welfare*, p. 138.

15. *Ibid.*, p. 140.

16. Alfred J. Kahn, *Theory and Practice of Social Planning* (New York: Russell Sage Foundation, 1969), p. 50.

17. John Romanyshyn, *Social Welfare: Charity to Justice* (New York: Random House, 1971), p. 380.

Chapter 2

REDISTRIBUTION

Social welfare is fundamentally concerned with the distribution into individual citizens' hands of the benefits of the society of which the citizen is a member. The word "benefit" is not to be used narrowly, for although it includes all manner of material goods, it also includes such service benefits as education, health care, and counselling, and such political benefits as the right to influence the form of the society.

However, social welfare programs are not the usual or most approved means of distributing these benefits in our society. The usual way to obtain any of these benefits is to pay for them, and the means to pay are obtained either from one's accumulated wealth or from one's labour. Social welfare programs provide an alternate means of distributing these benefits; but why is an alternative needed? There have been three principle answers given to this question.

1. *Poverty.* Some people are simply too poor to purchase the goods and services that provide the basis for a reasonably normal life in our society. The various poverty studies, in particular the 5th Annual Review of the Economic Council of Canada, the Report of the Special Senate Committee on Poverty, and the reports of the National Council of Welfare, provide a good guide to the extent of poverty in Canada and the underlying causes.

2. *Societal benefits.* Many types of social expenditure benefit the society as a whole as well as the individual who receives the immediate return. Education, child care, health services, etc. benefit not only the individuals who receive the service, but also the total social condition. Economists use the term "externality" for such benefits. Because everyone benefits, everyone has an interest in seeing that expenditures on these services are maintained at adequate levels.

If payment for health care were an entirely individual matter, some individuals would spend too little and their ill health would result in infection spreading to others, lower productivity, etc. Furthermore, some types of health expense, such as sanitation, would be neglected because no individual could provide them.

Societal or "external" benefits are thus an important argument for using social welfare rather than "market" means of distribution.

3. *Efficiency.* Although some types of service *can* be provided by a "market" mechanism, the market may not be the most efficient means of providing the service. Pensions are provided by life insurance companies but because of such factors as people changing jobs, people making inadequate plans, companies becoming bankrupt, and companies having high expenses due to sales costs and other administrative overheads, private plans may not be the most efficient or reliable means of ensuring that everyone receives a pension. A compulsory, monopolistic, non-profit plan – a social welfare plan – should be inherently more efficient and able to provide higher benefits for a stated premium. A comparison of health services and costs between Canada and the United States supports this argument.[1]

In the development of social welfare programs, these three arguments are used in combination with each other. Thus the argument for medicare is partly that some people cannot afford the price of health, partly that the whole society benefits, and partly that a universal government plan is the most efficient means to these ends.

Of these three basic reasons for government expenditure on social needs, only the first fundamentally involves a "redistribution" of resources from rich to poor, sometimes termed a "positive" redistribution. The argument concerning societal benefit only

results in a positive redistribution when the social need being
served is particularly prevalent among the poor. However, if the
social need is for, say, more doctors, lawyers, or school teachers,
a subsidy may be given to higher education that results in a negative redistribution. That is to say, the society may convey increased benefits on already affluent groups. Redistribution thus
occurs from poor to rich. The argument concerning efficiency is
a neutral argument that does not support any particular redistributive direction.[2]

Positive Redistribution as a "Deviant" Economic Institution

Positive redistribution serves the basic purpose of decreasing inequalities. People are able to obtain goods and services for themselves that they could not have afforded on the basis of their
incomes or wealth. This redistribution has a stabilizing and com-
plementary relationship to market economic processes because it
prevents those processes from leading to the point at which individuals have to choose between starvation or revolution. However, the scale of redistribution needed for this purpose continues
to require public scrutiny and debate because it is thought that
the person who is protected from market changes is less motivated
to be productive.

Welfare redistribution is deviant because it contradicts the most
basic tenets of "market" economic ideology. The "market" exchange is viewed as being a "free" exchange. No one is forced to
accept employment, to purchase particular goods, to give money
or service to others. Instead, all decide which economic exchange
they wish to engage in and the totality of their "free" actions
establishes the values of the contributions of each. This ideology
neglects the effects of monopoly, difference in knowledge of opportunities, etc.; it nevertheless remains a fundamental part of
normal economic exchange expectations. In contra-distinction,
the "welfare" exchange is compulsory.[3] The attempt to attain
welfare purposes on the basis of the free "philanthropic" giver
and the independent, self-determining beneficiary failed. The welfare exchange, as foreseen by the Webbs in the minority report
of the British Poor Law Commission 1905–09, is typically com-

pulsory. It is compulsory on the giver through taxation and on the recipient as he or she is assigned a social insurance number, "covered" by medicare, given family allowances, or made the enforced recipient of the services that the society considers will aid that person's rehabilitation.

Second, the market exchange is viewed as being based on a *quid pro quo*. That is to say, there is a *real* exchange. The worker contributes his labour and receives in return his wages. The consumer uses his money to obtain the goods and services he needs. The owner obtains a rent for another's use of his property. In each case, the exchange is a mutual one. In the case of welfare, however, the so-called "exchange" is a fraud. What good or service does the community as a whole, or any particular individual within the community, obtain for a public assistance grant? Nothing. The more appropriate term for this transaction is "transfer" rather than exchange. It is this basic affront to the values of economic ideology that is the source of the constant demand that the able-bodied "work for welfare." Surely, it is thought, the community should get some positive contribution in return for the payments it is making.

Lastly, the "market" exchange of Western industrialized societies is fundamental to the creation of inequalities. The exchange is not, in fact, an equal one, but favours those who, through their accumulated position in the market (capital), are able to create the terms on which others work and for this service obtain part of the power of the others' labour for themselves. The "market" exchange is thus effectively a transfer of men's efforts from those who are least competitive (the poor) to those who are favoured in the competitive process by the possession of real properties or capital (the rich). But the welfare transfer is fundamentally favourable to the poor. The need for the transfer is created by poverty and serves to reduce poverty. However, C.B. Macpherson draws to our attention the fact that:

> . . . the offsetting (welfare) transfer within the welfare state can never, within capitalism, equal the original and continuing transfer. This is fully appreciated by the strongest defenders of capitalism, who point out, quite rightly, that if

welfare transfers got so large as to eat up profits there would be no more incentive to capitalist enterprises, and so no more capitalist enterprise.[4]

Thus the welfare transfer is secondary in Western industrial societies to the economic exchange mechanisms.

The necessity for its existence must therefore be established. The welfare transfer requires both ideological and political justification. The assertion of this justification has a direct effect on the form of social welfare programs, and hence on the recipients of social welfare benefits.

There have been five principal arguments used to justify the welfare transfer: need; compensation for loss; insurance against risk; investment in human potential; and economic growth. Each in turn, when translated by legislation into a program, has a determining effect on eligibility criteria for program benefits.

Need

One may regard "need" as the most fundamental of the arguments used to justify the welfare transfer. The concept of "need" is a central one in social welfare thought and, indeed, in everyday life. Nevertheless, the concept has some subtleties worth exploring. Foremost of these is the distinction that must be drawn between "needs" and "wants." "Want" implies a purely private assertion by a person; "need" adds the notion of necessity and hence obligation on the part of others to respond. However, the "others" are free to allow or reject the need. Rejection in effect converts the alleged "need" back to the category of being a "want" because no one has agreed on its necessity or accepted any obligation. Allowing the "need," on the other hand, legitimized it. Thus, "needs" are the subjects of social and not private or individual definition.

Society is active in the process of setting boundaries as to what constitutes "need." In the early stages of the development of social welfare institutions, such boundaries were characteristically narrow, for example, to particular demographic groups, aged, sick, widowed, orphaned; to particular geographic locations – parish, city, province, etc.; and to particular financial circumstances. In the later stages, there was a marked trend to broaden the boundaries of need, so that programs operate more at the level of nation-states than of local units, assume average needs rather than demand demonstration of need from those who seek benefit and expand coverage to more inclusive demographic groups. These trends all are favourable to the social welfare ideal of equality of treatment. Indeed, part of the justification for a guaranteed annual income is that such a program would recognize "need" *per se* rather than the need of particular groups.

"Need" should not be defined exclusively in money terms. Social welfare institutions are also involved in making welfare "transfers," usually of services, to people whose need is social. Thus, some children's programs, such as day care, are justified by the "need" of children for adequate opportunities.

Where the justification for a program is the "need" of the intended beneficiaries, it follows that eligibility will be determined by whether or not the "need" exists; the simplest case is where a need is *assumed* to exist, as with such programs as Old Age Security and Family Allowances. Such programs are sometimes termed "demogrants." Every Canadian citizen within the designated age limits of the program is assumed to be needy and the transfer is made without particular inquiry as to whether discrete individuals are in fact needy.

The more typical approach to the determination of eligibility based on need is to conduct an inquiry or "needs test" into the individual's circumstances to determine whether, within the meaning given to need by the program in question, need exists for this individual. Such inquiries are characteristic of public assistance and public housing programs. The determination of need at the level of the individual inevitably requires consideration not only of his or her financial circumstances, but also of his or her dependencies. More need has to be recognized in the circumstances of a man and woman living separately than in the case of a man and woman living together because in the latter case they share a roof. The inquiry to determine need thus is necessarily extensive, involving the review of matters that most people treat as being their private affairs. Furthermore, an element of discretion is desirable in such reviews because of the variability of individual circumstances; one teenager might be expected to live in his parents' house as a dependant while for another such might not be appropriate. Discretion in the determination of such social aspects of need gives considerable power to social assistance workers. The applicant for such help can learn to manipulate the way he or she presents personal need and in so doing tends to become dependent on the worker and the program.[5] The exercise of discretion creates a situation in which the rights of applicants become ambiguous. Such programs are typically non-contractual with entitlements being expressed in general language in the legislation.[6] The determination of need at the level of the individual is also a time-consuming, expensive, and administratively complicated task. The "needs test" has been, and remains, one of the characteristics of social welfare programming.

A distinction is sometimes drawn between a *means* test and a *needs* test. The means test is perceived as being a more arbitrary form of the needs test in that attention centres only on the individual's resources, e.g., income, assets, etc., and not on his requirements. However, for the purpose of this discussion, the distinction is not an important or significant one. Both types of test involve a similar type of process to determine eligibility and have a similar impact on applicants. Recently the *income* test has been introduced. While similar in effect to means and needs tests, the income test disregards resources other than income in establishing a measure of need. The income test is used in the Old Age Guaranteed Income Supplement program.

In some social welfare programs, the financial circumstances of applicants are not the most relevant aspect of need determination. Particularly where programs, such as correction and mental health, are thrust upon their beneficiaries by force of law, the process to determine need becomes clearly one in which the society makes a judgement (a formal legal judgement) that the person is in need of special attention. A similar situation often exists in the admission process to such institutions as children's treatment centres. The need of the child is determined by an assessment process that seeks to identify the form of the child's alleged pathology and whether aid can be given by the treatment centre. These tests are no less tests of need than the financial tests discussed earlier. Their distinguishing characteristic is that they use social-psychological rather than social-economic criteria for the decision.

Compensation

The concept of *compensation* as providing a justification for welfare transfers introduces a quasi-market notion into the discussion that was absent from the discussion of need. In the affairs of Western society, this concept is rooted in law. If one suffers a disservice through either the deliberate or the careless act of another, one is entitled to sue and obtain compensation through the courts. Thus, if one is the victim of a motor accident, the careless party is forced to make a lump-sum settlement determined by a court process that attempts to measure the extent of the financial loss. Unlike need, compensation is based in the common law tradition of jurisprudence, inherited from Britain.

The familiarity of this concept and its acceptability within the ideology of the economic marketplace have interested those who would advance the cause of social welfare. Hence, Richard Titmuss identifies several types of disservice individuals suffer, to whom our society could make a welfare transfer on the basis of the concept of comparison.

> (1) As partial compensation for identified disservices caused by society (for example, unemployment, some categories of industrial injuries benefits, war pensions, etc.).
> (2) As partial compensation for unidentifiable disservices caused by society (for example, "benefits" related to programs of slum clearance, urban blight, smoke pollution control, hospital cross-infection, and many other socially related disservices).
> (3) As partial compensation for unmerited handicap (for example, language classes for immigrant children, services for the deprived child, children handicapped from birth, etc.).[7]

In practice the concept of compensation has found relatively little use in the development of Canadian social welfare programs. The clearest example of its use is in the provincial programs of

Workers' Compensation which, commencing in 1914 in Ontario, have provided contractual benefits to disabled workers and to their dependants. The Workers' Compensation program is funded by employers' contributions, each employer being required to pay on the basis of the accident record of his employees. The program in turn provides a measure of protection to employers from the individual suits that they might otherwise have to face.

The settlement made by the family court in situations of desertion, unmarried motherhood, etc., could also be classed as being a type of compensation. However, this latter type of compensation indicates some of the difficulties involved in applying the concept. The concept works reasonably well in the case of workers' compensation because the companies responsible for funding the program contribute to a common fund from which payments are made. It is much more difficult to force individuals to pay. They may not have the means, they may not be located, they may incur other dependencies that must also be met. If they are sent to jail for failure to pay, the intended beneficiary still has received no benefit. Thus, such programs are full of enforcement problems. Indeed, one can conclude that the lack of application of the concept of compensation is a product of the difficulty of determining responsibility and obtaining compliance.

There has been some looser use of the concept of compensation in the establishment of specific programs devoted to population groups that have suffered some general types of disadvantage. Thus, part of the argument for special services for veterans is that their military service has resulted in an effective loss of earning power, seniority, etc., not to mention the specific losses resulting from identifiable injuries. A similar argument is used to justify special social services for native peoples today. Native peoples are viewed as being a group who should receive special compensating advantages to overcome the results of past discrimination and neglect.

Insurance

The concept of insurance as justification for welfare transfers, like the concept of compensation, has been taken over from the ideology of the economic market, but its use has been much more extensive. The market use of the concept of insurance implies that the chance of a foreseeable risk, fire, accident, or death is assessed. On the basis of the assessed chance, and on the value of the loss incurred, a premium is charged to all who wish to protect themselves. If the foreseen contingency occurs, the insurer pays a settlement to the insuree. The system is a voluntary one in that neither insurer nor insuree is forced to enter into a contract. The system is designed in such a way as to be financially viable or the insurer goes bankrupt. There are no welfare transfer functions in the system for, although some receive benefits that others have paid for, the deliberate intention is to group insurees according to the nature of their risk so that each pays a fair premium for the protection he or she buys.

Social insurance uses some of these ideas but modifies them in significant ways to obtain a welfare transfer effect. The four best-known Canadian social insurance programs are Unemployment Insurance, the Canada Pension Plan, Medicare, and Hospital Insurance.

The principal ways in which social insurance differs from private insurance are as follows:

1. *Compulsion rather than free contract.* Government programs typically demand universal coverage. This ensures that there will be the maximum distribution of the risk and that no one will have to seek assistance from other government agencies because they privately decided not to seek insurance.

2. *Lack of "group experience" ratings.* While private insurance plans seek to relate benefits and risk closely to the individual insuree's situation, government insurance plans typically average all risks. Payment of premiums thus becomes a form of taxation, not particularly related to the chance of the individual becoming a beneficiary, and thereby produces a welfare transfer effect between those at risk and those not at risk.

3. *"Subsidy" elements.* While private insurance plans have to be actuarily sound, government insurance plans usually contain provision for subsidy from general revenues, which serves to increase the transfer effect. Thus if unemployment exceeded 4 per cent in

the 1970s, the unemployment insurance fund was subsidized from general government revenue.

4. *Increased range of "risks" accepted*. Unemployment is uninsurable as a "private" risk, partly because it is difficult (as the Unemployment Insurance Commission is aware) to control persons who are "unemployed" by choice, and partly because the risk of massive unemployment resulting from recession would threaten any private scheme with bankruptcy.

Social insurance accepts these risks, on the one hand, because a social purpose is to be obtained by protecting people against unemployment and, on the other, because the government will support payments from general revenue rather than allow the plan to become bankrupt.

5. *Benefits/contributions relationship*. In both private and social insurance a record of the contributions of those covered is kept and benefits are paid in foreseen circumstances. These features have particular importance in the process of determining eligibility. Eligibility for benefits is created by having an acceptable contributions record and by the occurrence of the foreseen contingency. In these circumstances, the applicant's right to benefit is contractually assured. Hence, no inquiry into other aspects of his personal or financial circumstances is necessary. The difference from private insurance is that in social insurance an acceptable contributions record is determined by social policy rather than by actuarial considerations.

An effect of these features is to create a situation in which certain needs are inevitably not recognized. The need of an individual whose circumstances are not those foreseen in the insurance provision or a person who does not have the necessary contributions record is obviously excluded from benefit. Further, some types of need-producing situations have not been thought to be "suitable" for insurance. Of these the most common "unsuitable" risk has been the risk of desertion, separation, or divorce and the similar risk of unmarried motherhood. In some Western European countries such as Denmark, these risks are covered by social insurance but in the English-speaking countries, they have been excluded and responsibility left with the individual.

Thus, social insurance has provided significant numbers of people with contractual benefits and obtained a high degree of public support. The principle of establishing a contractual base through a contribution record for the welfare transfer deserves restatement. It has proved itself acceptable to both beneficiaries and contributors in times of both prosperity and recession, moderating the tendency to change benefits because of short-term financial exigencies.

Investment

The concept of investment has been used relatively infrequently to justify welfare transfers. It is used in some discussions of the problem of poverty in which the problem is defined as one of under-investment in the human resources of the people who are poor. Thus, in the *Fifth Annual Review*, the Economic Council of Canada refers to "upgrading of human resources involved in combatting poverty."[8] The concept was also used to support the Relocation and Retraining programs of the Department of Manpower and Immigration and the extensive subsidies provided to education programs generally.

A different use of the investment approach in the design of welfare transfers was found in the Opportunities for Youth and Local Initiative Programs, and, in the reference in the federal Working Paper on Social Security, to: "a community employment program. Its purpose would be to provide socially useful employment to people who have been unemployed for an extended period of time . . . ."[9] These programs would appear to occupy a position intermediate between work and welfare. A major element of welfare exists because the programs' existence is justified by unemployment and eligibility is determined partly on the basis of need ("unemployed for an extended period of time"). On the other hand, they are designed to produce a return to the society, and the debate focuses partly on what in fact constitutes "work." Because of the intermediate nature of the programs between work and welfare, there is reason to hope that the transfers that occur may be more acceptable than is the case with the more visible welfare transfers in which society sees no return. However, the use of the ideology of "work" and "investment" for this function has its own effects on eligibility determination.

An investment ideology results in programs designed to concentrate resources on those who will benefit most. This diminishes the degree to which the programs are responsive to need and thereby decreases their effectiveness as welfare transfers. Indeed, it is questionable whether there is any welfare transfer effect in some social programs, such as higher education, where the primary approach to eligibility for benefits is based on a human resource investment ideology and a competitive process to determine who will be beneficiaries.

Economic Growth and Stability

Arguments have been advanced for welfare expenditures on the grounds that such expenditures will themselves contribute to economic stability and growth. Samuelson and Scott[10] suggest that welfare expenditures could be manipulated so as to increase total spending power in times of economic recession and thereby contribute to improved economic performance. A similar argument is advanced by Galbraith in *The Affluent Society*,[11] and a similar argument would appear to be implicit in Social Credit's "social dividend" theories. The purpose of the welfare state is services, including making "liberal capitalism more productive economically and more just socially." As confidence in economic growth has diminished, the argument has become one of ensuring that a "safety net" of social measures exists to ensure a foundation of economic and social stability.

The post-war Family Allowance program was accepted partly because it was seen as a way of providing for greater stability of consumer demand and hence as an asset in avoiding the recurrence of the pre-war depression. However, one cannot identify any welfare transfer program in which economic growth and stability policy are the primary determinants of levels of benefit and eligibility.

This review of the five approaches to justifying welfare transfers has treated them in the order in which they contradict market ideology. The greatest contradiction is present in the discussion of need; partial accommodations are made in the discussions of compensation and insurance; and full accommodation is obtainable in the discussion of investment and economic growth. The greater the degree of accommodation, the less the welfare transfer that is justified. These dynamics have additional effects on the maintenance of public support for welfare transfers and on the extent to which the programs stigmatize their beneficiaries. However, before proceeding to these subjects, we should introduce the distinction between selective and universal approaches to redistribution.

Selective vs. Universal Transfer Mechanisms

A *selective* transfer mechanism is one in which beneficiaries are determined by individual consideration of their circumstances. All means tests, needs test, contribution records, and the like are instruments of selectivity. A *universal* transfer mechanism is one in which beneficiaries are determined on the basis of some recognized common factor and without consideration of their individual circumstances. Examples of selective transfers are public assistance and public housing. Examples of universal transfers are Old Age Security and Family Allowances. Each of the approaches to making transfers has its own distinctive advantages and disadvantages.

1. *Administration*. Universal transfers are simple to administer. Beneficiaries and benefit levels are determined by the use of such simple and stable discriminators as age, sex, number of children. Hence administrative costs are low, and automatic and anonymous means of distribution – computers, mail service – are readily adopted.

Selective transfers are administratively complicated. There is the difficult and individualized task of considering personal need and circumstance. Changes as individual situations vary with time and fraudulent declarations also create problems. There is the difficult task of interpreting to public and beneficiaries how individual circumstances may lead to the different treatment of persons whose apparent situations are similar. An "unemployable" with a back injury may look as healthy as an "employable" without an injury.

Discrimination of this type has been the subject of numerous appeals and may be challenged in the courts on the basis of the Charter of Rights. Discrimination of this type is arbitrary as to where to draw the line between one category and another. For these reasons, selective transfers are expensive to administer, requiring a well-trained staff of social service workers. Developments in regulation specificity and computer capacity are improving the administrative ability to adjust benefits to individual need, maintain accountability for decisions, and provide evidence of contract and hence the right of appeal. Nevertheless fundamental problems remain either in the mass of detailed regulation required or in the lack of sufficient controls on discretion.

2. *Attention to need.* Universal transfers are necessarily based on some concept of assumed average need.[12] (Although when one considers the approximately $330/month Old Age Security payment or the $32/month Family Allowance payment, one may wonder what the standard is.) As a consequence, universal transfers usually miss unusual needs. The lower the general level of universal payment the greater the extent it will require supplementation because of the existence of special circumstances not recognized in the concept of "average need."

Selective transfers are by design attentive to individual needs and circumstances. The mechanism thus deliberately permits the accommodation of those whose circumstances are not typical. Moreover, selective transfers can be designed to provide positive discrimination in favour of particular populations who may have suffered a past injustice, for example, native persons. Such special populations are inevitably lost in universal transfers.

Finally, where the transfer is of a service, such as Medicare, education, or counselling, there is a tendency for an institutional "creaming" effect to take place within universal approaches. Thus, health services best serve a rather stoic, undemanding person who is unconcerned about time and will put up with the inconvenience of doctors' and hospitals' schedules. Similarly, education services serve best a rather controlled, receptive person with a good memory. To provide good services to people who do not have these service-related characteristics requires positive and selective discrimination by the service workers; for example, doctors may need to go to people rather than wait for people to come to them. Universal services only obtain this positive discrimination by introducing a measure of internal selectivity.

3. *Transfer efficiency*. Given a limited amount of funds to be transferred, it is a lot more efficient to give the whole of the amount to those who are judged to be in need, by a selective mechanism, than to distribute the amount to all persons regardless of need. In other words, it is easier to limit the transfer to only a portion of the recipients.

This was essentially the argument used by the government of Canada in its 1970 proposal to modify the Family Allowance program by graduating benefits in relation to income:

> Greater emphasis should be placed on anti-poverty measures. This should be accomplished in a manner which enables the greatest concentration of available resources upon those with the lowest income. Selective payments based on income should be made, where possible, in place of universal payments which disregard the actual income of the recipient.[13]

In theory, a universal program can obtain a similar distribution of benefit to a selective one by "recapturing" benefits from people who do not need them through the income tax system. In practice, such recapture is usually only partial and requires circulating funds twice through people's pockets. As a result, universal transfers have been the subject of intense scrutiny as an inefficient way of extending benefits to those that need them most – and a misallocation of resources to those who do not need them at all.[14]

4. *Stigma*. All social welfare programs have a tendency to stigmatize their recipients, principally because welfare support continues to be viewed as an admission of failure on the part of the beneficiary. Nevertheless, universal transfers have the effect of sharply reducing the stigma. When benefits are received by everyone, no one has to define himself as being in greater need than any other. In the terminology of Wilensky and Lebeaux,[15] the payments are "institutional." Conversely, selective payments sharply distinguish the "giver" from the "receiver." Furthermore, the receiver is individually distinguished by his or her having to deal personally with the administrative apparatus of selectivity, e.g.,

the public assistance department. In the terminology of Wilensky and Lebeaux, the payments are "residual." The consequence is that the stigma associated with receipt is sharply increased.

Given the competing advantages and disadvantages of selective and universal transfer mechanisms, it is apparent that both are needed. Where there is a widespread need, universal payments (or those seen as being universal, which are linked with the income tax system to increase their redistribution effect) are preferred because of their lack of stigma and administrative simplicity. To reach special populations and special individual types of need, selective payment and selective services are necessary.

Transfers, Stigma, and Public Support

In the discussion of universal and selective transfer mechanisms, the subject of *stigma* has already been mentioned.[16] Stigma means the conferring of a negative repute or social status on the stigmatized individual, and would appear to be endemic in social welfare programs. Why this should be the case is not altogether clear, although it appears to be related to the aforementioned "deviant" nature of the welfare transfer. The degree of stigma generated by social welfare programs is much greater in needs-related programs than in those programs that compromise with market ideology by adopting a compensation, insurance, or human investment justification for their existence. The two principle effects of stigma are the social control effect and the public support effect.

1. *The social control effect.* Stigmatized persons are, unfortunately, second-class citizens. As such, they learn to expect that a variety of social conditions usually enjoyed by others, such as reasonably adequate income, will be denied. The recipients come to view their social situation as one that is deserved, if not personally, at least by other members of their class. Thus, it is typically found that stigmatized populations hold very negative stereotypes of one another. This, in turn, makes it difficult for them to work together politically to obtain change in the society around them.

As individuals, it has the effect of making them amenable to the idea that they should accept with gratitude whatever the society should offer them. Thus work, at whatever wages and under whatever conditions, should be accepted. Work offers an escape from the stigma of welfare. In turn, the stigma of welfare assists in maintaining a considerable population in low-paid and unattractive occupations. As the Senate Committee on Poverty found, a majority of the poor are in the work force. The stigma of welfare assists in keeping them there. Thus, stigma has a functional use in helping to reduce the extent of the welfare transfer.

Furthermore, the stigma has the effect of providing a justification for a series of erosions of normal social rights. At the less severe end of a continuum of such erosions, one has the effect of the classification "client," with its presumption that it is the client who should be changed through rehabilitation or work opportunity programs.

In the middle of the continuum of erosions of citizenship rights are various administrative incursions into the freedom people normally enjoy. Thus, in the past, welfare recipients have been denied full freedom to spend their welfare transfer income according to their own judgement. They have been prohibited from owning a car, renting a telephone, or visiting a beer parlour. If they offended these administrative policy guidelines, then the guidelines would be enforced by denying the recipient cash and by issuing vouchers to control spending patterns.

In the severe part of the continuum are the extreme measures of depriving citizens of the right to vote; requiring that they live in designated places (poor houses, jails, mental hospitals); subjecting them to physical mutilations (sterilization); and breaking up families (neglect proceedings under child welfare legislation).

At different, and recurrent, points in the history of social welfare programs, these "social control" effects of stigma and the means to achieve them have been given explicit sanction in public policy. At other times, they have been concealed but remain as implicit contradictions of aspects of the welfare ideal. As a result, welfare measures have been accompanied by a continuing "double message," contradicting formal statements of objective and the values explicitly asserted.

2. *The public support effect.* The welfare transfer is an institutionalized form of gift. Thus, who gives and why are central to social

policy. The most positive and, for welfare ideals, most supportive answers to these questions are based in the consciousness of sharing a common fate with one's fellow citizens. For this reason, the most positive approaches to the development of social welfare in modern society have occurred during times of war. The British welfare state was founded in the experience of a nation that came to accept the principles of pooling and sharing during the emergency situations of World War II. T.H. Marshall, using a similar line of argument, identifies modern social security measures with the concept of citizenship.[17]

The paradox of welfare transfers is that, *de facto*, they tend to destroy this sense of common cause. The effect of stigma on public support is to divide citizens into two separate social classes, the "givers" and the "receivers." The givers are identified with industry, self-support, and beneficence, while the receivers are identified with laziness, dependence, and self-interest. The welfare transfer thus creates alienation and undercuts the basis of its own public support. The transfer based on a shared citizenship is debased by the dynamic into a transfer based on the principle that those who are the givers are justified in expecting that the recipients conduct themselves on terms dictated to them. A transfer based on a gift thus becomes a transfer viewed as a means of social control.

The history of the development of social welfare programs has thus been marked by cycles in which high ideals are declared – the Welfare State, the War on Poverty – followed by periods in which the ideals are eroded and forgotten. In such periods the social welfare transfer is viewed as a "burden" rather than as a desirable social expenditure. The form of this cycle in Canada is reflected in Appendix 2; for example, the 1940s were a period of substantial reform and review, which contrasted with the failure and chaos of the 1930s and the indifference of the 1950s;[18] likewise, the achievements of the 1960s in some measure led to the conservative reaction of the 1980s.

Transfers and Taxation

Although taxes do not necessarily result in welfare transfers, one cannot leave the subject of welfare transfers without some mention of the subject of taxation. The graduated income tax has a basic effect on the distribution of income, making the post-tax income distribution more egalitarian than the pre-tax income distribution. This result is not a welfare transfer in itself; there is no direct "gift" effect. However, the revenues raised by the graduated income tax may be used to support a welfare transfer, in which case the combined effect of the graduated tax and the welfare transfer changes the income distribution in a more egalitarian direction to a greater degree than would be achieved by the welfare transfer on its own.

Thus, a properly graduated taxation system (in which those with the highest incomes pay a higher percentage of their total income in taxes) is an important support to egalitarian welfare transfers. The Canadian tax system does not obtain this ideal. The effective total tax incidence is remarkably even so that all income classes part with approximately the same fraction of their total income in taxes.[19] This is a result of the fact that the progressive graduations of the income tax system are almost completely counteracted by the regressive impact of sales taxes, housing taxes, social insurance premiums, import duties, etc. In all of these indirect taxes, the poor pay a higher proportion of their income than the better off.

A tax system, however well designed, does not obtain a transfer effect unless its revenues are used to convey a gift. In recent years, there has been a considerable amount of discussion of the advantages and disadvantages of making such a gift-conferring function an integral part of the taxation system. This discussion has been carried on under the title of *negative income tax* proposals. One of the foremost advocates of such a system in Canada was the Senate Committee on Poverty. The discussion of negative taxation proposals became highly technical and our present purposes will have to be satisfied by summarizing the main arguments that were presented.[20] The principal arguments in favour of negative taxation proposals included the following.

1. *Means of selectivity*. The graduations of the income tax system, particularly the personal exemptions, represent a type of income test, an income test that is well accepted and universally applied.

The use of this testing mechanism for establishing need and making payments would represent a major simplification from the present situation with its separate administrative structures, provincial public assistance departments, and special needs tests.

2. *Anonymity.* Because everybody, rich or poor, already completes an income tax return, no special visible distinction would accompany the act of seeking assistance. This should lead to the program reaching people who at the moment are deterred by the stigma that accompanies application for public assistance.

3. *Assistance to the working poor.* There are a large number of people whose working income is below accepted poverty lines. This population of potential beneficiaries has been poorly reached by public assistance programs, partly because of earnings limits on public assistance that make work unrewarding and partly because of the stigma of public assistance. A negative taxation program would provide a means of automatically supplementing the incomes of this group.

In summary, it is argued that a negative taxation program would obtain some of the advantages of both universality and selectivity. However, four problems with such programming prevented its introduction.

1. *The benefits, rate of reduction, costs conundrum.* Since some people will have to be dependent on the program for their total income, the benefit level of any program should provide support at least at the level of poverty. In addition, the program should be designed in such a way as to provide an incentive for any individual to work. That is to say, any individual should retain a reasonable proportion of his earnings.

The problem is that a combination of these factors tends to lead to programs that are excessively costly. Thus, if a poverty line of $16,000 per year is adopted for a family of four, and if an earner is allowed to retain 50 per cent of his earnings, then income subsidies for families of four are extended up to the $32,000 per year income level (see Table 3).

Extending subsidies up to the $32,000 level involves such a high proportion of the total work force that the program becomes very costly. However, reducing costs involves either increasing the rate

TABLE 3: *Four person family: $16,000 poverty line, 50 per cent rate of reduction*

Earned Income	Negative Tax Income Reduced 50 Per Cent of Earned Income	Total Income
$ 0	$16,000	$16,000
10,000	11,000	21,000
20,000	6,000	26,000
32,000	0	32,000

of reduction (and thereby reducing work incentives) or lowering the poverty line and permitting those at the minimum level of support to live in poverty.

This dilemma was judged irresolvable in the early 1970s within a level of public expenditure that was politically accepted.[21] In the 1980s resolution is no easier, as the number of beneficiaries has grown while revenues to support public expenditure have not kept up with inflation. Attempts to solve this dilemma continue and will be discussed in Chapter Six.

2. *The tax base.* If the advantages of integrating taxes and transfers are to be achieved, then the tax base should be one that is attentive to the extent of people's need. Unfortunately, the existing tax base has been designed to treat different types of income in different ways. Thus persons engaged in business can reduce their taxable income by charging various types of expense against their total income. Their taxable income is therefore not a good measure of their comparative command over resources as compared to the taxable income of a person with a salary.

The Carter Commission on Taxation documented such inequalities and made proposals to correct them. However, the tax system serves many existing purposes that define established business conditions for entire selections of the society; beneficial treatment of farm incomes is a good example. Withdrawal of these features would result in major unproductive business dislocation. After much lobbying, this was recognized in the Income Tax Act, 1981, and in subsequent revisions to tax policy. If we now add a negative tax program to this base, we find ourselves supplementing the incomes of some who are already well off but whose present income is exempted from taxes.

Correcting this situation involves either beginning again to reform the ways taxation treats income or separating the negative tax program from ordinary taxes. The first approach was disastrous to at least one finance minister and remains politically difficult. The second approach removes the advantages of integration that are central to the case for the proposal in the first place.

3. *Administrative.* All selective programs have their administrative complications. In this case, income tax declarations are normally completed annually. However, individual situations vary from month to month. Hence, negative tax payments based on a previous year's earnings will only meet the need of those whose situation is stable from one year to the next. For others, the payments will be either inadequate (where their income is declining) or overly generous (where their income is increasing). Furthermore, people will move back and forth from one category to another as their monthly incomes vary.

If the total system is not responsive to these monthly changes, then large problems of overpayment and underpayment occur. On the other hand, providing a system that is responsive to need on a monthly basis involves a major modification of the income tax system and the addition to it of a corps of payment adjusters. These changes would tend to destroy the anonymity that is seen as one of the advantages of the proposed program.

4. *Work incentives.* An argument against the introduction of an automatic payment system is that it would result in a reduction of work incentive. This is a long-standing concern in relation to both unemployment insurance and social assistance. A major reason for this perception is that both programs require a person to be unemployed so as to receive benefit. In fact, evidence to support this contention has not been produced, except in anecdotal form. However, public perception has a continuing direct effect on public policy through polling and direct contact with politicians.

Social welfare benefits are designed to reduce inequalities and to create a more equal social order, but this role remains contentious. Social welfare measures have been developed by pleading a series of "special-case" situations and arguing that these situations could not be met by the usual mechanism of economic exchange. These special-case pleadings – need, compensation, etc. – have the effect of directing thinking toward the economic market so that its role as the "normal" means of support and exchange is retained. Furthermore, this perception of normality is conducive to social welfare measures performing functions that guide beneficiaries toward market employment. Hence, social welfare measures increase the supply of labour. On occasions, coercion is obvious – refusal of benefits unless employment is accepted – but more usually coercion takes the form of persons accepting such employment to avoid the stigma of welfare.

The stigmatizing consequences of the social welfare transfer are compounded by the use of selective, case-oriented means of distributing benefits – yet no other means to reaching individualized types of need have been found. Universal measures are based on assumed average need and, where services are delivered, have "creaming" characteristics that impede an equal distribution of benefits. Attempts to find an alternate distribution mechanism, possibly through combination with the tax system, have had partial success, as with the increasing integration between federal benefits and taxes for both the elderly and children. However, consensus on a more complete integration – and hence major restructuring and simplification – has not been achieved.

The reasons for this lack of achievement include both policy and administrative concerns. Both are capable of technical resolution but at the cost of dislocating existing patterns of benefit. The problem of implementation is thus a political one awaiting new ideas, consensus, or courage. The net effect is that egalitarian ideals have not been achieved as effectively as they might have been, given the resources available.[22]

Notes

1. Robert G. Evans, "Hang Together or Hang Separately: Universal Health Care in the Year 2000," *Canadian Public Policy* (June, 1987).
2. For an expanded discussion of the concept of redistribution, see Adrian Webb and Jack Sieve, *Income Redistribution and the Welfare State*, Occa-

sional Paper on Social Administration No. 41 (London: Bell and Son, 1971).

3. The compulsory nature of the welfare transaction can be viewed as a result of the decision to go beyond Pareto-optimality and attempt to obtain a morally determined view of social justice (see discussion of equality in Chapter One.).

4. C.B. Macpherson, "The Real World of Democracy," *Massey Lectures, 4th Series*, CBC, 1965, p. 48.

5. For a good discussion on the dynamics of such dependency, see David Woodsworth, "Agency Policy and Client Roles," *The Social Worker*, 37, 4 (November, 1969).

6. For example, the following discretionary clause in the Social Development Act of the Province of Alberta: "6. The Director *may* provide to an employable person in need of assistance (I) a social allowance (II) advice or instruction . . . ."

7. Richard M. Titmuss, *Commitment to Welfare* (London: George Allen and Unwin, 1968), p. 131; Brian Abel-Smith and Elizabeth Titmuss, eds., *Social Policy* (London: George Allen and Unwin, 1974), Chapter 5.

8. Economic Council of Canada. *Fifth Annual Review* (Ottawa: Queen's Printer, 1968), p. 117.

9. Canada, *Working Paper on Social Security in Canada* (Ottawa, 1973), p. 25.

10. Paul Samuelson, *Economics* (Canadian edition) (Toronto: McGraw-Hill, 1966).

11. J.K. Galbraith, *The Affluent Society* (London: Penguin Books, 1958), pp. 238–44.

12. Ramesh Mishra, *The Welfare State in Crisis* (Brighton: Wheatsheaf Books, 1984).

13. See Canada, *Income Security for Canadians* (Ottawa, 1970).

14. Walter Block, "The Case for Selectivity," *Canadian Social Work Review* (1981).

15. Wilensky and Lebeaux, *Industrial Society and Social Welfare*, p. 138. "Two conceptions of social welfare appear to be dominant in the United States today: the residual and the institutional. The first holds that social welfare institutions should come into play only when the normal structures of supply, the family and the market, break down. The second, in context, sees welfare services as normal 'first line' functions of modern and industrial societies."

16. For a detailed discussion, see Pinker, *Social Theory and Social Policy*, Chapter 4.

17. T.H. Marshall, *Class, Citizenship and Social Development* (Garden City, N.Y.: Anchor Books, 1965).

18. For an extended treatment of the cyclical nature of social welfare concerns in the United States, and their relationships to the society, see F.F. Piven and R.A. Cloward, *Regulating the Poor: The Functions of Public Welfare* (New York: Vintage Books, 1971).

19. Canada, *Poverty in Canada*, Report of the Senate Committee on Poverty (Ottawa, 1971), p. 46.

20. For a full discussion, see the following: Christopher Green, *Negative Taxes and the Poverty Problem* (Washington: The Brookings Institute, 1967); H.W. Watts, "Graduated Work Incentive: An Experiment in Negative Taxation," *American Economic Review*, LIX, 2 (May, 1964); Arnold Katz, "Income Maintenance Experiments: Progress Towards a New American National Policy," *Social and Economic Administration*, 7, 2 (May, 1973).

21. For example, see the Castonguay-Nepeuv proposals from Quebec in *Income Security*, Report on the Commission of Inquiry on Health and Welfare (Quebec City, 1971).

22. Canada, *Report* of the Royal Commission on the Economic Union and Development Prospects for Canada (Ottawa: Queen's Printer, 1985).

Chapter 3

COMMUNITY

Welfare is influenced by the idealized model of what a community should be like. Whereas Chapter 2 presented the conflict between welfare ideals and normative economic theory, this chapter deals with the conflict between these same ideals and the realities of socialization, social control, and political participation.

The ideals are simply stated: "Free men living in a community of free and equal men is the democratic ideal," writes John Romanyshyn.[1] These ideals have received tangible expression in the sociological literature, as well as in the social welfare literature, through attention to the ideals of the tightly knit small town or rural community. More than forty years ago, C. Wright Mills exposed how deeply the discussion in North America of social disorganization, and society's response to it, is affected by this concept of community, a concept he defined principally with reference to rural life.

In approaching the notion of adjustment, one may analyze the specific illustrations of maladjustment that are given and from these instances infer a type of person who in this literature is evaluated as "adjusted." The ideally adjusted man of the social pathologists is "socialized." This term seems to operate ethically as the opposite of "selfish"; it implies that

the adjusted man conforms to middle-class morality and mo-
tives and "participates" in the gradual progress of respectable
institutions. If he is not a "joiner," he certainly gets around
and into many community organizations. If he is socialized,
the individual thinks of others and is kindly towards them.
He does not brood or mope about but is somewhat extrovert,
eagerly participating in his community's institutions. His mother
and father were not divorced, nor was his home ever broken.
He is "successful" – at least in a modest way – since he is
ambitious; but he does not speculate about matters too far
beyond his means, lest he become a "fantasy thinker," and
the little men don't scramble after the big money. The less
abstract the traits and fulfilled "needs" of the "adjusted man"
are, the more they gravitate toward the norm of independent
middle-class persons verbally living out Protestant ideals in
the small towns of America.[2]

Urbanization and Community Ideals

Population movements in Canada during the twentieth century
have been dominated by migrations toward central Canada and
toward the West, and by a rural-to-urban migration. The combination of these trends has made urban growth the dominant
reality throughout Canada but with the pace of growth varying
between different metropolitan areas. Table 4 indicates the growth
of selected Canadian cities.

In the period 1901–71, the percentage of the total population
living in urban areas of 20,000 or over population increased from
approximately 17 per cent to close to 60 per cent. Between 1971
and 1981 growth slowed in the largest metropolitan areas, but
continued at high rates in the middle-sized communities in both
eastern and western Canada. Analysis of this urban growth process
indicates it is the product of Canada's economic development,
particularly its role as an exporter of commodities. Further, the
by-products of this growth have been seen in the identification
of a common set of problems, of which poverty, housing costs,
transportation congestion, environmental decay, social unrest, and
fiscal squeeze are most common.[3]

TABLE 4: *Population and % change in Population for Selected Metropolitan Areas, Canada 1901–1981* (population in thousands)

	1901	1911	1921	1931	1941	1951	1961	1971	1981
Halifax	51	58	75	79	99	134	183	222	277
Montreal	415	616	796	1086	1216	1504	2156	2743	2828
Toronto	303	478	686	901	1002	1264	1942	2628	2998
Winnipeg	48	157	229	295	302	357	476	540	584
Calgary	8	56	78	103	112	156	290	403	592
Vancouver	—	—	224	338	394	562	790	1028	1268
	Per cent Change in Population Since Last Census								
Halifax	—	13.4	30.6	4.1	25.5	35.8	37.3	21.3	24.7
Montreal	—	48.6	29.2	36.3	12.1	23.6	43.3	27.2	3.1
Toronto	—	57.7	43.6	31.3	11.2	26.2	53.6	35.3	14.1
Winnipeg	—	223.7	46.0	28.7	2.4	18.1	33.4	13.5	8.1
Calgary	—	570.2	39.5	33.0	8.1	39.7	85.8	38.9	46.9
Vancouver	—	—	—	51.3	16.5	42.7	40.6	30.1	23.3

SOURCE: Leroy O. Stone, *Urban Development in Canada* (Ottawa: Dominion Bureau of Statistics, 1967), p. 278; *Census of Canada*, 1981.

The identification of these "normal" features of urban life as problems is testimony to the lack of congruence between the realities of urban living and the ideals that are held. Thus the reality of urban living is that the majority of contact between people is impersonal, either random in that strangers pass one another in a crowd, or purposive in that some function is accomplished by these people meeting. Neither form of contact is in accord with the ideal that people should know and understand each other. The reality of bringing large numbers of people together is that their competition for available space will result in the poverty of some and the capital gain of others. Yet, housing costs are viewed as a problem, partly, at least, because the idea that Canada is a large country, with much vacant land, causes people to continue to question the high cost of urban land. The reality of bringing large numbers of people of different backgrounds and expectations together, breaking up their familiar patterns, asking that their young people learn to live in this new environment, produces conflict between groups and between generations. But social unrest is viewed as a problem because people continue to expect that differences should be resolved by face-to-face communication, tolerance, and understanding, or, if these means are inadequate, segregation.

Urban growth and individual affluence nonetheless continue to be viewed as indications of progress. Thus, the process that produces problems also imparts to them a surprising character. This has several important effects on the response.

1. *Residual responses.* Because the problems are surprising and unexpected, there is a tendency to design limited, specific responses to them, rather than to analyse seriously the problem's origins. Thus juvenile delinquency, a typical chronic urban problem, tends to be viewed primarily as the product of an individual dilinquent's personal disturbance and secondarily as a product of his or her parents' failure. The response is to design alternate parenting and controlling measures, such as probation. This is a limited view of the problem producing a residual, remedial response.

A broader view of the phenomenon takes into account the anonymous nature of urban life; the difficulty all youth has in orienting itself to the acceptable limits of social behaviour in such an environment; the impact of youths acting out upon strangers, increasing their tendency to be apprehensive and to take formal action. When these factors are taken into account, the response to delinquency needs to include the design of facilities to assist the socialization process and that will, in turn, absorb for the community some of the delinquent behaviour to be expected. This broader view of the problem produces more institutional and preventative responses, for example, good recreational services.

2. *Unplanned services.* The "surprising" nature of the problems stands in the way of effective planning responses. Instead, a series of *ad hoc* responses are typically begun, which do not treat the links between the various phenomena defined as problems. Thus, the interconnections between poverty, child neglect, and delinquency are lost. Instead, separate services are developed around each of the separate problem phenomena. Indeed, one family is soon in the situation where it receives unrelated services from a series of social agencies.

During the later 1950s, such families were viewed as being "multi-problem" families and received a considerable amount of special attention, both in the literature and in special demonstrations and research service proposals.[4] Later, it was realized that the problem was an unplanned social service delivery system that treated whole families in a fragmented and "multi-problem" manner. With this understanding, attention shifted from the families to the redesign of social service delivery systems.

3. *Scapegoat populations.* A third result of the unexpected nature of the problems of urban life is a tendency to make scapegoats of specific populations. An urban problem is identified with the scapegoat population and attempts are made to overcome the "problem" by driving away the "scapegoat."

Thus, it is to be expected that processes of migration will produce difficulties for the people who move. Urban centres encourage such movement and make use of the cheap and unskilled labour provided. However, such a population inevitably has service needs. They may be cash needs because the urban area ceases to need their services, consumption needs because their inadequate earnings lead to inadequate housing, overcrowding, and slum conditions, or educational needs because their high density results in crowded local schools.

The scapegoat response usually takes the form of keeping services poor in the hope that poor services will discourage the population from staying – or others from joining them. In more extreme cases, the scapegoat response involves the use of specific measures – refusal of service, eviction from housing, police harassment – to drive the scapegoat population away. In recent years, transient youth and native persons moving to urban areas have suffered from this phenomenon.

4. *Resistance to service costs.* Finally, there is a general resistance to service costs. The assumption of progress, growth, and affluence does not prepare the population to expect to pay a service price for the problems such growth produces, and the services are identified negatively with problems rather than positively with the quality of life.

Metropolitan-Small Urban/Rural Relationships

Some of the same processes and problems of metropolitan urban development also occur in smaller urban and rural communities.

Urban growth has resulted in the *de facto* creation of small towns that exhibit all the same problems as their larger metropolitan counterparts.

Each of the major metropolitan areas has an extended hinterland in which a series of populations work only because they are sent there by their employers. Thus, in a typical small town, there will be a local industrial population, often containing a managerial class that aspires to move or return to the large metropolitan area and a working class of immigrants, either from overseas or from Canadian rural areas. Serving these populations will be service workers, police, nurses, doctors, school teachers, social workers, many of whom will have few if any ties to the community but who instead view themselves as being in mobile professional careers. Finally, there will be a class of local owners and entrepreneurs.

Only this latter group (and they are a distinct minority) have a real investment in the local community. The other groups are likely to exhibit all the features of the cities from which they are drawn, compounded by their short-term commitments to their present location. The speed and ease of transport and communication also contribute to this tendency. The movement of people, and of their lifestyles, between urban and rural areas is continuous. As the urban populations are considerably larger, their effect on rural populations is greater than the reciprocal rural-to-urban effect.

Thus, although the origins of the conflict between rural ideals and urban realities are to be found in the major metropolitan areas, the conflict is now all-encompassing. Its features are exhibited as frequently in small towns, particularly growing small towns, as in the urban areas with which the small-town populations are associated.

Community Functions of Social Welfare

Part of the distinctive meaning of social policy is to be found in its concern for the integrity of life. Kenneth Boulding writes:

> If there is one common thread that unites all aspects of social policy and distinguishes it from merely economic policy, it is the thread of what has elsewhere been called the "integrative

system." . . . The institutions with which social policy is especially concerned, such as the school, family, church, or, at the other end, the public assistance office, court, prison, or criminal gang all reflect degrees of integration and community. By and large, it is an objective of social policy to build the identity of a person around some community with which he or she is associated.[5]

These ideas are further developed in writings addressed to the definition of the concept of a "welfare state."

. . . the resources of the nation can and must be used for what the Elizabethans called the "common weal," which is at once the basis and essence of the Welfare State.[6]

Indeed, they are carried forward by some writers into a discussion of the meaning of citizenship in modern societies.[7]

Roland Warren provides a systems analysis of community functions that will be used here as a basis for a review of how the conflict between rural ideals and urbanization has more specific effects on the systemic function of social welfare organizations. The principle community functions may be distinguished: production, distribution, consumption; socialization; social control; mutual support; and social participation.[8] It is evident that social welfare includes important functions in each of these areas.

Socialization

Social welfare services are evident in carrying out a variety of *socialization* functions, socialization being defined as "that process through which individuals, through learning, acquire the knowledge, values and behaviour patterns of their society and learn behaviour appropriate to their social roles."[9] This important sphere of social welfare activity is not only a dominant focus of much work with children, but is present in such fields of practice with adults as family therapy, debt and budget counselling, and marriage counselling.

A broad view of socialization must begin with consideration of the role of such primary institutions as the family and the church and the ways in which traditionally they have provided the means for individuals to learn mutually acceptable patterns of behaviour. This broad view can then be extended to include the role being played by established formal institutions, particularly schools, whose institutional role in socialization is fully accepted in the community. However, this range of institutions appears to have been inadequate to the learning need of persons in today's complex urban society. As a result, they have been supplemented by a variety of additional institutions, including the development (aided and abetted by commercial interests that also serve important socialization functions) of a teenage culture. They also include the deviant expressions of those learning needs in the conduct of delinquency and in the formation of delinquent groups. Finally, they include an array of welfare institutions distinguished from the institutions previously mentioned by the facts that they do not have a commercial motive and formally adopt a community-based (moral) view of behaviour between individuals. These welfare institutions can be further distinguished by the way in which they act as agents of socialization. The terminology of prevention[10] assists in such a classification.

At the primary preventative end of the continuum are the declared educational services, for example, family life education, sex education, drug information programs. These services are distributed broadly to the community as a whole and the case is increasingly made that they should be mandatory parts of the socialization all young people receive. Hence, arguments are advanced for including them in the curricula of school systems.

At the secondary level of prevention are the developing social utility services, such as day care and homemaker services, and recreational services such as Boys Clubs, which are intended to meet the needs of potential problem populations. These services are usually located to make them readily accessible to the populations who are perceived as most requiring them. Thus, if single-parent families are seen as having increased socialization needs, attention is given to making such services as day care accessible and financially feasible to this population. Further, the day-care service may be supplemented by educational programming dealing with the particular situation of single parents.

At a tertiary level of prevention are the case-specific services such as family therapy, debt counselling, and family planning clinics, all of which require that specific individuals come forward with service requests.

Beyond these services are those made mandatory on specific populations, e.g., correctional services and the committal aspects of mental illness services. However, with the addition of these mandatory powers to force services on people, it would appear that the emphasis on social control is sharply increased. Thus, although these services also perform socialization functions, they are discussed under the heading of social control.

Social Control

Important social control functions are performed by social welfare, social control being defined as the "process through which a group influences the behaviour of its members towards conformity with its norms."[11] The means used to obtain social control may be classified with respect to the type of power they use: physical, material, or symbolic.

> The use of a gun, a whip or a lock is physical since it affects the body; the threat to use physical sanctions is viewed as physical because the effect on the subject is similar in kind, if not . . . in intensity, to the actual use. Control based on application of physical means is ascribed as *coercive* power.
>
> Material rewards consist of goods and services. The granting of symbols (e.g., money) which allow one to acquire goods and services is classified as material because the effect on the recipient is similar to that of material means. The use of material means for control purposes constitutes *utilitarian* power.
>
> Pure symbols are those whose use does not constitute a physical threat or a claim on material rewards. They include normative symbols, those of prestige and esteem; and social symbols, those of love and acceptance . . . . The use of symbols for control purposes is referred to as *normative, narrative-social,* or *social* power.[12]

The most coercive social control agencies, the military and the police, are generally regarded as outside the orbit of social welfare, (although some aspects of police work, for example, in youth work, are similar in form and intent to the practice of social agencies). However, throughout its history social welfare has been associated with various total institutions – jails, mental hospitals, work houses, and the like – that are testimony to the coercive social control functions of social welfare.

There is a high degree of ambivalence with respect to the use of coercive power for social welfare purposes. On the one hand, the use of coercive power to obtain either the segregation and/or compliance of another person is an affront to the social welfare values of faith in man and democracy. On the other hand, the right of individuals to protection from their fellow men cannot be denied, nor can social welfare dissociate itself from the effects of social control measures on the populations singled out for sanctions.

The result of this ambivalence is seen in the peripheral role that social welfare organizations typically play with respect to the primary instruments of coercive social control, the police and the courts. The recognizable social welfare and social work aspects of such institutions as mental hospitals and jails are to be found in functions designed to mediate their relationships with the community. Thus, probation and parole programs with respect to correction and after-care programs with respect to mental illness facilities are typically regarded as part of social welfare. Furthermore, the internal programs of such institutions, which either serve to assist in the process of rehabilitation or have bearing on the internal democracy of the institution, are also regarded as parts of social welfare and may be staffed by social workers.

The use of utilitarian power for social control purposes, particularly the effects of the granting or withholding of welfare payments on the willingness of people to take low-paid and unpleasant work has already been discussed. A similar social control effect should also be noticed in the behaviour of social agencies dealing with the problem of narcotic addiction. The introduction of medication programs, e.g., methadone treatment, places such agencies in the situation of seeking to obtain social control over a deviant population by utilitarian means.

Although there is noticeable ambivalence in the social welfare literature around the use of utilitarian power for social control purposes, it is much more acceptable than coercive power. Thus, the institutions that use utilitarian power for social control are regarded as social welfare institutions and social workers frequently become their principal executives.

Normative or social power would appear to be the most acceptable form of power to social welfare enterprises. The most pervasive use of such power is found in the way social welfare enterprises ascribe status to their service populations. The symbolic ascriptions used – "on welfare," debtor, addict, neurotic, etc. – all have stigmatizing consequences. Social welfare agencies obtain change in service populations partly by their power to ascribe such statuses and then symbolically to remove them when the process of rehabilitation is complete. This use of normative and social power for social control purposes represents the point at which social control functions blend with socialization functions.

The difference in the degree of acceptability to social welfare values of the three types of power is related to the alienating characteristics of the use of power for social control purposes.

> The use of the coercive power is more alienating to those subject to it than is the use of utilitarian power, and the use of utilitarian power is more alienating than the use of normative power. Or, to put it the other way around, normative power tends . . . to generate more commitment than utilitarian, and utilitarian than coercive.[13]

Unfortunately the complex urban communities we have created exhibit social tensions and destructive behaviours we do not know how to control by normative or utilitarian means. Hence, coercive power remains essential. Nevertheless, the thrust of welfare values is toward the least possible use of coercive power for social control purposes. This in essence is what is being sought with respect to narcotic addiction. It is not known whether a program based on methadone treatment (utilitarian power) and education (normative power) would be as effective in restricting narcotic use as a coercive program, but it is known that such a program would be less alienating. Hence, social welfare spokesmen can be expected to remain its advocates.

This thrust is also apparent in the support consistently given to de-institutionalization objectives for the handicapped, retarded, mentally ill, and elderly. Everywhere the emphasis is on community living and on approximating normality, not on institutional control. In this field there has been a common interest among advocate groups, social workers, and broader government objectives of financial restraint – with substantial results in the reduction of institutionalized populations.

However, a caution must be recorded. The continued support, socialization, and control of de-institutionalized populations have not been achieved with consistency. The handicapped, retarded, and mentally ill have too often been confined by poverty and institutional neglect to the skid-row ghettoes of our towns, left to be served by churches and voluntary agencies. The resources needed to ensure "normalcy" include the community support of churches and voluntary agencies, but the budgets and professional staff needed can only be provided through consistent long-term government action. Means are needed to institutionalize this commitment and to speak for these minorities.

Mutual Support

It is to the mutual support function of community that social welfare must appeal for resources. At the level of the nation, mutual support is used to rationalize the use of resources, including the graduated income tax, to support social welfare; at the level of the philanthropic social agency, the appeal is directed at both the feelings of concern and of "noblesse oblige" that it is hoped the better-off have for the less fortunate. Finally, at the level of the co-operative self-help group, the community function of mutual support is brought into play.

The inherently alienating and anomic nature of the urban community poses a threat to the mutual support function of social welfare by eroding the sense of brotherhood and common community identity necessary to its performance. Unfortunately, the bureaucratic and professional means used to deliver social welfare programs contribute to the sense of separateness between peoples. The establishment of efficient, but impersonal, federated fund-raising mechanisms and the development of large, government social agencies that operate inevitably as bureaucracies contribute to this separation of helper from helped.

However, one should not underestimate the value of the substantial number of non-profit service groups that provide a substantial alternative to government direct action. Through voluntary service action in the Boys Clubs, Scouts, Kinsmen, and churches (to name but a few), a substantial and continuing contribution is made to community mutual support. A broad-based community framework exists that has a capacity of its own for non-partisan action on behalf of others. Governments have increasingly used this framework through contracting and privatization policies, which can lead to improved services in the sense that they are more efficient and better integrated into communities than direct government services.

Social Participation

Social participation as a systemic function of community receives considerable moral support from the social welfare ideal of democracy. People *should* exercise a right to be heard in relation to decisions that affect them; conversely, they should not be alienated from their surroundings.

This thrust in social welfare thinking was endorsed in the American War on Poverty, Office of Economic Opportunity programs under the heading of "maximum feasible participation." A similar ideal was expressed in Canada in relation to the social action goals of the Company of Young Canadians. In addition, the Department of the Secretary of State and the Welfare Grants Division of the Department of National Health and Welfare were active in supporting demonstration projects aimed to give poor people's groups a voice. The creation of the National Council of Welfare, with representatives of the poor forming half the Board, is additional evidence of the search for means to allow the participation of consumers in the design and operation of social welfare.

It has long been accepted that social welfare provides an opportunity for community participation to those of philanthropic means and high social status. Similarly, service groups provide a broad path to social participation to those community members willing to act personally for the collective good.

There have been many attempts to extend this ethic further so that the welfare consumers can also make a contribution to their own social development and welfare. In some communities strong grassroots organizations have provided a consistent means for the least advantaged citizens to make their views known. These organizations have been most successful where they have had control of the resources needed to ensure their continued existence. Where they have been dependent on government funding, problems of a political nature have tended to obstruct the achievement of their goals:

> The desire of the Canadian government to encourage participation at the grassroots is matched by its apprehension about the people who are animating the neighbourhood population. The recent fervor over the Company of Young Canadians, reflects this ambivalence, for the basic problem that emerged was not so much the adequacy of the C.Y.C.'s performance as the uneasiness with which leaders in and out of government responded to the left-wing postures adopted by some of its members.[14]

The group that readily accepts government grants all too often finds that the same grants can become the means of its social control.

The following cycle of events was observed in a number of centres in Canada in the sixties and seventies. A welfare rights group would be formed on a voluntary, unsupported basis. The group would receive advice from one of the Company of Young Canadians, the Department of the Secretary of State, or the Department of National Health and Welfare. A grant would be provided to the group so that it could rent an office, prepare a newsletter, and pay an organizer and its members' out-of-pocket expenses. The group, and particularly its newly appointed paid organizer, would become more vocal and visible. It would attract local media interest. The group would be critical of social welfare authorities and organize pickets, "sit-ins," confrontations, and the like. The local welfare authority's complaints at this treatment would be expressed through both bureaucratic and political channels. The granting agency would come under considerable pressure to curb the protest group's militancy. It would yield to pressure reluctantly, but conditions would be attached to the grant, such as different organizers and an insistence on co-operation with local welfare authorities and no disruptive tactics. The protest group would be split into a moderate, funded group and a militant, fundless faction. The subsequent internal quarrelling would destroy community respect and support for the group, which would eventually die.

Organizing the participation of the poor is endorsed as an ideal, but effective participation involves long-term commitment and a willingness to contribute and compromise as well as to demand. The more successful organizations of disadvantaged people appear to have been built on identities other than "poverty" or "welfare." It may be that these labels are too stigmatizing to be a basis for long-term community action. Thus, immigrants have always organized themselves around their ethnic origins, institutions, churches, and language – not their poverty. Similarly, native peoples are now reaching into their roots and are finding a heritage of pride and independence from which they can assert long-term goals for themselves as people. Womanhood, too, has become an important source of identification and pride. These strengthened senses of identity and pride provide a basis for independent organization and hence the ability to participate in political action.

The Nature of the Community Ideal

Throughout the previous discussion of community functions and their relationship to social welfare, there is the underlying issue posed by the basically conservative nature of the concept of community. "Conservative," in this context, means a normative thrust toward the retention of the known and toward the orderly transformation of institutions.

Further, there is a distinct bias in the direction of identifying community interests with the interests of the best-known and most articulate spokespersons. H. Lithwick points to the fact that the problems we habitually identify as urban, e.g., unsightly old housing, downtown congestion, lack of central park space, polluted downtown air, are principally the problems of an elite consisting of business people, media personnel, artists, and intellectuals.

> Because the elite, as defined above, are the articulate members of society, their problems have dominated the debate on the urban crisis. Thus, urban policies have been oriented to improving the urban environment, rather than improving the lot of urban residents. As a result, there has probably been a substantial redistribution of resources in favour of the elite, aggravating the problems of urban inequity.[15]

The concept of community therefore can have a normative bias toward established interests.

Given this bias, it is not surprising that social agencies appealing to a concept of community typically adopt the role of enlightened conservatives in their commentary on the social order. As such, they provide ways whereby the deviant individual or group and the society can accommodate to each other with the least possible change on the part of the society. The dilemma of the Commission of Inquiry into the Non-Medical Use of Drugs headed by Gerald Le Dain illustrated both the process and the typical conclusion. The three-way split in the commissioners' conclusions with respect to cannabis was particularly instructive.

The majority view expressed by Gerald Le Dain, Henry Lehmann, and Peter Stein took a compromising position typical of much social welfare thought. Cannabis was not to be legalized "because of serious ground for concern about its use," particularly expressed with respect to "the use of Cannabis by adolescents."[16] The "serious ground" referred to took the form of apprehension of the commission, which mirrored apprehensions of the community. Nevertheless, the majority of the commissioners could not treat lightly the fact that enforcement practices and penalties with respect to cannabis use were themselves a cause of serious social problems. Thus, the final recommendation was directed toward "the repeal of the prohibition against the simple possession of Cannabis"[17] but the retention of reduced sanctions against cultivation, importation, and trafficking.

Too radical for the majority was the much simpler position of commissioner Marie-Andrée Bertrand, who spoke for full legalization;[18] too repressive was the much simpler position of commissioner Ian L. Campbell, who recommended "retention of sanctions against possession as well as against trafficking."[19]

Effects on Social Welfare

The process of developing support mandates for social programs has entailed a compromise between the values of social welfare and the realities of community. The effects of this compromise are widely evident in the programs operated by social agencies. The following common features of these programs can be traced to this source.

1. *Ambiguous objectives.* The objectives of social programs are frequently ambiguous, may be deficient in both comprehensiveness and internal logic, and on occasion may not even exist at all. The majority report of the Le Dain Commission illustrated both the typical form and the origin of these deficiencies.

The effects of such ambiguity contribute to the problems of service duplication, resource inadequacy, interagency competition, and co-ordination. These effects will be evident in the discussion of social service delivery systems (Chapters Five, Six, and Seven).

2. *The community value tends to take precedence over the individual value.* A major source of ambivalence in social welfare programming results from the fact that the interests of individuals, and the interests of the communities of which they are a part, may not converge. The essentially conservative nature of the rural community ideal increases this dilemma. Thus social workers find themselves caught between one set of values telling them to put their clients first and another set telling them to defend, if not strengthen, community. The community-centred values tend to take precedence because they receive public and political support.

3. *The emphasis is on individual change rather than community change.* This derives directly from the emphasis on community rather than individual values. Where individuals and community conflict, it is much more probable that social welfare institutions will be used to obtain harmony by changing individuals than by changing com-

munities. The distribution of social workers between individually oriented changes and social change has always been overwhelmingly on the side of individual change. The resources devoted to changing individuals are many times greater than those for planning and changing communities.

Furthermore, attempts to change communities have not had a high success rate. One can go further and question where the mandate for such change came from. In a democracy there is a legitimated process of leadership selection that, at its broadest level, provides opportunities for community change. Any alternate route is likely to be challenged sooner or later and will be found to be lacking answers to the questions of mandate, authority, and accountability.

By the end of the 1970s the conservative reaction to community action resulted in a return to direct provincial control of services and withdrawal of federal funding from community participation and action.[20] These decisions now require re-examination, as isolating services from communities results in misunderstanding and destroys the community support necessary, for example, for continued long-term community acceptance of de-institutionalized populations. The solution to this problem may well be aided by the privatization policies now being advocated – these policies place service responsibility back in the hands of community-based groups.

The dynamics of community appear more amenable to welfare values than the prescriptions of normative economic theory. Nevertheless, the effects of those dynamics are seen in a series of decisions that substantially affect the translation of welfare ideals into reality and explain some of the discrepancies that exist between values and achievements.

The discussion of these last two chapters has endeavoured to keep economic considerations separate from community considerations. Conceptually and analytically, this has its uses. However, the reality of the development of social programs necessarily involves both sets of considerations. Thus, a typical day-care program has both community (socialization) and economic (redistributive) objectives. The socialization objectives include the provision of an enriched social environment for the child. The redistributive objectives include the provision of a financial subsidy to day care to permit the attendance of the children of the poor. In the analysis of any social program, the effects of both community and economic objectives require consideration.

Notes

1. Romanyshyn, *Social Welfare*, p. 291.
2. C. Wright Mills, "The Professional Ideology of Social Pathologists," *American Journal of Sociology*, xlix (September, 1942), pp. 175–76.
3. See N.H. Lithwick, *Urban Canada: Problems and Prospects* (Ottawa: Central Mortgage and Housing Corporation, 1970).
4. United Community Services, *The Area Development Project* (Vancouver, 1968).
5. Kenneth Boulding, "The Boundaries of Social Policy," *Social Work*, v, 12 (January, 1967).
6. Maurice Bruce, *The Coming of the Welfare State* (London: Batsford, 1961), p. vii.
7. Marshall, *Class, Citizenship and Social Development*.
8. Roland Warren, *The Community in America* (New York: Rand McNally, 1963).
9. *Ibid.*, p. 174.
10. Alfred J. Kahn, *Social Policy and Social Services* (New York: Random House, 1973), pp. 139–42.
11. Warren, *The Community in America*, p. 177.
12. Amitai Etzioni, *Modern Organizations* (New York: Prentice-Hall, 1964), p. 59.
13. *Ibid.*, p. 60.
14. Ben Lappin, "The Community Workers and the Social Work Tradition" (School of Social Work, University of Toronto, 1970, unpublished), p. 167.
15. Lithwick, *Urban Canada*, p. 18.
16. Canada, *Interim Report of the Commission of Inquiry into the Non-Medical Use of Drugs* (Ottawa: Information Canada, 1970), p. 301.
17. *Ibid.*, p. 302.
18. *Ibid.*, pp. 303–10.
19. *Ibid.*, pp. 310–16.
20. Brian Wharf, "Citizen Participation in Social Policy," in S. Yelaja, *Canadian Social Policy* (Waterloo, Ont.: Wilfrid Laurier University Press, 1978).

Chapter 4

POWER

Provision for social welfare, that is, the translation of welfare values into welfare programs, requires the exercise of power. The Canadian Tax Foundation attributed $20 billion to direct income security programs in 1981;[1] the Macdonald Commission attributed $60 billion to both direct programs and indirect tax expenditures in 1984. These redistributive expenditures themselves evidence power in operation. In addition, thousands of civil servants, administrators, social workers, and others are employed in social administrations, the purpose of which is to retain social control over deviant populations. All of these workers evidence power in one form or another.

Power is the essence of social welfare and this chapter will deal with principal features of the way the organization of power in Canadian society affects social welfare. As such, it will deal principally with the operation of the Canadian state.

In the following discussion the concept of the Canadian state should be distinguished from the concept of a Canadian government. Canada possesses not one government able to exercise power over welfare but a multiplicity of governments – federal, provincial, and municipal. Furthermore, important powers are held by the courts and by the administrative bureaucracies created by the act of making social provision.

The concentration here on the state and social welfare should not be read as implying that the state has a monopoly of power with respect to welfare. However, the following review of the alternatives to state power makes the dominance of such power readily apparent.

Three alternatives exist: philanthropic organizations, co-operative organizations, and entrepreneurial or corporate organizations. First is the role played by *philanthropic organizations*, including all those organizations supported either by united funds and community chests or by their own private campaigns. The total financial resources raised by such means in Canada have in recent years approximated $300 million, less than one per cent of state expenditures. As a consequence, the major issue during the last thirty years confronting the allocation committees of united funds and the administration of the philanthropic social agencies has been what useful supplementary roles might be performed – supplementary, that is, to the major roles played by the state.

This has been the principal question faced by such planning studies as the Vancouver Chest and Council's Priorities Study (1964) and by the Winnipeg Social Audit (1971).[2] The answers provided by such studies include programming designed to supplement government activities: (1) by supporting services not receiving government support, for example, the recreational programming of YMCAS, YWCAS, Boys Clubs, Neighbourhood Houses; (2) by supporting services designed to increase the responsiveness of state services; and (3) by pioneering new services to previously unserved problems and populations.

These are not unimportant activities. Nevertheless, each function is, in its own way, a secondary function in a state-dominated field. Further, as such services are perceived as important to the general welfare, the organizations that provide them have been successful in obtaining state funds given in the form of contracts for service, grants, etc. In the course of time, 95 per cent or more of the budget of such nominally "philanthropic" organizations as children's aid societies have been derived from such sources. This development was frequently the prelude to the complete assumption of responsibility by government.

During the early 1980s an attempt was made by neo-conservative governments to reverse this trend. The 1983 B.C. restraint program was accompanied by rhetoric on the role of voluntary agencies. It was assumed that as government services were reduced, voluntarism would flourish, filling the gap. Despite valiant efforts to provide services withdrawn by government, the resources were not and are not there.

Second, there is the role played by *co-operative organizations*. Included under this heading are such organizations as Alcoholics Anonymous, organizations of ex-prisoners, low-income citizen groups, and counter-culture organizations for transient youth and drug problems. This is an alive and vital section of the social welfare enterprise, but it is relatively powerless in terms of control over resources. What power it has is basically directed toward making government services more responsive to the interests of particular groups of consumers of those services. The viability of this sector was increased considerably in the 1970s through its use of a variety of government grants – Opportunities for Youth, Local Initiatives Programs, National Health and Welfare, Welfare Grants – to extend its ability to provide services. In the 1980s these grants have been either "capped" or withdrawn. Furthermore, receipt of grants has proved to be a prelude to restrictive conditions of receipt, whereby the organization's ability to provide service to its clients is made conditional on its curbing advocacy actions that place government in an unfavourable light.

Finally, there is the role played by *entrepreneurial* or *corporate organizations*. These include such private services to individuals as marriage and family counselling for which the individual pays a fee. The practitioner supports himself in private practice. These services are organized primarily on a medical model and practitioners usually advocate the extension of government medicare-type coverage to their practice. Also included under this heading are such entrepreneurial activities as competitive tendering for contracts to provide services or to evaluate programs. This sector of non-government activity has grown substantially – aided by government policies of privatization. However, the source of such contracts is almost exclusively government, hence the apparent independence of the entrepreneurial or corporate organization that obtains its income from service contracts is largely illusory.

The dominance of state power is seen in the way the roles played by these three alternatives to state power – philanthropy, co-operatives, and corporations – are determined by how state power is used. The dominance of the state in social welfare matters is also fundamentally desirable. Social welfare involves the exercise of considerable coercive, utilitarian, and normative powers. It is a mark of civilized society that coercive power is unified – which, in an industrialized society, implies a state function. Further, establishment of social policy involves moral choices. It is fundamentally desirable that such choices at policy, program, and administrative levels are accountable to the society. This is achieved through the state exercising major authority over social welfare. For these reasons, all students of social welfare have to concern themselves with the processes by which the state makes decisions.

The Constitutional Context

The Canadian state is a federal state, the constitution of which provides formal sanction for the existence of a federal government and ten provincial governments. Power for social welfare functions is divided between the federal government and provinces. In specific terms the British North America Act, now incorporated into the Canadian constitution, states:

91. It shall be lawful for the Queen, by and with the Advice and Consent of the Senate and the House of Commons, to make Laws for the Peace, Order and good Government of Canada, in relation to all matters not coming within the Classes of Subjects by this Act assigned exclusively to the Legislatures of the Provinces; and for greater Certainty, but not so as to restrict the Generality of the foregoing Terms of this Section, it is hereby declared that (notwithstanding anything in this Act) the exclusive Legislative Authority of the Parliament of Canada extends to . . .

    2. The Regulation of Trade and Commerce
    2A. Unemployment Insurance
    7. Militia, Military and Naval Service and Defence
    11. Quarantine and the Establishment and Maintenance of Marine Hospitals

24. Indians, and Lands reserved for Indians

25. Naturalization and Aliens

27. The Criminal Law, . . .

28. The Establishment, Maintenance, and Management of Penitentiaries . . .

92. In each Province the Legislature may exclusively make Laws in relation to Matters coming within the Classes of Subject next hereinafter enumerated; that is to say,

6. The Establishment, Maintenance, and Management of Public Reformatory Prisons, in and for the Province

7. The Establishment, Maintenance, and Management of Hospitals, Asylums, Charities and Eleemosynary Institutions, in and for the Province, other than Marine Hospitals

16. Generally all Matters of a merely local or Private Nature in the Province

94A. The Parliament of Canada may make laws in relation to old age pensions and supplementary benefits, including survivor's and disability benefits unrespective of age, but no law shall affect the operation of any law present or future of a provincial legislature in relation to any such matter.

This formal division of powers has been interpreted as providing to the provinces primary jurisdiction over social welfare. The combined effect of Sections 91 and 92 resulted in the provinces having all the general powers in the field of social welfare that are not included in the specific list of federal powers included under Sections 91 and 94A. This interpretation has been established as a result of the federal government seeking increased powers, certain of the provinces opposing such powers, and the issues of division of powers ultimately reaching the courts.

The role of the courts, and specifically of the Privy Council, was seen when, in 1937, the federal Employment and Social Insurance Act was deemed *ultra vires*. In that instance the Attorney General for Ontario brought action against the Attorney General for Canada. The Supreme Court of Canada ruled 4 to 2 in favour of Ontario. Canada appealed to the Privy Council and the judgement of the Supreme Court was upheld. In 1940, the legislative authority for unemployment insurance was obtained by the federal government through the adoption of a constitutional amendment specifying parliamentary jurisdiction (Section 91, subsection [2A]).

Forewarned by this sequence of events, the federal government sought and obtained a constitutional amendment in 1951 giving it authority to make laws in relation to old age pensions (Section 94A). This authority was extended in 1964 to cover survivors, disability, and supplementary benefits, allowing the introduction of the Canada Pension Plan. The power of the Parliament of Canada to make laws affecting social welfare has thus been limited by the constitution and the courts. However, this sequence of events serves to raise the questions of why the federal government should seek such powers, and why, in turn, certain of the provinces should oppose them.

The principal reasons for greater federal powers over social welfare were stated by the government of Canada as part of the background preparation for the 1968 constitutional conference.[3] Dealing with income security measures, the principle reasons given were:

1. *Income redistribution*. The federal government asserted a role in redistributing income nationally, benefiting the populations of poorer provinces at the expense of the wealthier. Only the Parliament of Canada could provide for such a redistribution, hence the need for federal powers.

2. *The sense of community*. The range of social welfare income security measures, family allowances, old age security, unemployment insurance, etc. is viewed by the federal government as contributing to a sense of national unity. Receipt of cash benefits by persons is seen as one of the most tangible benefits conferred by a government. The federal government wishes to exercise this power.

3. *Portability*. The Canadian people move frequently between provinces. It is undesirable that benefits vary sharply between provinces. Such variations would tend to deprive some people of benefits they might have expected and hence would tend to impede the movements of people.

4. *Economic policy*. Because income payments made by the federal government affect the total demand for goods and services, they are a part of the means used by the government of Canada to

stabilize the economy. Thus the federal power over economic policy requires the exercise of welfare powers.

5. *Service equality*. In the field of social services, the federal government was prepared to concede a primary role to the provinces.
However, a national interest was asserted in social services, that
of ensuring a reasonable measure of service equality between
provinces. This goal reflected one of the central objectives of federal social policy, first asserted by the Royal Commission on Dominion-Provincial Relations (1940):

> Not only national duty and decency, if Canada is to be a nation
> at all, but equity and national self-interest demand that the
> residents of these areas be given average services and equal
> opportunities, – equity because these areas may have been
> impoverished by the national economic policies which en-
> riched other areas, and which were adopted in the general
> interest.[4]

To these five reasons, two additional ones can be added. As a
result of the establishment of a Charter of Rights within the Canadian constitution, Canadians have been given constitutional
assurances that require Canadian – implicitly federal – interpretation and administration. Language rights and provisions for freedom of movement are two such examples, the latter having the
effect of rendering *ultra vires* a variety of provincial residency conditions that formerly restricted welfare rights.

The last reason for direct federal action is federal visibility. Federal leaders during the 1970s and early 1980s were concerned to
ensure that the policies and programs carried out with the support
of federal fiscal powers were known to be federal actions. The
federal presence in the form of logos, signs, press releases, and
specific actions was seen as necessary to maintaining popular support for both the federal state and for the government of the day.
Programs that permit that visibility to be reduced through provincial administration were viewed as deficient from the federal
political perspectives, however effective were their results. Conversely, inefficient and ineffective programs were continued because they were supported by visible pro-federal groups.

These reasons for the assertion of a federal power with respect to social welfare are in no way peculiar to Canada. Indeed, the history of the development of social welfare programs throughout the Western industrialized world suggests a general tendency toward the extension of the welfare powers of national governments. Distinctive to the Canadian experience has been the opposition of certain provinces to this extension and the effects of that opposition. The principle reason given by certain provinces for opposing the exercise of federal powers are as follows:

1. *Provincial diversity.* Canada is one of the largest countries in the world. The distinct regions and their distinct peoples have differing welfare needs. Attention to such needs and to the consequent policy choices with respect to priorities is best obtained by retaining provincial jurisdiction over social welfare. At different times, different provinces have established precedents in programming, for example, the introduction of medicare in Saskatchewan in 1962, which would not have been possible if the provinces lacked jurisdictional power.

2. *Distinct linguistic and cultural identities.* The government of the province of Quebec has viewed itself as the guardian of the language and culture of the French-speaking minority within Canada. The government of Quebec has thus sought to safeguard a distinct sense of community that can be viewed as competing with the Canadian sense of community. Further, social policy has been viewed as playing a central role in the maintenance of French language and culture.

In extreme form, this view was part of the case for an independent Quebec. However, the same line of argument has been used consistently by the government of Quebec to oppose extensions of federal powers, with the result that Quebec has been the most consistent province in its opposition to an extended federal role.

3. *Fiscal reasons.* The governments of the wealthier provinces, specifically Ontario, British Columbia, and Alberta, have not always viewed favourably the argument for federal income redistributions. The federal argument implies that funds would be raised in the wealthier provinces and transferred to the poorer provinces.

Provincial politicians have to restrain themselves from appealing to the narrow self-interest of their electorate to oppose such a transfer. Inevitably, such restraint is not always apparent.

4. *Administrative efficiency and simplicity.* The effect of federal actions – in combination with provincial action – has been to produce major administrative burdens on both levels of government. The actions of two governments, often with conflicting political mandates, have resulted in contradictory programs and policies. Government at one level can have objectives of stability and reliance on the private sector while the other level of government has policies of incentives and direct government action: each tending to contradict the objectives of the other. Within the administration of joint programs these political contradictions result in major conflicts and competitiveness between federal and provincial bureaucracies. However, the net result is a largely wasted effort, with public resources consumed in purely administrative competition to no net result.

5. *The logic of single responsibility.* The development of comprehensive institutional social services is obstructed, it is argued, by the divided nature of jurisdiction over social welfare. In that more comprehensive services are desirable it is essential to locate responsibility clearly with one level of government. Furthermore, the existing divisions of power obstruct the proper accountability of governments for the services they render by confusing the electorate as to responsibility. Governments at both provincial and federal levels are able to avoid issues by claiming the other government level was responsible.

For both these reasons, single responsibility for social welfare would be preferred. As the general power presently exists at the level of the provinces, it is argued that single responsibility at the same level would be the preferred way to unify power over social welfare.

Given the sharply opposing nature of the federal and provincial reasons for wishing to assert powers over social welfare, and given, too, the primary position, established by the British North America Act and its judicial interpretation, of the provinces, it is not surprising that constitutional amendments increasing federal powers have been infrequent.

Instead of seeking constitutional amendment, the federal government has sought to extend its effective jurisdiction over social welfare through the use of those powers that it already holds under the terms of the British North America Act. This has included an expansive intepretation of the powers granted the federal government in Sections 91 and 94A and the use of the spending power of Parliament to make payments to individuals and conditional grants to provinces. These means toward extending the federal power will now be reviewed.

1. *Use of existing federal powers.* The federal government has made extensive use of those welfare powers it has been able to develop on the basis of the existing constitution. Thus, a wide array of employment services and training subsidies has been developed on the basis of the powers of the federal government with respect to the economy and on the basis of the unemployment insurance amendment. The federal responsibility for the militia and for military service has been the basis for the organization of extensive welfare services for veterans. Similarly, the federal responsibility for Indians has been used, somewhat less comprehensively, in the development of welfare services for native peoples. The federal responsibility for naturalization and aliens has been used to develop services for immigrants and also to provide support to a variety of minority groups under the general heading of "citizenship" services. The federal responsibility for the criminal law and for penitentiaries has been used in the development of national parole services.

2. *Spending power and individuals.* The government of Canada has asserted the right to make payments directly to individuals. Thus, Family Allowances were introduced in 1945 without constitutional amendment. However, while asserting this right, the government of Canada has introduced little legislation of this nature. Instead, constitutional amendments have been sought. This could be the result of apprehensions that, if challenged in the courts, such powers would not be upheld. The introduction of a guaranteed income program under this power could lead to such a challenge.

3. *Conditional grants.* The most important means used by the government of Canada to extend its influence over social welfare

have been conditional grant programs (for example, Canada Assistance Plan, Hospital Insurance, Medicare, and Public Housing provisions of the National Housing Act). A conditional grant program is one in which the federal Parliament approves legislation permitting the payment of federal funds to provinces in support of provincial welfare programs. Such programs are also referred to as "shared cost" programs.

A conditional grant program has a significant effect on the use of provincial powers. To be eligible for the federal grant, the province has to design a program that meets federal requirements. Provinces have been consistently reluctant to refuse such federal grants, largely because their electorates were already contributing to such grants through the federal taxes they were paying.

The federal government has thus been able to use conditional grants to influence provincial priorities and programs. The result is seen in the development of a similar array of basic social welfare provisions throughout Canada. The problems of the conditional grant approach to obtaining federal goals are numerous. The less wealthy regions and their provincial governments benefit less from such programming than the more wealthy regions whose provincial governments can better afford the provincial contribution to program costs.[5]

Conditional grants have had the generally undesirable effect of diffusing government accountability for social welfare programs. Instead of clear responsibility residing at either the federal or provincial level, it rests with both. In practice this leads to negotiation between governments behind closed doors. Thus, important social welfare decisions are made on the basis of intergovernmental compromise and without the benefit of debate in a single legislative forum.

In addition, administrative, legal, and fiscal complexity increases with such programming. Governments at the provincial level use their resources to seek the widest possible cost sharing, while at the federal level the definition of eligible expenditures is narrowed to restrain costs. Complex agreements on eligible costs are negotiated — only to provide the grounds for dispute as to whether all costs attributed to the agreements were in fact incurred in the manner claimed: lawyers, administrators, accountants, and auditors defend the positions of governments at both levels, travelling extensively to meet and pursue their mandates. Yet the cost of this totally unproductive exercise within the Canadian state has to be carried as an administrative expense by the Canadian taxpayer although it contributes nothing to the goals of welfare.

The seriousness of these objections to conditional grants is compounded by their extent. Particularly in the less wealthy provinces, these grants comprise such a high proportion of total provincial revenue that the independence of the provincial legislature can be said to be substantially decreased. Nevertheless, conditional grants have provided the means whereby social welfare services have been extended, with federal support, despite the existence of constitutional obstacles to a federal role.

There have been attempts to reduce the use of shared-cost programming and reduce the administrative burden. The transfer of tax points to the provinces under the "Established Programs Funding" agreement provided federal support to health and higher education while avoiding the need for a shared-cost administration review. However, such an approach fails to ensure the application of federal resources to the designated programs and obscures policy requirements, leading in turn to the erosion of federal political support for the objectives originally sought. This saga of federal-provincial constitutional politics continues unabated, and with the Meech Lake Accord (1987) it enters a new era.

The Meech Lake Accord would appear to increase provincial authority because it provides the provinces with a constitutional right to opt out of new cost-shared programs, *while continuing to receive an attributed share of expenditures* provided the province enacts its own program "compatible" with federal objectives. Widespread use of this authority would undercut the ability of the federal government to use shared-cost programs to undertake social policy objectives. However, the federal authority to undertake direct actions through its expenditure powers continues, and thus Meech Lake provides the context for further federal-provincial discussions aimed at establishing clearer jurisdictions for the two levels of government. If agreement could be reached that the federal government should have full responsibility for redistribution – because of the close relationship to economic policy and the need for equity throughout Canada – then the way would be clear for the provinces to assume full responsibility for personal social services. Such an agreement would be a major simplification of policy and administration for both fields of service – and a major means of reducing administrative costs.

The Influence of Electoral Politics

The influence of electoral politics on Canadian social welfare policies and programs is exercised within the context of the divided jurisdiction over social welfare between the federal and provincial governments. This division of jurisdiction affects the power of any government, federal or provincial, to pursue its policy aims. Thus electoral politics, that is, the choice of the party to govern by the people of one province or by the federal electorate, does not have the same direct impact on policies and programs that can be expected in a unitary state.

The election in 1963 of a Liberal government, headed by Prime Minister Pearson and committed in its electoral platform to the establishment of the Canada Pension Plan, led to extensive federal-provincial negotiation. The federal government needed to secure a constitutional amendment to introduce the plan. To obtain this concession, changes in the original thrust of the government's intention were negotiated. These included the establishment of a separate parallel plan by the province of Quebec (the Quebec Pension Plan) and provision for the establishment of a pension fund that would be invested in provincial government bonds, providing the provinces with a dependable source of capital.

The situation of a provincial government elected with a clear mandate for social reform is constitutionally more explicit. However, securing financial resources for the support of programs usually requires that a provincial government enter into negotiations with the federal government. While such negotiations are being conducted, the introduction of new programs and policies is delayed, and failure in negotiation may lead to their abandonment. This is not to suggest that electoral politics are without influence on social welfare. It does imply that political compromise between governments of different political persuasions is the characteristic route to change. The resulting programs show the marks of such compromises.

Further, it is not possible to distinguish one political party as being exclusively the proponent of social welfare ideals while another is characterized exclusively by opposition. Instead, each party can rightfully claim to have made a significant contribution to social welfare. The concluding stages of debate at both provincial and federal levels are frequently characterized by multi-party support for social welfare measures.

Despite these modifying influences on the expression of a clear welfare ideology within the field of electorial politics, significant differences exist between the major political parties.

The New Democratic Party has been the most consistent advocate of social welfare in the Canadian political spectrum. The party's political statements have, more clearly than other parties', committed it to the welfare ideal of the redistribution of income, wealth, and power. When elected to office (only achieved in British Columbia, Saskatchewan, and Manitoba), New Democratic governments have shown a willingness to introduce social welfare programs not legislated anywhere else in Canada, or indeed in North America. An example of an initiative of this type was the enactment by Saskatchewan of a provincial medicare program in 1962. The effects of these initiatives have extended beyond the provinces in which they were enacted. The federal government has been co-opted to their support and other provinces have tended to establish similar provisions at later dates.

In the federal Parliament, in which the New Democratic Party has consistently held a minority of seats, the party's spokesmen have been the advocates of social welfare programs. Long before Liberal or Progressive Conservative governments have introduced social welfare legislation, the spokesmen of the New Democratic Party and its predecessor, the Co-operative Commonwealth Federation, have brought the need of Canadians for such programs as pensions, medicare, housing, and income guarantees before the House of Commons. Indeed, some New Democratic Party MPs, for example, Stanley Knowles, earned the respect of all for their integrity and for their dogged pursuit of welfare ideals.

These consistent long-term objectives have been challenged in the 1980s and the NDP has found itself in the position of an opposition party defending the status quo from government-initiated reform. The challenge for the NDP as we look toward the 1990s is to be the friendly critic of welfare institutions, providing support to the ideals and objectives of welfare while recognizing institutional problems and resource limitations.

The Liberal Party can rightfully claim to have comprised the federal government when nearly all significant social welfare legislation has been passed by Parliament. Furthermore, committed Liberals are proud of their party's record in the welfare field. Judy LaMarsh writes of the Department of National Health and Welfare and of her being asked to be minister (1963–65):

> It is a department to a Liberal that is cherished indeed. Such greats in their time as Paul Martin and Brooke Claxton had served in that portfolio. To any Liberal, the subject matter dealt with in National Health and Welfare are "gut" issues – basic to their whole philosophy of the role of Government in modern society.[6]

Although very significant social welfare programs have been legislated by Liberal governments, there have also been periods of neglect and disinterest. Indeed, the political spokesmen of the Liberal Party appeal on occasion to the alienating aspects of welfare transfers in their search for political support. For example, during the 1972 federal election, Prime Minister Trudeau was sharply critical of the beneficiaries of unemployment insurance. He appealed to the "backlash" sentiments of the electorate rather than defending the progressive nature of the reforms made by his government during its first term of office. The record of the governments led by Trudeau generally was one of rhetorical support of welfare ideals accompanied by increasing bureaucratization of welfare functions. Sometimes it seemed that the true beneficiaries were increasingly the service staffs rather than the needy groups within the society.

At the provincial level, Liberal governments have shown a variety of attitudes toward social welfare legislation. Some Liberal governments, such as the Saskatchewan Liberals under Ross

Thatcher, have run against the welfare proposals of their New Democratic Party opponents. Other Liberal governments have established positions of leadership in the introduction of social welfare programs in their own province and in the influence they have brought to bear on the federal government. Liberal governments in Quebec have shared this emphasis. The comprehensive and substantial social reforms resulting from the Commission of Inquiry into Health and Welfare (the Castonguay-Nepeuv Report, 1971) are a good example.

The Progressive Conservative Party has had less opportunity to legislate social welfare programs at the federal level, largely because it has formed the government for only eleven (1957–63, 1979, 1984–88) of the post-war years. During these years, no substantial welfare programs were enacted. There were temporary programs (Winter Works in 1960) and minor programs (National Welfare Grants in 1962); and the foundation was laid for substantial subsequent reforms in the appointment of the Royal Commission on Health Services (1961), the Royal Commission on Taxation (1962), a commission on Old Age Pensions, and by the national day-care study (1986).

As an opposition party, the Progressive Conservatives have shown a tendency to disavow the progressive ideals expressed on occasions by their leaders. In 1969, the party's research bureau conducted a study of the guaranteed income that concluded with an emphasis on the feasibility and desirability of such a plan. The party leader, Robert Stanfield, attempted to have the plan endorsed by policy conference only to find it replaced by a compromise resolution to provide assistance for the unemployable and work incentives for the unemployed: scarcely "progressive" but certainly "conservative."

Those provinces that have had Progressive Conservative governments for extended periods, such as Ontario, have also shown a cautious attitude toward social welfare programs. Thus, the opposition of Ontario to the federal medicare program was not only based in the province's desire to protect a field it viewed to be part of provincial jurisdiction. It was also an expression of conservative political philosophy. Despite the fact that at the provincial level Conservative parties have held office more frequently than Liberal parties, it is not possible to find examples of provincial Conservative parties that have shown a strong commitment to welfare. Given the emphasis of the 1980s on restraint, it is surprising that there has not been stronger federal leadership aimed at restraint and simplification. However, the Canadian federal Conservatives have exercised great caution in the welfare field, leaving it to the provincial parties to articulate and apply restraint.

The remaining political parties that have received substantial electoral support, that is, Social Credit in Alberta and British Columbia and the Union Nationale, Créditistes, and Parti Québécois in Quebec, contributed principally to the Conservative critique of welfare institutions. (The Parti Québécois is an exception, being more like the NDP than other parties.) These parties have tended to be built around the distinctive leadership of major independent politicians. Thus, the party labels are not necessarily a good guide to the policies advocated. The Social Credit government of British Columbia under W.A.C. Bennett was less sympathetic to welfare ideals than the Social Credit government of Alberta under Ernest Manning. The Union Nationale government of Quebec under Maurice Duplessis was hostile to social welfare measures, while the Union Nationale government under Jean-Jacques Bertrand was cautiously reformist.

The 1983 Bennett government in B.C. will long be remembered for the reputation it established for cutbacks and mass firings of civil servants. The rhetoric was of removing the state from areas of activity that should be left to families and to charitable institutions. The effect of this rhetoric and of its hasty application contributed to widespread opposition to the Bennett government, an opposition that was defused by Bennett's resignation.

The Influence of the Bureaucracy

Provision for social welfare has required the creation of substantial administrative departments at each of the federal, provincial, and municipal levels of government. These departments are the result of political decisions and become the recipients of the powers needed to carry out these decisions. Whereas the elected governments are invested with the formal powers of the state, the actual day-to-day operations and the power that derives therefrom are held by the bureaucracy. The billions of dollars and the thousands of civil servants and professional social workers involved represent a very substantial vested interest.

The division of powers between federal and provincial governments increases the power and influence of the bureaucracy. It also has the effect of removing political decision-making with respect to policy from elected assemblies to intergovernmental negotiations between federal and provincial bureaucracies. In 1973, the federal government published the Working Paper on Social Security in Canada and called for the participation of the provinces in "a joint federal-provincial review of Canada's total social security system."[7] The ministers of welfare with their officials met to agree on general principles for the review but the actual task of conducting the review and preparing policy options was the work of officials. The influence of officials on the scope of choice in policies was thus considerable.

Federal and provincial civil servants have a substantial common interest in working together competitively on such a task. The competition referred to is collegial, with its primary goal being the reputation for understanding and astuteness of the individual. The career civil servant works within the context of existing social welfare programs. The day-to-day dealings necessary for the conduct of the large conditional grant programs require the maintenance of working agreements and relationships. Individuals involved share similar backgrounds, usually in social work or public administration, participate in career patterns that move from provincial bureaucracy to federal bureaucracy, and share similar values and goals with respect to social welfare programming. This creates a situation in which innovation and change tend to be preceded by informal discussion and persuasion rather than by political confrontation.

The non-political claim of the Canadian civil services, both federal and provincial, reinforces the influence exercised by the bureaucracy. Power and influence are held by officials whose tenure is secured by invisibility and whose seniority is secured by the respect of their peers. The Department of National Health and Welfare has been a major and enduring influence on the development of social welfare. The senior officials of the department sought to influence the course of social policy through various types of activity.

1. *Federal-provincial meetings.* Federal-provincial meetings of officials have been held regularly. They have been necessary to ensure the proper operation of shared-cost programs but they have also served as a forum for the exchange of ideas and experiences and for a process of education.

2. *Consultation.* Consultation between federal and provincial officials has extended both the transfer of ideas and the resolution of program issues.

3. *Support for progressive provincial initiatives.* Where provinces engaged in progressive experiments and/or changes in programming, the officials of Health and Welfare Canada have endeavoured to obtain federal fiscal and political support.

4. *Demonstration programming.* Federal officials have actively encouraged the development of new approaches to social welfare programming through demonstration grants. The Welfare Grants division, established in 1962, has been a major focus for such activities.

5. *Research and education.* The Welfare Grants division has also been used to support research and social service education. Officials of Health and Welfare view weakness in these areas as damaging to the quality of social welfare provision.

6. *Support to national agencies.* Federal officials have recognized that the monopolistic nature of their own agencies had perils of its own. To support a free exchange of ideas, support has consistently been provided to the Canadian Council on Social Development and to other Canadian national welfare agencies.

Until the mid-1960s the major direction of influence appeared to be from federal to provincial officials. The federal officials were, in essence, introducing new programs to their provincial counterparts and organizing them so that both federal and provincial officials would give similar advice to their respective ministers. By these means, agreement could be achieved in the federal-provincial meetings at the ministerial level through which social policy in Canada was made. Such an approach to social reform tended to be closed, cautious, and secretive. An idea thrust prematurely into the political domain was likely to be divisive. Because effective change required federal-provincial co-operation, such divisiveness was avoided wherever possible.

The character of the bureaucracy's influence has had a major impact on the translation of values into provision. An elite corps of senior federal officials, aided by some of their provincial counterparts, provided an enduring and consistent force for social welfare reform. On the other hand, such factors as consideration for one another's interests, a preference for change through education and agreement, and avoidance of political controversy tended to produce a process of slow change.

Since the mid-1960s some provinces, notably Quebec, Manitoba, Saskatchewan, and British Columbia, have advanced substantial social welfare reform proposals of their own. These can be viewed as products of the more knowledgeable and able provincial social welfare planning sections that have been developed. These independent provincial proposals have tended to produce a more open debate of policy options. They have also resulted in more specific and different objectives that have made a co-operative approach to welfare administration difficult to achieve.

In addition, emphasis has increased at both federal and provincial levels on staffing policies that focus on management expertise rather than sectoral knowledge in senior staff. This emphasis has been accompanied by policies of moving senior staff between ministries. Both sets of staffing policies have made it more difficult for civil servants to bring a consistent influence to bear on social policy.[8]

Special Interest Groups

On occasion, special interest groups have perceived new social welfare provisions as infringing on their established interests. Where this has happened, there has been a marked tendency to fight back and to attempt to obstruct or alter the new provision. Although such attempts have often failed to attain their major objective, they have nevertheless left their imprint on the final form of social legislation. Three examples of such episodes will illustrate the characteristic pattern.

The introduction of Medicare in Saskatchewan in 1962 and in Quebec in 1969 was marked by physicians first threatening to withdraw their services and then actually withdrawing them. Of the two physicians' strikes, the one in Saskatchewan was the more seriously fought, largely because Saskatchewan was the first example in North America of what was referred to as "socialized medicine." In each case, the strike was less than 100 per cent successful in ending medical practice. Further, the strikes ended and medical practice was resumed without any occurrence of the serious consequences of which doctors warned, such as a mass exodus of physicians from the province. Nevertheless, the physicians appear to have been bought off. Their already high incomes have become higher under Medicare. The fee-for-service basis of payment, which physicians consider protects their independence of practice, has been retained, and there has been no serious attempt to reform the delivery of medical service or to ensure equitable geographic or socio-economic distribution.

The introduction of the Canada Pension Plan was marked by the opposition of the Canadian life insurance industry. Judy LaMarsh provided an entertaining account of a group of insurance company presidents visiting her with the intention of persuading her not to proceed with the legislation:

> We had no real meeting of minds at all, although the discussion was polite enough, because I could not understand their bland assumption that we would renege on our election promises, and they could not make me see that it would be better all round, and less disruptive of business, if we just forgot the whole thing.[9]

Having had an unsympathetic hearing, the life insurance industry went on to lobby in national and provincial capitals. Advisers from the industry tried to bring influence to bear through those Conservative premiers to whom they looked for support, specifically John Robarts in Ontario and Duff Roblin in Manitoba. In the end, the campaign failed to prevent the legislation of the Canada Pension Plan.

However, some effects of this campaign remain. Judy LaMarsh herself pointed out that the Canada Pension Plan was designed with the expectation that private insurance plans would be "stacked" over the government plan. This is another way of admitting that the government plan would provide a rather low level of benefit so that the interests of the private insurance industry would not be seriously hurt. In addition, the right of individuals to deduct life insurance premiums from their pre-tax earnings was retained and subsequently the amount deductable was increased.

The third and final example was more successful from the perspective of the special interest group involved. During the ministry of John Munro, the National Welfare Grants program of the Department of National Health and Welfare was used to fund a considerable number of welfare rights groups in Canadian metropolitan areas. The idea behind this funding was that people on welfare should have rights with respect to the services they receive and that the exercise of power to obtain such rights would have useful effects in reducing alienation. These ideas were imported from the American War on Poverty, Office of Economic Opportunity, Community Action programs. As was to be expected, the welfare rights groups organized protests, organized sit-ins in welfare offices, published newsletters, sought publicity in the press, and generally tried to influence public assistance programs by harassing and cajoling local and provincial officials.

The vested interest involved in this case was part of the welfare establishment itself and it proved capable of defending that interest. The support of local politicians was obtained. The minister had to confront angry MPs from his own party and angry Liberals from his own constituency. Grants were cut back, conditions were attached to their use, and no enduring program supporting such groups was created.

These three examples illustrate the influence of special interest groups. Direct internal observation of the day-to-day business of government indicates that the influence of such groups is more pervasive than these examples suggest. Their success more often results in social reform *not* taking place than in the reversal of existing programs. It is, of course, difficult if not impossible to study what obstructive action occurs in secret. Hence, the role of special interests remains cloaked in speculation.

Consumers of Service

The "power" of the consumer of social service remains a subject of major concern. The democratic ideals of social welfare and the concern with alienation – which is linked in the sociological literature to powerlessness[10] – make it desirable that consumers possess power with respect to institutions that affect them. These ideas have received widespread endorsement and there has been a very considerable number of local "client" organizations formed. At the national level, conferences of poor people led in the 1970s to the establishment of such organizations as the National Anti-Poverty Organization, National Indian Brotherhood, National Association of Public Housing Tenants,[11] and National Council of Welfare.

At the same time, the concept of citizen participation in social welfare received considerable attention.[12] The concepts of citizen and consumer are linked in this literature, possessing both similarities and differences. Both terms are capable of broad application. All are citizens, but all are also consumers of social services – sooner or later. Both concepts are used in endorsing the need to find means to influence social welfare organizations. The intention in both cases is to reduce the effects of bureaucratic and professional power and hence make the consequent provisions more democratic, more responsive to need. There is also a similarity in the meaning commonly given to the concepts of "citizen" and "consumer" in the context of social welfare programs. The citizen or consumer spoken of is often thought of as being one who is poor and unrepresented at present in decision-making. Thus, the concept of "citizen" and its use in these discussions overlaps that of "consumer."

Nevertheless, there are differences. The concept of "citizen" has a broader meaning than that of "consumer." Any adult person is equally a "citizen," but the consumption of social services is unequal between citizens. When the concept of citizen participation is used, it tends to lead in the direction of the establishment of community councils representing the whole range of interests present in a community. Of these groups, "consumers of service" is but one. To apply the concept of citizen participation requires that the "others" be identified. In practice, the resulting councils tend to be composed of consumers, plus local professionals such as school principals, members of the clergy, and local businessmen. The logic or "representative" nature of this selection is difficult to defend.

On the other hand, "consumer" is linked to other contemporary developments. The consumer of many services, public and private, has received attention in recent years, largely the result of the realization that organizations are much more powerful than those who consume their services. As a consequence, consumers need to develop means to exercise countervailing influence or their interests will tend to be manipulated rather than attended. In all sectors, public or private, goods or services, the search for the means to organize and obtain that influence has yet to produce significant results. The grassroots mechanisms of consumer boycotts and the political mechanisms of consumer affairs departments have appeared. However, they are still searching for the means to become effective and are not in the position of influencing established power.

The consumer of social services is particularly vulnerable to the general weaknesses of consumers. He or she confronts a bureaucratic organization that views itself, and is viewed by most citizens, as expessing the "goodwill" of the public toward the disadvantaged. The assumption that good is being done represents a major obstacle to the consumer's criticisms being heard. Indeed, the more characteristic attitude toward such criticisms is to view them as evidence of the consumer's pathology. Undercutting the position of the consumer of social services is his stigmatized identity. The consumer is a "client" who needs help; or he is a prisoner who should be punished and rehabilitated; or he is "mentally ill" and needs treatment; or he is an "unemployed employable" who needs to be motivated and trained to be a productive member of society. Futhermore, this terminology is a nicer way of expressing much more sharply stigmatizing identities such as "criminal," "crazy," "welfare bum." This combination of "good" social agencies and stigmatized consumers makes it likely that consumer protest will be depreciated.

The consumer of social service is also weakened by the monopolistic nature of social services. There are literally no alternatives to receiving service from the designated social agency. In many cases, clients are the captives of either the agency's formal coercive powers (in the case of probationers, parolees, children-in-care, and mental health committals) or of its utilitarian powers (for people on public welfare or living in public housing). These powers can be used, and have been used, to discourage the organization of effective critical groups of social service consumers.

Finally, effective consumer organization involves the development of the means to question the monopoly of information and understanding that the service organization possesses. Such means involve money and autonomy of decision-making as to which issues should be pursued. Yet all too frequently, the only source of funds to support such organizations has been government itself. This leads to a situation in which:

> Harmony exists so long as the community organization is content to operate on the funding body's terms, but when the organization seeks autonomy, the relationship breaks down. The rupture is hastened by the fact that . . . a successful community organization frequently ends up biting the hand that feeds it.[13]

No one gains from such conflict. The consumer organization serves usually to entrench opposition rather than to obtain change, and public support for both consumers and service organization is weakened.

Thus, it is not surprising that the power and influence of social service consumers are severely restricted and circumscribed. Indeed, the limited power they exercise comes not through any strength of organization they possess but rather on the basis of professional understanding of their situation. The enlightened professional realizes that lack of power tends to create alienation and dependency in the consumers, while arrogance and unresponsiveness grow in the serving organization. To avoid these effects, the professional supports the idea of organizing consumers. However, the resulting organization owes its existence to professional goodwill rather than to consumer strength.

Two exceptions to this professional base for consumer (client) advocacy are worthy of note – women's organizations and native peoples' organizations. The women's organizations are broadly based with support from all sections of the women's socio-economic spectrum (approximately 50 per cent of the wealth and income levels of the corresponding male spectrum). Women have always been disproportionately the clients of social service organizations. But seeking recognition of the problems of women, rather than the problems of welfare consumers, results in a stronger, more positive identity being established.

The native organizations have also had to face the problem of the relationships between their cultures and social welfare. For native peoples social welfare has been a major means of applying alien social policies to their cultures. The initial application has usually been well meaning but ignorant and misguided, as in the development of residential schools. Unfortunately, the damage from this first imposition is not easily undone and a second wave of services is developed to combat the problems created by the first. Native peoples are today seeking ways of separating what remains of their cultural institutions from this cycle. One of the meanings of self-government is government of cultural and social policy. Some native organizations have assumed responsibility for child welfare and others are building their capacity to do so.[14] A greater willingness to respect native culture and institutions in Canada has provided a favourable context for this change. The task faced by native peoples in finding social policies to restore and invigorate their culture is substantial, yet the progress being made demands respect. The establishment of independent organizations of native peoples is a major development in the political relationships that are expressed in welfare policies and institutions.

The Media

The media are a potential source of influence on social welfare. Indeed, they are sometimes seen as the primary route to progressive social reform. The adoption of welfare ideals and social welfare programs is seen as being rendered slow and uneven by the attitudes of politicians. Politicians reflect the knowlege and attitudes of those who elect them. Social change should thus begin with change in public attitude. It is up to the media to play the critical role of presenting the facts and their "true" interpretations.

The National Council of Welfare's study, *The Press and the Poor*,[15] explores how the media treat poverty. The findings suggest that the media tend to maintain rather than alter contemporary attitudes toward the nature of poverty and social welfare. Several reasons for this tendency are suggested. The media are often monopolies – one-newspaper cities abound in Canada, for example. But the media are also expected to be responsible, to avoid the one-sided pursuit of partisan issues, and to present all sides of an issue. Where this task is done well, the result is to confirm existing understandings of issues. In addition, there are tendencies, not deliberate or malicious but inadvertent, that tend to make media coverage of poverty shallow. These include the relatively unimportant nature of the community involved, the control of most information by bureaucracies that are hostile to the disclosure of their internal affairs, and the tendency to view the situation of the poor in "we-they" terms. Because of these tendencies, the media do not always obtain their impartial ideal but instead tend to reinforce existing stereotypes and misunderstandings.

For these reasons, one can dispute whether the media, in fact, represent a progressive source of influence with respect to social welfare. Indeed, the evidence would appear to be that the influence tends to be regressive. The National Council of Welfare's study begins on a note of seeking to ensure that the media perform a role of "burying" the "cherished myths" with which the public regard poverty, and it concludes:

> Canada's press is not today providing that relevant information. On the contrary, the information it is providing, and the way it is providing it, is reinforcing those myths. Instead of shattering icons, as its self proclaimed role would have it do, it is encouraging their preservation. By failing to properly play the role it has appropriated to itself, it is not only failing the five million Canadians who are poor; nor is it failing only the general Canadian community; but as an institution overwhelmingly composed of honest and sincere practitioners, it is failing itself.[16]

Elites and Social Welfare

The classical view[17] of the distribution of power is that it is concentrated in all societies in the hands of an elite. The elite rulers
of the society control all important decisions within the society,
protect their own interests and power, and enjoy the benefits
derived therefrom. This view contrasts sharply with the most widely
held view of Western industrialized democracies, that they are
characterized by a high degree of diffusion of power. This diffuse,
pluralist[18] model of the way in which political systems work suggests that society is effectively organized into a series of competing
interest groups. Each group is able to defend and to obtain some
adjustments with respect to its particular interests and no group
is in a position to unilaterally impose its interest on others. Aspects
of both views can be seen in the ways in which different Canadian
elite groups relate to social welfare.

In his analysis of social class and power in Canada, John Porter
distinguishes a series of elites: an economic elite; a labour elite;
a political elite; a bureaucratic elite; and an ideological elite composed of the media, higher learning, and clergy.[19] Of these elite
groups only one, the *bureaucratic elite*, would appear to play a
central role in the operation of social welfare institutions. The
economic elite can be viewed as being usually hostile and, at best,
tolerant toward social welfare institutions. Porter writes:

> The Chamber of Commerce and the Canadian Manufac-
> turers' Association are together organized corporate capital-
> ism, if not at prayer, at least in an intense passion of ideology.
> At meetings and in briefs to governments the way to salvation
> which is presented is through competitive free enterprise. All
> measures toward welfarism are seen as the road to ruin. Higher
> profits, higher incomes, and lower taxes to provide initiative
> at the top are seen as essentials to social progress . . .[20]

The effects of the economic elite's influence on social welfare
appear to lie principally in their power to restrict the extent of
the welfare transfer. The egalitarian approach to taxation proposed
in the Report of the Royal Commission on Taxation (1966) trig-
gered a period of intense lobbying by economic interests seeking

to protect incentives and productivity. The subsequent Proposals for Tax Reform (1969), the results of the inquiries by the Senate and House of Commons committees (1970), and the amended Income Tax Act (1971) all led away from the egalitarian thrust of the original proposals and tended to restore incentives and restrict measures that would have supported welfare ideals. Of 333 briefs presented to the Senate committee and 543 briefs presented to the House of Commons committee, less than ten expressed welfare ideals. A similar response followed Allan MacEachen's 1981 budget, showing again the ability of business interests to organize a strong, effective response when its interests are affected.

The influence of the economic elite on individual specific measures, for example, Medicare or pensions, also appears to be substantial. The earlier discussion of the influence of interest groups at this level suggests that their power is limited, once a government is committed to change, to being able to obtain recognition of their interest rather than being able to prevent legislation. The lack of positive support for social welfare by this elite has an effect that is as damaging as outright opposition.

The *labour elite* contains allies with respect to the furthering of welfare ideals. The Canadian Labour Congress, in particular, aims to support the process of social reform:

> In the deliberations of labour conventions since 1898 there have been changes, sometimes in subject matter, sometimes in emphasis; but there has always been a persistent theme of concern with social issues which affect all citizens. The trade union movement, from its beginning until the present, has seen itself as a spokesman for ordinary working people in those matters.[21]

Social welfare, however, is not a central concern of labour in Canada. In turn, Canadian social welfare legislation has been less attentive to the relationship between social welfare and wages than in those Western countries, such as Australia, in which the labour movement has played a more substantial role in the government of social welfare.

Porter's analysis of the *political elite* suggests that "the underprivileged classes have never produced a political leader at the federal level." Canadian politics is affected substantially by "avocationalism" (political careers are interstitial in business or legal careers rather than being vocations in their own right) and by the fact that the complex structure of federalism tends to convert potentially partisan political issues into issues of administrative politics between bureaucracies. In turn:

> Avocational and administrative politics leaves the political system relatively weak as a system of institutional power. With a political elite of substantially middle class origins the dynamics of social class which give rise to conservative and progressive social forces have never worked themselves out within the political system. Perhaps it is from looking at their politicians that Canadians get the impression that their society is a middle class one. Neither the corporate elite, nor the very wealthy, have much to fear from middle class politicians. It is more likely that the politicians hold the corporate elite in awe.[22]

For these reasons, the political process has failed to bring the same degree of sharpness to the debate concerning welfare ideals as is found in those states, for example, the United Kingdom, where a political elite has been developed based on socio-economic class interests.

The bland nature of the coverage of issues that derives from the monopolistic nature of the *media elites* control of newspapers and television has already been commented on.

In 1965 Porter wrote that the *higher learning elite* contributed little to social criticism and had little impact on the society outside its walls in English Canada. French-Canadian higher learning appeared to have a more dynamic relationship with the society of which it is a part. However, such writers as Marcel Rioux[23] and Yves Martin[24] or, indeed, Pierre Trudeau, have concentrated their attention on nationalistic issues rather than on issues of social class and inequality. Neither tradition was thus particularly productive with respect to the development of a distinct Canadian welfare ideology. However, the isolation of higher learning from social welfare programs was not complete, and since 1965 there has been substantial growth in informed academic analysis of social welfare. This has been most noticeable in the growth of Marxist criticism and analysis of welfare. The results of this analysis are academically challenging but removed from the policy and administrative issues faced in social welfare administration. The impact of the analysis on the actual conduct of welfare administration is dispersed by this distance. The bureaucracy has a critique but no practical way to apply its lessons.

Whereas the higher learning elite has influenced the bureaucracy, the *religious elite* has had a distinct influence on the electoral politics of social welfare. However, there have been very strong regional and provincial characteristics to the way in which this influence has been exercised. On the Prairies, with the exception of Alberta, the Social Gospel of the Protestant churches, the agrarian populist sentiment, and the hostility to eastern business interests provided the context for the emergence of the one consistent supporter of welfare ideals in the Canadian political spectrum – the Co-operative Commonwealth Federation (now the New Democratic Party). The early leaders of the CCF-NDP, among them Woodsworth, Douglas, Knowles, were drawn principally from the ranks of the clergy. The United Church continues to be a source of progressive thought. In Alberta the same social forces, combined with fundamentalist rather than Social Gospel traditions, provided the context for the development of the Social Credit Party, which has tended to support individualism rather than welfare collectivism. In Quebec, the Roman Catholic Church viewed itself as the protector of nationalism and to this end sought and obtained control over the institutions of health, education, and welfare. It was not until the second half of this century that Quebec began the task of legislating the secular social institutions, responsible to state political processes, that are characteristic of western industrialized societies.

Thus, although the impact of churches on social welfare in Canada has been considerable, the influence has not been in one direction but has rather contributed to substantial differences in approaches to social welfare between different regions of Canada. At the national level, no unified influence exists.

This review of the relationship of elite interest groups to social welfare tends to support a pluralist-democratic view of Canadian society. An apparent process of competition between elites is only partially resolved. The partial resolution and the continuing process of competition explain in part the incomplete application of welfare values, which is characteristic of social welfare enterprises.

The forms that conflict takes and the existing alliances between the bureaucratic elite and parts of the labour elite, political elite, and religious elite exclude a major party from the discussions. The consumer of social services has no elite to represent him. Those who develop social welfare programming usually see themselves as the benevolent and understanding allies of the poor. However, they are concerned in the end to preserve the status quo by welfare means rather than to seek fundamental reform of society.

Notes

1. Canadian Tax Foundation, *The National Finances: An Analysis of the Revenues and Expenditures of the Government of Canada* (Toronto: Canada Tax Foundation, 1981).
2. Canadian Council on Social Development, *Case Studies in Social Planning: The Winnipeg Audit* (Ottawa, 1971).
3. Canada, *Income Security and Social Services* (Ottawa: Queen's Printer, 1969).
4. Canada, *Report* of Royal Commission on Dominion-Provincial Relations (Ottawa, 1940), Book II, p. 128. "These areas" refers principally to the Maritime and Prairie provinces, which were particularly hard hit during the Great Depression.
5. For a general discussion of conditional grant mechanisms, see Donald Smiley, *Conditional Grants and Canadian Federalism* (Toronto: Canadian Tax Foundation, 1973); for a discussion on their effects on social welfare programs, see D. Anderson, MSW thesis (University of Calgary, 1974).
6. Judy LaMarsh, *Memoirs of a Bird in a Gilded Cage* (Toronto: McClelland and Stewart, 1968), p. 49.
7. Canada, *Working Paper on Social Security in Canada*, p. 2.
8. Richard Splane, "Social Policy Making in the Government of Canada: Reflections of a Reformist Bureaucrat," in Yelaja, *Canadian Social Policy*.
9. LaMarsh, *Memoirs*, p. 90.
10. Melvin Seeman, "On the Meaning of Alienation," *American Sociological Review*, XXIV, 6 (December, 1959).
11. Canada, *Directory of Low Income Citizen Groups in Canada* (Ottawa: National Council of Welfare, 1973).
12. See, for example, James Draper, ed., *Citizen Participation* (Toronto: New

Press, 1971); Paul C. Vrooman, "The Power Dilemma in Citizen Participation," *Canadian Welfare*, 48, 3 (May-June, 1972); Jim Apostle, "A Question of Autonomy," *Canadian Welfare*, 48, 4 (July-August, 1972); R. Doyle, "Perceived Effectiveness of Citizen Participation," *The Social Worker*, 41, 4 (Winter, 1973).

13. Apostle, "A Question of Autonomy," *Canadian Welfare*, 48 (4).
14. The Nuchahlnuth Tribal Council and the Spallumacheen Band, for example, have entered agreements with the B.C. government that provide for delegations and recognize child welfare functions. For a full account, see Brian Wharf, *Toward First Nation Control of Child Welfare* (Victoria: University of Victoria, 1987).
15. Canada, *The Press and the Poor* (Ottawa: National Council of Welfare, 1973).
16. *Ibid.*, p. 46.
17. See, for example: Gaetano Mosca, *Ruling Class* (New York: McGraw, 1939); Vilfredo Pareto, *Mind and Society* (New York: Dover, 1935).
18. See, for example, R.A. Dahl, *Pluralist Democracy in the United States: Conflict and Consent* (New York: Rand, McNally, 1967).
19. John Porter, *The Vertical Mosaic* (Toronto: University of Toronto Press, 1965).
20. *Ibid.*, p. 306.
21. Canadian Labour Congress, *Labour's Social Objectives* (Ottawa, 1973).
22. Porter, *Vertical Mosaic*, p. 412.
23. Marcel Rioux, *Quebec in Question* (Toronto: James Lewis and Samuel, 1971).
24. T.B. Bottomore, *Critics of Society: Radical Thought in North America* (New York: Random House, 1969), p. 113.

Chapter 5

HUMAN SERVICE

ORGANIZATIONS

The establishment of social welfare policy objectives and programs has required the development of major administrative and service organizations. These are known as human service organizations. Examples include hospitals, welfare agencies, universities, public schools, and Children's Aid societies. Indeed, the presence of such organizations is seen as "a hallmark of modern society." These organizations have the task of translating the policies, values, and ideals of the welfare state (both manifest and latent) into specific administrative and professional acts. On the one hand, they provide access to service, distribute benefits, and create special statuses; on the other, they deny access to service, maintain social control, and stigmatize their clientele: "The individual's loss of power to human service organizations is a fundamental characteristic of the welfare state."[1] The human service organization is responsible for the delivery systems of the welfare state, and the realities of such organizations' activity has given the welfare state the reputation for bureaucracy with which we are familiar. If the student is to understand the characteristics of social welfare, then the study of the organizations and systems that deliver welfare is inescapable.

The establishment of social welfare policy objectives is but the first step toward ensuring that the welfare of people is in fact achieved. Objectives have to be expressed, not in the general language of policy, but in the much more specific and precise language of services to be delivered to specific people under specific conditions defined in operating procedures. Furthermore, the services have to be made available to people. Hence the importance of the concept of a "delivery system," the means whereby provision is in fact made.

As such, the delivery system is in an intermediate position between the processes whereby goals are established (and the influences that bear upon such goals) and the utilization of social services. These processes involve four levels of interest, termed "domains" in organizational theory.[2] The first domain is the *policy* domain, where government is exercised and public accountability held. In this political domain the highest value is placed on public image and social justice in the form of "fairness." Issues are typically decided in this domain by bargaining and negotiating (where powerful parties are involved) or arbitrarily (where the interest being treated is powerless). The final test of effectiveness is usually by voting at the ballot box.

The second domain is *management*, where the organization is established and controlled. The highest values here are control and co-ordination, with equity being treated as an organizational principle necessary to control rather than as a policy principle of social justice. The organization is bureaucratic, using established principles of division of labour, specialization, procedural description – with mechanization through electronic processing rapidly displacing paper systems of records and communications.

The third domain is the *professional* domain, where the organization has face-to-face contact with its clients. Here the highest values are autonomy and self-regulation. The professional seeks the recognition of colleagues and, through professional association, asserts independence of ethics, judgement, and action. The engagement with clients is individualistic and specific.

The fourth domain (usually considered to be outside the organization) is comprised of the *clients*. The clients are usually unorganized and are there to be processed. Their values, motivation, resources, knowledge, and behaviours are the targets of the enterprise.

Needless to say, the interests of these distinct domains usually differ. In fact, the wonder is not that they differ but that they are successfully linked at all in a joint enterprise. The linkages have been characterized as "loose coupling" – that is, considerable dissidence, conflict, and negotiation exist at the boundaries between each domain. The linear bureaucratic work modes of the management domain are at odds with the indeterminate human processing of the professional domain and both are incompatible with the negotiating and bargaining of the political domain. In the end the effectiveness of the enterprise depends on the ability to develop shared purposes and an appropriate structural and technological fit.

This is not to say that all coupling between domains is loose. In a typical social assistance agency, the objectives of the agency will include the manifest objective of making provision for those who are destitute and the latent (sometimes manifest) objective of making such provision in a manner (and at a level) that provides an incentive to recipients to seek employment. Those who administer and deliver service share in these general objectives but have others of their own, particularly self-protection from the public criticism that comes from fraud or laxity in administration. These objectives require tight coupling in the financial administration function, a tight coupling now achieved by electronic processing, direct-entry systems.

The consumers of service share few of these objectives. They are faced with the reality that the service delivery system serves to retain them in a state of inequality by a combination of minimum provision and conditions of receipt that provide them only with a choice of types of inequality.

Tension between domains is the most fundamental internal issue in the provision of social services. This tension is increased where the social services pursue regulatory functions with respect to their consumers and where they are given in a "total institution" context. Conversely, it is decreased where consumers exercise choice in service receipt and where services are given in the community. Using these two variables Adrian Webb[3] developed a classification table for social services:

TABLE 5: *Classification of Social Services*

Client – Organization contact	Goal Orientation		
	Regulatory	Adaptive	Service (non-regulatory)
Total Institutions	Prisons	Psychiatric Hospitals	General Hospitals
Quasi-total institutions	Attendance centres	Hostels for mentally disordered	Boarding schools
Non-Total Insti-tutional { Expressive contact	Probation	Some child-care functions	Day schools Medical services
Instrumental contact	Unemployment Insurance and "work opportunity" programs		Guaranteed Income Supplement for elderly
No contact	Pollution regulations	Hospital insurance	Old Age Security FamilyAllowances

In the non-total institutional category, "expressive contact" refers to face-to-face contact, as in counselling relationships; "instrumental contact" refers to the more anonymous forms of direct social service delivery.

The value of this means of classifying social services is that it identifies those services in which the conflict between consumers, deliverers, and policy-makers is most severe. As one traverses the table from the upper left-hand corner to the lower right, one moves from services in which there is severe conflict to services in which there is harmony.

The ideals of social welfare and the ethics of the social work profession would suggest that the primary orientation of professionals should be toward service. The social welfare ideal is of equality and the professional ethical obligation is "To regard the welfare of the individuals, the group, and the community he serves as his primary professional duty." Nevertheless, the professional also seeks to exercise his powers in this situation and power is manifestly not in the hands of consumers of social services. Thus, administrator, professional, and delivery system each seeks to build its own power base and to protect its boundaries. Protecting the boundaries involves avoiding political and public controversy and is accomplished partly by participation in many aspects of policy-making, partly by the assertion of social control over consumers, and partly by drawing a curtain of secrecy around the delivery system's operation. This secrecy is presented publicly as necessary to protect client confidentiality, but in fact it protects both the administrative and professional domains from public review and scrutiny. Few actions will get a social worker dismissed faster than speaking out in public.

The power requirements of the delivery system do not suggest that a politically partisan role, fighting for the interests of their clients, is wise or desirable. However, the political role that is desirable is not a neutral one. The role is one in which the delivery system seeks to extend its own power with respect to both policy processes and consumers.

The means to this end is through mastery of the technical features of social service delivery and through control of information. Social service delivery has become a complex technical operation. This complexity is a product in part of a complex social order, but it also arises from the variety of different conceptual and value positions from which to view the social order. It is also a product of the availability of choices between different ways of making provision, and of the complexities of managing an organization with a variety of functions and a variety of types of personnel. Complexity has also been increased unnecessarily by political and bureaucratic competition, confusion, lack of attention to planning, and poor management. As a result, it is not uncommon to hear that many social services are poorly designed and managed. Humanistic concern for the individual tends to be lost in attention to technical detail: ability to manipulate the technical aspects of delivery provides a power base for professional self-centredness and rivalry, and complexity has been mystified as a way of protecting power and influence.

Social Service Delivery: Organizing Concepts

Systems theory provides a means of analysing the complexities of social service delivery through clarifying conceptually distinct processes and systemic features. In reality, these processes and systems features are interrelated and interact, but understanding of them is enhanced by distinguishing their separate and distinctive characters. The following classification scheme, which is admittedly incomplete, focuses attention on four systems processes.

1. *Goal establishment*: the processes whereby objectives for specific social service provisions are established.

2. *Design*: the processes whereby a design is elaborated as to how provision *should* be made in accord with our understanding of how objectives or goals may be achieved.

3. *Implementation*: the processes whereby a design is put into effect.

4. *Consumption*: the processes whereby the recipients of social services receive services that affect their lives.

These four processes are viewed in combination with three boundary features of social service delivery systems.

1. *Political boundaries*: the types of influence that act, or should act, on systems processes. They can be sub-categorized according to source (consumers, service deliveries, public at large) or to type of power exercised (utilitarian or normative).

2. *Conceptual boundaries*: the role of ideas, or concepts, in establishing the territory that social service occupies. Frequently there is competition between different ways of conceiving the same basic phenomena. A boy of thirteen beats up and robs an old man – is this a problem of parental neglect, a problem of the boy's mental health, a problem of criminal delinquency? The different ways of conceiving this phenomenon result in different service patterns. Because numerous social phenomena cannot be easily classified, there is competition between service systems as to which sets of definitions are to be applied.

3. *Size/scope boundaries*: the quantitative boundaries of service. How many require service? What resources are needed to serve them? Where are they located? etc.

The result of combining the four processes with the three boundary dimensions is a matrix, each cell of which provokes distinctive questions (Table 6).

There is a normative thrust of the systems approach to the examination of social service delivery systems. This thrust is to-

TABLE 6: *Matrix: Social Service Delivery Systems*

System Processes	System Boundary Features		Size/Scope
	Political	*Conceptual*	*Size/Scope*
Goal establishment	What constituencies have a direct interest in service goals? Are they influential? How?	What concepts are relevant to the definition of this phenomenon? Are several definitions feasible? How clear and precise are the concepts used?	How many are affected by the phenomenon, problem, etc.? Where are they located?
Service design	How is choice made between different service designs? Who is represented in such choices?	What is the range of possible service design?	What do different service designs require by way of resources, etc.?
Service implementation	How is administrative discretion exercised? To whom are administrators accountable?	What latent functions have to be performed by the service?	What resources are in fact available? How are they used?
Service consumption	How are beneficiaries determined? Who influences the choice of beneficiaries?	What concepts shape the conditions of receipt of service?	Who obtains what service?

ward congruence; the theory leads us to expect that there will be logical and rational relationships among goal, design, implementation, and consumption. However, the review of the context of social service delivery and the distinct, separate interests of the public at large and the deliverers and consumers of service suggest that such congruence will not always be found.

This same idea can be expressed by using the systems concept of homeostasis. The social service delivery system exists in an environment containing separate and distinct sets of interests. At any one point in time, there exists a homeostatic balance among these separate interests, which is achieved only by various types of accommodation that show up when consistency or congruence between different parts of the system is lacking. The tensions within the system are both a source of instability and a source of change.

The maintenance of incongruence between different parts of the system also indicates how power is used within the system. The potential instabilities of the homeostatic balance are stabilized through the uneven distribution of power between system parts and processes. Control of this homeostatic balance is a central purpose of executive-level management. When change is sought then sanction is given to those domains and values within the system that value the change. At other times these values are repressed and each domain grumbles about the other over lunch or coffee. The problem of a strong or charismatic personality within the system is that such a person tends to attract forces for change in a manner that may make control impossible for the executive.

Bolman and Deal direct attention to four different ways of seeing and managing organizations.[4] The *structural approach* directs attention to organizational form and rational processes, such as policy directives. The *human resource approach* focuses on human needs within the organization. The *political approach* deals with power and conflict, while the *symbolic approach* concerns itself with myths and ceremonies. Integration between the domains calls for skill in the use of all four of these approaches to management.

Goals

The term "goal" is used to identify the end purposes of the human service organization delivery system. Statements of goals are to be found in general statements of organizational mission and in statements of general purpose for programs and organizational units. The statements to be found in such official documents deal only with the goals that are acceptable for public viewing. There are usually other goals that are just as real but are concealed from public view.

Westerlund and Sjostrand suggested the following typology for the goals of human service organizations. *Honorific goals*: These goals credit the organization or program with benign and desirable qualities and are the type that political leaders can be eloquent about. An example for a child welfare agency would be "strengthening family life." *Stated goals*: These are more at a working level for the organizations; they are designed to produce a shared understanding within the organization that can guide it in setting objectives and making decisions. An example for a child welfare agency would be "protecting children" or "receiving reports of neglect or abuse." *Repressed goals*: These are goals that are pursued but which would not stand up if confronted with public scrutiny or the organization's stated values or self-image. An example for a child welfare agency would be "deterrence." Parents are rightly scared by the agency's power and intrusions and the agency uses this fact to deter neglect. *Tabu goals*: These are goals no one talks about but which are known to exist. For the child welfare agency, one such goal might be, "If you cross us by going to the media, we will make life difficult for you."[5]

Goal Establishment

The goals or objectives established at the political level provide only general direction for the development of social services. An increased degree of specificity is essential to the actual delivery of services. The process of goal establishment thus works across the dividing line between policy and program. Table 6 directs attention to conceptual, quantitative, and political aspects of the process of establishing goals.

1. *Conceptual aspects.* The general goals established by policy processes have the following usual forms: problem-centred goals, service-centred goals, and population-centred goals.

a. *Problem-centred goals.* A social problem (e.g., alcoholism, narcotic addiction, delinquency) is defined and a social agency is established to deal with the problem. The social agency is then faced with the important issue of how to deal with the problem – or even how to think about the problem. There are invariably a series of competing views with respect to any social problem, views reflecting ideological and value differences and involving different concepts in their formulation. The following overview of concepts used to define the social problem of narcotic addition is not intended to be all-inclusive, but it does illustrate a usual range of choices.

i. *Psychological*. The problem can be viewed as a learned behaviour. Individuals have learned to obtain satisfaction through the use of narcotics. Also, from a psychological perspective, the problem can be seen as a manifestation of unresolved interpersonal conflict. The individual is using narcotic addiction to act out hostility toward some significant figure, such as a parent or spouse.

ii. *Sociological*. The problem can be viewed, as well, as a product of patterns of association between peoples. Certain groups of people (medical professionals and counter-culture and criminal underworld groups being the most common) have access to narcotics. The problem of narcotic addiction derives from entering one or another of these groups. From each of these groups a certain percentage become addicts.

iii. *Micro-economic*. The problem can also be defined as a product of rapacious micro-economic behaviour. A product, narcotics, is covertly advertised and the population of users is exploited for economic gain.

iv. *Political-institutional*. The problem can be seen as a matter of political-institutional definition. We have decided to exclude narcotic use from the range of permissible behaviours and have developed a set of institutions around that decision. If we were to accept narcotic use as an acceptable private behaviour, the problem as we know it – an illicit, criminal phenomenon – would cease to exist.

These choices between different ways of conceptualizing the problem of narcotic addiction are not mutually exclusive. Nevertheless, a social agency has to make some decisions as to which view of the problem it is going to adopt as primary. The primary view taken of the problem will affect the type of services the agency develops. Where there is conflict between different service approaches the primary view will determine the outcome of the conflict. In each case the adoption of a view of the problem leads to the identification of a target for change.

b. *Service-centred goals*. The objectives of a social agency may be conceptualized around a service rather than around a problem, and may take the form of the provision of day-care services, homemaker services, information services, counselling services, etc. In each case, the agency is faced with the issues of the purpose to be served by the service and hence the population to be served.

The purpose of a service like day care can vary considerably. The service may be viewed as a baby-sitting service that allows mothers to work, confident that their children are being well cared for; as a developmental, pre-school education experience for the children; or as therapeutic, correcting behaviour problems. These different views of day care will lead to different types of staff, different staff/child ratios, and different populations of children being seen as primary. The social agency thus has to make a goal decision from among these different views of the purpose of day-care services.

c. *Population-centred goals.* The objectives of a social agency are usually expressed in terms of a population that may be ethnic (native peoples), institutional (veterans), or geographic. However, the population to be served is only synonymous with the total population in those cases where the service is truly universal, for example, Family Allowances. In all other cases, the target population is a sub-population within the total population. This sub-population is defined in problem- and/or service-centred terms.

2. *Size/scope aspects.* As indicated above, each of the concepts used to define the objectives of a social program has implications for the establishment of the size of the target population. The ease or difficulty of this task varies with our ability to express concepts in quantitative form. For some programs, such as family allowances, this is a straightforward matter. The population the program is intended to serve can be defined by demographic concepts of age, citizenship, residence, and, for older children, school attendance.

However, many of the concepts used in determining problems and service purposes do not yield to such ready quantification. The process of quantification becomes one of establishing arbitrary boundaries in order to estimate the size of the phenomena within the boundaries. Thus, if the problem is poverty it is possible to establish boundaries, with respect to income or expenses, that define a population as being poor. Using income statistics, the size of that population can be estimated. The process remains an arbitrary one because the income and expense boundaries are matters of social judgement. The characteristic way of asserting the existence of such boundaries is by reference to an authority, such as the Economic Council of Canada or the Senate Committee on Poverty.

Furthermore, some of the concepts used in defining problems and purposes are so diffuse that even arbitrary quantifications appear pointless. For example, the concept of pre-delinquent behaviour is sometimes used to indicate the target population of delinquency prevention programs. But what precisely is pre-delinquency? There are times when everybody has contemplated, indeed engaged in, criminal acts. Yet it is scarcely useful to identify the total population as being pre-delinquent. On the other hand, any more restricted boundary appears to be so arbitrary as to be of no real use.

There are pressures from within the human service organization to consistently expand the boundary. Several factors contribute: the self-interest of professionals and administrators in having serious problems to deal with; the fact that the penalty for keeping out a client who needs service is more severe than the penalty for taking in a client who does not need service. The child welfare agency will be criticized more for failing to apprehend the child who is subsequently abused than for apprehending the child who has not been abused but is thought to be "at risk." As a consequence it is usual to find human service organizations surrounded by unserved needs, typically 45-50 per cent greater than the needs that can be met with available resources.

3. *Political aspects.* The conceptual and quantitative aspects of establishing goals are responsive to public conceptions of the issue and to bureaucratic and professional shaping of those conceptions. The public, whose views are reflected in the political elite and who in turn may reflect the views of other elites, cannot be ignored in the goal-establishment process. A delivery system cannot achieve stability unless its goals are broadly acceptable to the public. The apparently inevitable instability of community development and social action programs evidences the difficulty of developing services that are change-oriented. The difficulty of obtaining a humanistic approach in public assistance programs – where the public's notion of acceptability is shaped by the work ethic – also indicates

the need for basic congruence between a delivery systems goal and the public's view of its purpose.

On the other hand, the management and professional domains are deeply involved in establishing goals. This is partly because of the complexities and ramifications of decision-making, partly because control of these issues is important to delivery system stability. Management and professional interests acquire this influence principally through their control of sources of information and analysis. This power can be used, and is used, to shape public understanding of an issue – and to oppose other understandings. The testimony presented to the Commission on the Non-Medical Use of Drugs is a case in point. Each of the interested parties was skilful in marshalling evidence that supported its own point of view. Thus, enforcement agencies would present data on crime both directly and indirectly related to drug abuse; social agencies would proffer data on demand for counselling and public information services; and medical agencies would appear with data on pharmacological effects and demand for hospital beds.

Management and professional control of the process of goal establishment influences how the conceptual and quantitative issues are resolved. The differences of conceptual approach are largely the property of different professional groups. Thus the issue as to which conceptual approach is to be dominant tends to be settled through the process of inter-professional rivalry and politics. In some instances, several different professional groups may be sufficiently adept at obtaining political support for their case that a multiplicity of service empires is created. Hence, the field of child relationships to community norms is contested among the concepts of juvenile delinquency (police and corrections professionals), child welfare (social work), mental health (psychiatrists), and education (teachers).

The effect of management influence is seen in the need to obtain clarity and precision as to who is to receive what service. All organizations need to defend the rationality of their actions and bureaucracies are expected to be impartial in their relationships to the public. If such impartiality cannot be achieved through the clear definition of purpose, population, and means, then it is usually achieved through the establishment of arbitrary limits to service. Furthermore, such limits, once established, will be rationalized in part by the precedent of their establishment, precedent itself being an acceptable argument within a bureaucracy for the settlement of boundary issues.

On the other hand, the consumer is commonly isolated from the goal-establishment process. This is particularly true of those social service organizations in which there is conflict between "common weal" and "service" orientations. The definition of consumers as a population to be regulated and controlled denies the idea that they should be active in shaping their controls. Where there is a closer identity between common weal and service orientations, as in services to the blind, the service populations may be more active in influencing goal establishment. Even in such instances consumers remain substantially the creation of the servicing organization. Only where consumers form a co-operative and directly employ their own social service staff, as has been achieved by some aboriginal organizations, do consumers become a major party in the process of establishing goals.

Service Design

The process of designing the service is distinct from that of goal determination by virtue of its focus on intervention, specifically with how services should operate. The issue of how services should operate is distinct, too, from the issue of how they actually operate. Thus service design is distinct from service implementation.

The processes of goal establishment and service design are intermingled in the actual development of a service. For example, sensitivity to a social problem's existence is affected by the existence of alternatives. The development of a series of techniques for transferring income from those who are better off to those who are poor has increased our sensitivity to the problem of poverty by increasing our realization that the problem can be solved. Nevertheless, the distinction between issues of objective and issues of means (intervention) is useful in the analysis of social service delivery.

1. *Conceptual aspects*. The means of intervention are not inevitably determined by the concepts used to establish goals. A goal may

be established using a concept such as deviance. The service design may take the form of individual services oriented to decreasing the deviance of individuals, community services oriented to decreasing the deviance of groups, e.g., delinquent gangs, or the service design may aim to revise public understanding and tolerance of difference. All three approaches are congruent with the goal of decreasing deviancy, but they have very different change targets and involve different types of intervention.

The distinction between remedial and preventative approaches to social problems is a distinction of this order. Given that a social problem, such as child neglect, is identified primarily with individuals, it does not follow that intervention should be concentrated on those same individuals. The problem of child neglect could be approached by the provision of basic parental education both in schools and through the media – this would be considered a primary preventative approach to the problem. The problem could be approached by providing an array of basic social support services to provide parents with an opportunity to learn improved parenting behaviours – this would be considered a secondary preventative approach. The problem of child neglect could be approached, as it frequently is, as a problem of saving children from their delinquent parents.

These service design choices involve the adoption of specific concepts of the target system and of the means of intervention. There is a close interconnection between these two. Means of intervention can be classified by target system. Social work practice, for example, has been considered to include casework, group work, and community organization.

Furthermore, the service design choice requires a well-rounded knowledge as to how specific interventions are supposed to operate, and hence the interventive theory. The ideal in this regard is that: "The proponents of any treatment technique or method that is planned and goal directed rather than haphazard, should be able to state in advance what its goals are, and what specific techniques are to be employed to bring about behavioural change."[6] Unfortunately, such clarity is not commonly achieved. One of the major problems of service design lies in our inability to compare the effects of different interventions on social problems. In this circumstance, the choice of intervention may be unduly subject to trends, fads, professional rivalries, and the like. In the development of social services there was often not a conscious, conceptualized, and rationally argued choice of service design. Yet, the absence of conscious choice does not mean the absence of choice. The decision to develop individual services for neglected children rather than community services to support their parents may not be a conscious and deliberate one. It is an implicit choice nevertheless. Part of the service provided by the consultant or analyst of social provision is to assist delivery organizations to understand the implicit choices they have already made and to explore alternatives. A major challenge today is to revisit these historic decisions and examine them in the context of current issues and professional knowledge.

2. *Size/scope aspects.* The choice of a service design at a conceptual level leads to quantitative aspects of choice. The first consideration here is whether the service is intended to be comprehensive with respect to the phenomena with which it deals or whether it is intended to be a partial or demonstration service.

Comprehensive service designs require that a rational relationship exist between the size and scope of the problem, the goals of the service, and the resources that are sought for service operation. Child protection services targeted toward abusive parents aim to be comprehensive. The unambiguous intention is that no child should be subject to deliberate and permanently damaging physical abuse. The service thus needs to determine as best it can how many such children will likely exist in the area and population it serves. This can be done approximately on the bases of demographic data and epidemiological data on child abuse.[7] Having established an order-of-magnitude figure for the population to be served, the delivery system has to review the means that exist for systematic contact with that population (referrals from physicians, hospitals, schools, day-care centres, etc.). In turn the resources, money, facilities, and staff needed to reach and serve the population are determined.

However, comprehensive service designs are comparatively rare in social service delivery; partial or incomplete designs are much more common. Partial service designs only intend to serve part of the phenomena with which the service is concerned. This partial nature of service may be part of the design itself in that essentially arbitrary limits are established with respect to service based on the resources that are available to the agency. Thus, a family service agency may intend to serve only that number of clients to whom its social workers can provide a quality service. The partial nature of service coverage may, however, be implicit rather than explicit in that the agency maintains the fiction of serving everybody who needs service but makes no realistic estimate of the resources needed to provide such a service. Such partial service designs were once viewed as a developmental phenomenon, with the service eventually growing toward comprehensive coverage. Now they are more often the product of restraint and cutbacks that have left behind a series of services no longer able to address fully the problems they once did. Partial service designs sometimes have a representative character. For example, community development or community action programs are not intended to organize all the citizens of a community. Rather, they are intended to organize a representative group of citizens who will act as spokesmen.

The demonstration or experimental service designs common in the 1970s were similar to partial service designs in that they did not intend to provide a comprehensive service, but they had the added feature of exploring new service approaches. The implicit, sometimes explicit, understanding was that a successful demonstration program would be followed by a comprehensive program. In practice this rarely occurred.

The existence of many partial designs (the field of personal social services, counselling, information, etc., and of social utilities, day care, homemaker services provides many examples)[8] is one of the central problems of social delivery. The problem is all the greater because it is concealed by the lack of clear statements as to what comprehensive services are desirable, an unwillingness to admit the partial nature of services that have been developed, and the heritage of poorly rationalized cutbacks that are the heritage of restraint.

The size/scope aspects of service design involve two additional problems that make the development of clear specifications of what resources are needed difficult. The existence of these problems contributes to the existence of partial service designs.

The first of these is the issue of standards. The quality of data that exist with respect to service standards remains inadequate. Professional organizations have sought to establish service standards for particular types of service. Thus, a worker in a family service agency may be viewed as carrying a full load when he has twenty family therapy cases and is spending one hour per week with each. However, the standard is rarely based on objective analysis – the worker considers that twenty such cases form a full caseload, and this becomes the standard. The standard is not the product of discriminating choice between service methodologies that may involve differential contact patterns, nor is it responsive to differential worker qualifications and experiences. It may not even be based on economic considerations of worker salary, client payment, etc. Even so, such a standard is better than the complete absence of standards to be found in some fields of social service delivery: for example, what standards exist for a community development worker?

The broad model of intervention has the following form:

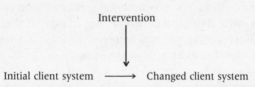

Hasenfeld distinguishes three major ways in which human service organizations work on client systems: people processing, people sustaining, and people changing.[9] In people processing the change being made is to the status of the client in relation to the society. The client's status is changed through a one-step or two-step process. In one-step processes the client is simply labelled in a way that has future social consequences. The consequence can be positive, as when a degree is awarded, or negative, as when a criminal record is established. In a two-step process the client goes through an intermediate state, e.g., "treatment" prior to final labelling. In people-sustaining intervention the human service organization has the job of providing direct benefits to the client. These can take the form of money or can be in the form of residential care and sustenance.

Only at a third level, people changing, does the human service organization claim to have effected change in its clientele. This is frequently associated with people processing and is the prelude to the second step of people processing – removing the initial label and announcing to the world that change has occurred.

Shulman and others have made this the subject of major research programs that have begun to develop objective knowledge of human service-client system interactions.[10] At the same time as this process of building knowledge is going on, major changes are being made in the intervention process. The careful dissection of the interventive process is leading to an ever-increasing degree of task differentiation, procedural specification, and work differentiation. This process has been referred to as the industrialization of social work practice, is seen by some as a threat to the autonomy of professionals, and can lead to challenges to the need to have professional credentials.

This has been aided by the development of electronic data processing and its application in human service organizations. The computer presses practice in the direction of dissection into a series of yes/no decision points, all of which become potential focii for mechanization and control. The "craft" of social work is seen as disappearing and a mechanistic, decision-oriented, people-changing system is emerging. Mastering this system requires a depth of understanding of information technology. The social worker's expertise, which was once thought of principally in terms of worker/client relationships, must now be recognized as being equally concerned with information, decision-making, and case management. This changed understanding requires that social workers face the fact that they are instruments of power. Timms recognizes the effect of this understanding when he writes: "unless social workers' power is regulated by law in accordance with the principles of natural justice, social workers may themselves be the major obstacle to the implementation of welfare rights."[11]

3. *Political aspects.* Issues of service design are seen to be a management and professional matter. The required technical knowledge places these issues beyond the scope of reasonable debate in

the policy arena. Indeed, one of the reasons professionals are needed in the social services is to relate the complexities of design choice to the broad decision made in the course of policy deliberation. Less reasonably, the consumers of social service are typically thought of as not possessing the knowledge or intelligence to make a substantial contribution to the discussion of service design issues. As in the case of goal establishment, a negative judgement is more likely to be made with respect to those services that have regulatory as opposed to service objectives. The common weal orientation leads to a devaluation of the contribution that could be made by those who are consumers of service.

The political issue of who participates in design choice is thus largely a professional matter and the subject of intense rivalry among professions. Making logical choices is complicated by the fact that different interventive methodologies are in the hands of different professional groups. Thus psychologists are supreme with respect to the whole arena of testing and learning theory; medical psychiatrists command access to drug-based methodologies of individual change; and social workers regard both psychologists and psychiatrists as being too narrowly concerned with intrapersonal dynamics and missing thereby the effects of environment and interpersonal dynamics.

The uncertainties of the debate about strategies of intervention in relation to goals and of the size and scope of service operations tend to be resolved through the process of interprofessional rivalry. In each service delivery system, one professional group has become dominant. That group determines the major forms of intervention to be used, the subordinate role to be played by members of other professions, and the types of analysis and research to be conducted. Interdisciplinary approaches rarely mean equality between disciplines; the more usual meaning is that one discipline has been successful in getting other disciplines to work with it in a subordinate relationship.

Once a professional group has become dominant in a delivery system it is very difficult, if not impossible, to replace it by another. This means in turn that differential strategies and design choices that involve crossing disciplinary boundaries (and thereby changing the discipline that is dominant in a particular system) are equally difficult to pursue. Where the need for a change of strategy is overwhelming it is more probable that the dominant discipline will be modified, so as to maintain its dominance. Thus, the overwhelming evidence that casework services would never end poverty resulted in a modification of the discipline of social work – with increased emphasis on community and policy processes.

Partly because of these entrenched professional positions, management expertise has increasingly been seen as necessary to make the choices between professions that professionals are incapable of making. This has served to ensure that bureaucratic rationality is incorporated into service design in the name of sound administration. Services that are predictable in their effect are favoured over those that are less certain. For example, professional workers are favoured over charismatic individuals because they can be interchanged with each other, replaced, or dismissed without affecting institutional stability.

In addition, strategies aimed at changing the powerless are to be preferred over political battles with the powerful. Such battles may result in the agency losing its mandate for the problem – hence the bureaucratic bias toward changing individual clients rather than seeking change in society and the rules of its social institutions.

Cabinet Submissions

Within government the political aspects of goal establishment and service design are visibly expressed in the policy submissions made by ministries to their ministers and to cabinet when programs are added, changed, or withdrawn. Their purpose is to ensure the accountability of the management domain to the political.

The typical submission covers the following subject fields: (1) *Goals.* In one sentence, what is the proposal intended to achieve? (2) *Background/discussion.* This section provides context and is the opportunity to review alternatives, indicate prior reviews, frame policy options open to government. (3) *Legislation.* What is the law as it relates to this proposal and what legislation or regulatory action (if any) is needed to make a change? (4) *Financial.* What will the proposal cost or save, and what second-order financial consequences can be estimated? (5) *Staffing*. Are more staff needed, or will staff be saved? Are there opportunities to staff by contract rather than by direct government staffing? (6) *Intergovernment*. The relationship to other government levels, federal, provincial, or municipal, is examined with particular attention to boundary jurisdictional relationships. (7) *Public reactions/information plan*. How will the public react – including differing reactions by major segments of the public? A strategy for "selling" the change is often suggested. (8) *Implementation*. If the change is approved, what major steps follow and how long will they take? (9) *Recommendation*. What is the minister's recommendation to his colleagues in cabinet?

The policy submissions of government are not available for study in Canada.

Service Implementation

Service implementation is the study of what actually takes place. The focus of attention is on the real behaviour of the delivery system rather than on its ideal, or designed, behaviour. The uncertainties of design, referred to above, create situations that are resolved *de facto* in the process of providing service. Where features of the design may be contradictory, implementation will tend to favour one side of the design contradiction. Furthermore, there may be factors in the systemic environment that the design does not take into account, for example, a hostile client population. The delivery system cannot disregard such realities merely because they ought not to exist, and the service that is provided develops features of its own that respond to these realities.

This variation is accommodated systemically through the loose coupling of the domains. The discretion gained by the professional domain permits street-level bureaucrats to develop relatively autonomous services that adapt stated policies to delivery realities. In so doing the issue is raised of what is an "acceptable" modification of policy. Here there is no guidance to be had in creating a situation of both power and vulnerability at the same time.

1. *Conceptual aspects*. An important concept in the discussion of service implementation is the distinction between manifest and

latent service functions. Attention to the processes of goal establishment and service design has been primarily concerned with
the accomplishment of manifest or declared purposes of the social
service delivery system. Delivery systems, as indicated above, have
to handle a reality that may not be fully congruent with the goal
and design statements. Indeed, the analysis of the tension between
objectives from different domains would indicate that such contradictions are inherent features of social service delivery systems.

Latent functions are concealed in these contradictions. The expressed goals of the public welfare system may be to provide the
basic means of subsistence and incentive for independence. The
measure of success in accomplishing both functions in the public's
view is seen in the limiting of public welfare expenditures. However, the delivery system can also obtain this effect by restricting
grants, by making processes of application difficult, by pressuring
recipients to take poorly paid and unpleasant work, or by restricting the number of applicants by stigmatizing them. Such behaviour is not officially sanctioned as the purpose of the service but
it can be tacitly sanctioned in the process of service implementation. Thus, to stigmatize clients, to maintain people in minimal
states of subsistence, and to support sweatshop working conditions
are all latent functions of the social service delivery system.

Latent functions are not unintended secondary consequences;
they are part of the objective reality of social service delivery.
Some of them (the support to low-wage employment) may be
functionally necessary for other concerns (non-unionized busi-
nesses). Others may become part of the broad public and political
expectation of the delivery system (for example, that its clients
should regard themselves as second-class citizens). On occasion,
latent functions may receive deliberate sanction by being formally
incorporated into service goals. The British poor law reform of
1834 made the poor law deliberately more stigmatizing,[12] and
pressure to introduce such deliberately regressive features into
social welfare policy remains.[13] Part of the discussion about the
desirability of a guaranteed annual income was concerned with
whether such a program would perform the latent functions of
income security programs. The neo-conservative position on the
revision of social services gains much of its strength from the

articulation of latent functions, providing a mandate for incremental systems change that strengthens the performance of these functions.

Latent functions are by definition concealed (or partly concealed). Revealing latent service delivery functions, including how they are performed and sanctioned and whose interests they serve, is essential to the full understanding of any social service delivery system. A strength of Marxist analysis is that it exposes such functions to critical examination. Both latent and manifest service functions, in fact, have to be implemented by somebody. The analysis of service implementation thus involves use of the whole discipline of administration. Such a treatment would deal in some detail with intra-system processes, the internal management and control of information, the means adopted for feedback, and the means of system accountability.[14]

2. *Size/scope aspects.* The size/scope aspect of service implementation is concerned with the issue of what resources are available and how they are to be used. At the level of service implementation, resources appear to be chronically inadequate. This inadequacy has a substantial basis in relation to standards. The maintenance of large numbers of Canadians in poverty indicates that there is a gross discrepancy between the size of the desirable and the size of the actual welfare transfer that is made. The gross discrepancy between the availability of such social utility services as day care, and the need for such services, is further evidence of the extent of resource inadequacy.

Some areas of social service delivery suggest that the inadequacy of resources may be more apparent than real, and some social service fields appear to suffer more from structural problems than from gross inadequacy of resources. In the field of health care, for example, resources are extensive, but attention to remedial rather than preventative aspects of care, attention to the professional frontiers (e.g., cancer research) rather than to the bread-and-butter needs of native peoples for basic health care, the underuse of some personnel (e.g., nurses) and the overuse of others (e.g., physicians) all tend to produce a situation in which some populations are poorly served and resources to serve them *appear* to be chronically inadequate. Job placement, retraining, manpower services would appear to suffer from similar difficulties, as would some aspects of services to children (e.g., the overlapping jurisdictions of child welfare, mental health, school, and probation agencies).

The issue of resource use cannot be left without a brief discussion of the concept of efficiency, as applied to social service delivery systems. The existence of competing claims on resources and the resulting resource scarcity suggest that the most efficient possible use is desirable. But what exactly is efficiency in the context of social service delivery? The cost/benefit analysis school[15] treats efficiency in terms of resources necessary to obtain a specific result. Thus, efficiency is defined in terms of results and the means used to achieve those results. Such an approach has considerable utility. The various resources used – payments, personnel, buildings, etc. – can all be treated as costs and related to the objectives being sought. Differences in the cost of different approaches are thus made clear. However, there are major weaknesses in our knowledge of the relationship between the means and ends of social service delivery. Furthermore, we frequently lack any measurement of the achievement of results. Thus we tend to lack the means of knowing when we are being efficient and when we are not. Doubtless this leads to much inefficiency.

Given this unfortunate state of affairs, there is a trap, too, in the single-minded pursuit of efficiency. This pursuit leads to a concentration of attention of those aspects of social service delivery that are definable and measurable at the expense of those that are not. Such an approach distorts the nature of services provided. For example, within a public assistance department a unit is established to collect money from putative fathers and separated or divorced husbands. Such a unit has a ready-made yardstick of efficiency – the amount of money collected at what cost. This unit can use arguments as to "efficiency" to expand its staff and extend its collection services. Yet from any overall view of a public assistance agency's functions, the "collection" aspects would appear to be much less important than the provision of counselling and rehabilitative services to the agency's clientele. The lack of an efficiency measure for these services can lead to their being perceived as having less priority than "collections" for additional resources. The internal allocation of resources within the delivery system can thus be distorted. Similar effects can readily occur in other delivery systems.

The difficulty of defining efficiency in the social services is one of the major features that distinguishes social administration from business administration. Moral responsibility, the central phenomenon of social welfare, cannot be costed. The objectives of social administration go beyond cost/benefit analysis to concern for the fulfilment of public trust and moral responsibility.[16]

3. *Political respect.* As with service design, service implementation is dominated by the politics of professions and management. The main features are so similar that their repetition is not necessary. However, two minor features of the politics of implementation are not included in the previous discussion: the politics of working relationships between persons of different status and the role that consumers are seeking in the administration of the delivery system.

The process of professional competition for delivery system "ownership" ensures that interdisciplinary work will involve the subordination of one discipline to another. However, at the operational level such a subordination may not be functional. Its existence obstructs the use of the secondary discipline and may result in the impossibility of obtaining employees from members of the discipline. This is particularly the case when a low-ranked profession (e.g., social work) wishes to establish an interdisciplinary team involving higher-ranked professions (e.g., psychiatry). Similarly, the establishment of a bureaucratic organization ensures that certain persons will occupy positions of high status and others will occupy positions of low status.

Again, at the operational level such a subordination may not be functional. The workers and clerical staff will have a first-hand knowledge of the impact of services not available to persons of higher status. As a result, the status differentials will tend to obstruct the use of information and may result in the perpetuation of useless and wasteful practices.

The preferred management model[17] to obtain a better use of human resources is a participative or consultative model. Such a model has the related advantages of fostering employee morale and commitment to the delivery system's objectives. Where there are sharp differences concerning objectives either within the service or resulting from the tension between domains, then more authoritative management styles tend to result. They result from the process of resolution of difference through reliance on ascribed status and professional identity. As a consequence, the best examples of good interdisciplinary teamwork are found in those organizations, such as child guidance clinics, that do not have major regulatory functions. In contrast, those organizations with considerable regulatory responsibilities (penitentiaries and mental hospitals) are characterized by hierarchical organization, lack of interdisciplinary work, poor morale, and high turnover of professional staff.

It is debatable whether this relationship between regulatory functions and management style is necessary. It may be that the relationship is the product of the desire of senior management to avoid controversy in those services that are already controversial because of the tension between service to clients and the public good. The authoritarian management style may be the product of the delivery system's self-protective aspects rather than a necessary means to obtaining its regulatory objectives.

In the 1970s there was interest on the part of consumers in participating in the internal deliberations involved in service implementation.[18] The democratic and humanistic values espoused in welfare ideology would appear to have been very favourable to such a development. Why, one wonders, was it not achieved? The reason lies in the prior existence of professional and bureaucratic dominance. The most that is acceptable is some sharing of this power. Indeed, one can perceive a hierarchy to exist between: (a) no sharing and no client participation – which remains by far the most common pattern; (b) establishment of advisory committees – which involve the recognition of some value in client contributions but maintain judgement as to their value entirely in bureaucratic and professional hands; (c) participatory structures in which some clients play roles on such bodies as agency boards and task groups.

Participatory functions should be favoured not only for value reasons but also because they would appear to be the most conducive to mutual understanding, flexibility, and change. However, this is offset by the complication they introduce into domain relationships, particularly as they are not bound to confidentiality by political, management, or professional values.

Service Consumption

Social services are intended to affect people. The test of any social service program is ultimately what it accomplishes in the lives of those who are its consumers. The process of social service consumption is thus the most critical part of the whole delivery operation. The most significant types of service evaluation are those that deal with the basic question, "Did this service obtain its objectives?"

Changing people is not easy. The objectives of change are not always clear and the means of change are far from being universally effective. Evaluative studies of social casework services, group work services, and psychiatric counselling services[19] are characterized principally by their recurrent conclusion that little change results from even the best-designed systems. Furthermore, although some social service delivery systems are in the process of helping people change in ways that they have agreed to, many social services are engaged in trying to change people against their wishes. Regulatory forms and some adaptive forms of social service have this feature.

1. *Conceptual aspects.* The major conceptual aspects of service consumption deal with the concept of consumer (or client). Thus it is realistic to expect that some social service delivery systems will create their consumers. For example, services that provide subsidized housing create a group of public housing tenants. For other types of service, the creation of clients may be an unexpected secondary consequence of service designs. A child in school cannot get along with his homeroom teacher. The teacher refers the matter to the principal, who involves the child guidance clinic. The child is singled out and the parents are interviewed by a social worker, a psychologist, and a psychiatrist. The child comes to be perceived by his parents, by the school, and by his peers as having a behaviour problem. A client is thus created. The means of delivering social services label the recipient, particularly in those

instances where a pathology or problem is the basis for service design and service use. The more problem-centred delivery systems that exist, the greater the number of persons who will be labelled by the system and become part of the system's property. Herein lies the dangerous possibility of a delivery system that grows on a self-created demand, ever seeking to use greater resources, to label more people, and then asking again for more resources to continue the cycle.

The delivery system defines its consumers through its processes of beneficiary determination, which are responsive to the objectives of the service and are basically designed to ensure that the service is delivered to those, and only those, who are intended to be changed. Neil Gilbert suggests that terms of eligibility may be classified according to four princples. (1) *Attributed need*. Eligibility is conditioned on belonging to a category or group of people having common needs that are not being met by existing institutional relationships. (2) *Diagnostic differentiation*. Eligibility is conditioned on court or professional judgements of individual cases where special goods or services may be needed. (3) *Compensation*. Benefits are allocated on the premise of equity restoration as a social right. (4) *Means-tested need*. Eligibility is determined by evidence regarding an individual's inability to purchase needed goods and services.[20] These four principles are not mutually exclusive but may be used in combination with each other.

Each eligibility principle leads to the definition of a distinctive type of social service consumer. Consumers defined on the basis of attributed need or compensation can be expected to possess their status with a greater sense of social right than consumers whose status is defined either by proof of their financial inadequacy (means-tested need) or by the superior judgement of a professional (diagnostic differentiation). These two latter bases for consumption have the effect of attributing an inadequacy to the consumer and their use corresponds to the delivery of social services that intend to regulate and/or change the consumer despite his wishes.

A consumer who is defined by a process that attributes an inadequacy to him receives stigmatized social status. The possession of that reduced status may have the effect of making the consumer more amenable to change. Thus, the admittedly difficult task of changing persons against their wishes leads to the process of stigmatization. In turn, the stigma that many social service consumers carry provides a ready means to conceal some of the inadequacies of social service delivery systems. The lack of resources to provide people on welfare with an adequate standard of living is concealed, but it reappears in the form of the assumption (and sometimes services built around the assumption) that people on welfare manage their funds poorly. The lack of change in behaviour resulting from intensive counselling is concealed but it reappears in the form of "client resistance." The lack of adequate work opportunities to permit the handicapped consumer to be independent is concealed but it reappears in the form of deprecating client hostility and lack of motivation.

The client is caught in the contradiction of delivery system design. The formal objectives may value independence of client motivation but the reality of service delivery tends to favour the malleable and dependent client. The client is thus caught in a double bind. If he acts independently then his access to the discretionary favours his social workers can confer is reduced. If he acts dependently then he is blamed for failure to become independent.

The client is faced with delivery system behaviours that appear to have a scientific and rational basis. The detailed tables used to calculate public assistance budgets and the linguistic complexity of some social therapeutic diagnostic statements are two examples. All too often, the appearance conceals either political decisions with respect to the extent of need that will be recognized or professional uncertainty and imprecision. In either case, the consumer is left with the appearance of substantial response to his problem but not the substance. His failure to change is then attributed to his pathological state. These switches between positive and negative reinforcement are not accidental. It is by these means that the human service organization applies carrot and stick to the client.

2. *Size/scope aspects.* The size/scope aspects of service consumption suggest the need for evaluation as to whether the intended consumers are the actual consumers. Where the consumer defines

himself by a self-initiated application process, then the issue is one of the proper "take up" of benefits. All persons eligible for public benefits should receive them. However, even a cursory examination of income statistics for any province in Canada will show that significant numbers of people who receive no assistance are living at income levels *below* those required for eligibility under public assistance.

This should be viewed as a discrepancy between the intended size and scope of the service and the realities of delivery, and measures to correct the situation should be taken. There are perils here on both sides. On the one hand, the reasons for the lack of take up of benefits – specifically, the stigmatized status of the consumer – can be exploited in the interest of restricting the extent of the social welfare transfer and the demand on services. On the other hand, an attempt to serve all potential beneficiaries when, in fact, the boundaries of need are ill-defined can lead to a self-serving expansion that contributes to social problems rather than solving them.

3. *Political aspects.* Service consumption is politically the most vulnerable part of social service delivery enterprise, partly because it provides a tangible measuring point as to whether objectives have been obtained, partly because the process is a visible one, and partly because all three parties – public, service deliverers, and consumers – can be seen to have legitimate interests as stake.

As with other political aspects of delivery system dynamics, those factors favouring professional and bureaucratic dominance would appear to be substantial. However, there are two major balancing mechanisms, the courts and an independent political system.

The role of the court is particularly important where recognized citizenship rights are being removed or modified. The criminal court or the family court provides the client with opportunity for a due-process examination of the facts, independent from the human service organization. Obtaining such rights is dependent on access to counsel.

The second balancing system is less well developed. Aboriginal peoples provide the best examples. Until 1963, the Department of Indian Affairs was supreme in its bureaucratic authority over

Indians. Through the introduction of community development programming directly on reserves, native people were encouraged to confront the bureaucracy that nominally served them but in fact served the society by segregating them and keeping them quiet and dependent. Walter Rudnicki writes:

> The genie was let out of the bottle – and there has been no end of trouble with the Indians since. Today they are organized nationally and provincially, they engage their own professional and technical staffs to lobby governments with well prepared briefs, they hold press conferences and sometimes march on legislatures, they have challenged major economic developments such as the James Bay Project, the Mackenzie Pipe Line and eventually perhaps the Tar Sands Development – they are claiming back large tracts of the country, including most of British Columbia – and they take no back-talk from any government bureaucrat. It is not uncommon now to see government officials waiting deferentially, hats in hand, in one of the outer offices of a Provincial Indian Association.[21]

Once such a consuming group develops an organization and a budget of its own it will not long be satisfied with dealing with the immediate issues of service consumption. It will seek a voice in the processes of goal establishment, service design, and service implementation.

There has been increasing recognition by government that the closed bureaucratic/professional nature of social service delivery system design and implementation is undesirable. The politics of consumer groups and the effects such groups have on service delivery systems may be the means to obtain more humanistic and responsive services. The political dominance of bureaucracy and professionalism is being challenged but is far from being displaced.

Issues of Multiple Delivery Systems

Up to this point, we have dealt with the concept of *a* delivery system. This represents a major simplification. The reality is a multitude of delivery systems, many of which are independent of each other and differ from each other on any of the dimensions that have been discussed.

In a typical Canadian urban community of approximately 400,000 persons (Calgary, Alberta – mid-seventies), the Calgary Community Resource Index for 1974 was a book with 363 pages.[22] Approximately eighty-three distinct services were identified – some being so general (financial services, child welfare) as to contain within each of them a series of separate service functions. These services were provided by 125 separate social agencies. Of these, seventy-five identified themselves as offering individual counselling, forty-eight identified themselves as offering group services, thirty-two provided family counselling, and twenty-four provided employment counselling. The potential consumer would appear to have faced some confusion as to who would serve him.

Some basic preventative and social utility services were provided by a relatively few agencies: only two agencies offered family planning services; only two provided a homemaker service; only two provided a meals service to the disabled or elderly; and only eight offered a day-care service. Where one organization provides several services, each service may operate as a semi-independent delivery system unit. For example, the City of Calgary Social Service Department provided both income and probation services as two largely independent services, unified principally at the level of delivery system politics but quite separate in terms of concept and size/scope dimensions.

The result of this complexity is seen in the existence of very considerable inter-system issues in social service delivery. These are the familiar social service delivery problems of duplication, co-ordination, referrals, service gaps, integration, and information.

1. *Duplication.* Duplication refers to the situation where multiple delivery systems are addressing basically the same problem and person. It may be the product of different types of politics or different concepts of the problem. For example, the family with marriage problems resulting in the problem behaviour of a four-teen-year-old boy can consume social services from any of the following major organizations: a family service agency; a mental health agency (voluntary); a mental health department (govern-

ment); a probation department; a child welfare agency. Further, there are a host of minor organizations, including independent practitioners of psychiatry, social work, psychology, or law, who may be involved. Each of these separate types of delivery varies in its goal, design, implementation, and consumption processes and in its political, conceptual, and size/scope boundary features, and, from the point of view of the consumer, some are alternatives to others.

Duplication does not imply an excess of resources. It is frequently the case that resources from the perspective of each of these delivery systems are inadequate. However, duplication makes it impossible to discern whether the existing total resources are too great, adequate, or inadequate. In addition, duplication certainly leads to social service delivery systems devoting very considerable resources to inter-system boundary maintenance and inter-system political activity.

2. *Co-ordination*. Co-ordination views the issues of duplication at the level of implementation rather than at the level of goal establishment or design. The co-ordination of social services is the practical problem faced by service administrator and worker, and this is usually expressed in terms of the lack of co-operation or co-ordination of some other part of the service delivery enterprise whose services they need but cannot get.

With the failure of attempts to obtain comprehensive social service reform in the late 1970s, increased emphasis has been given to co-ordination through the development of mandate relationships between organizations and of detailed protocol agreements. These have been accompanied by a major increase in case conferencing. The conclusion is that effective co-ordination can be achieved but the cost in terms of staff time is high. However, a failure to attend to such co-ordination results in contradictory behaviours being expected of the client and self-defeating results.

The major policy issues raised by these arrangements is that the need for co-ordination is a product of delivery system multiplication and duplication. Co-ordination offers no basic answer to these problems.

3. *Referrals*. Referrals are the behaviour manifested by this complex system at the level of the individual consumer. The consumer

can expect to be referred from agency to agency as each agency determines that the prospective consumer does not fit its mandate and tries to find a replacement.

It has been estimated that 40 per cent of clients do not follow through on such referrals. Hence, a good many clients are lost in the complex of referrals between delivery systems. Referrals can also represent a type of "sharp practice" in that the separate parts of the delivery system can each discharge their responsibilities for a particular client by sending him elsewhere. The client, or consumer, is placed in an unserved limbo by such action. The agency to whom referral is made is not obligated to serve him while the agency that has made the referral may have, in theory, completed its services.

4. *Service gaps*. Duplication does not imply comprehensiveness of service. Duplication in some sectors is completely compatible with the presence of large service gaps in other sectors. The multiplicity of case-oriented services for family problems indicated in the discussion of service duplication is completely compatible with the lack of development of preventative services relevant to such problems.

The politics of service delivery system development have led to considerable competition between separate systems and separate professions for some types of activity and neglect of the development of other areas of activity. This leads in turn to distortion in the ways in which need is perceived with the developed service sectors producing much evidence of demand for their services, but with no agency or organization producing evidence of demand for services that have been neglected. Sometimes service gaps may only be detected by international comparison.[23]

5. *Integration*. Integration of existing parts of the social service delivery system into fewer and more comprehensive systems offers the only fundamental approach to the issues of duplication, coordination, and so on, and permits a simplification and rationalization of boundaries between systems. Yet, little integration has been achieved. The reason for this lack of achievement is principally that the existing service delivery sytems defend their own identity and obstruct integration. The social service field has no parallel to the corporate takeover. Integration can only be brought

about by the exercise of power and authority from beyond the existing systems.

Table 6, which was introduced in the form of a series of questions, can now be elaborated by indicating the use of specific concepts and by the addition of multiple-system issues. (See Table 7.)

TABLE 7: *Matrix of Social Service Delivery Systems: Major Concepts*

System Processes	System Boundary Features			Inter-System Considerations
	Political	*Conceptual*	*Size/Scope*	
Goal establishment	Public "common weal" Professions Bureaucracy	Social problems Social utilities Service populations	Extent of problem or service population	Duplication Complexity Integration Service gaps
Service design	Professions Bureaucracy	Target systems Preventative/ remedial interventive method	Comprehensive/ token demonstrations Effectiveness, standards, required resources	Duplication Complexity Integration Service gaps
Service implementation	Bureaucracy Professions	Manifest/latent functions Management (and administrative concepts)	Resource adequacy Resource use	Co-ordination Referrals
Service consumption	Public/ Professions/ Bureaucracy/ Consumer vulnerability	Consumer unintended consequence "Sharp practices"	"Take up" Effectiveness Evaluation	Consumer information "Lost" consumer

This chart indicates where in the preceding discussion particular concepts have been applied. Many of the concepts are capable of broader application than to the single "box" on the matrix in which they are located.

Future Issues for Human Service Organizations

Human service organizations have become more than the vehicles of social program delivery. They are now major social organizations with internal agendas for change that are as significant in affecting social welfare as are the historic bases of income redistribution and community relations from which social welfare developed. Human service organizations are now a third force in their own right. Furthermore, they are in the midst of major types of internal change that in turn affect the social welfare goals, design, implementation, and consumption. The following major issues, which have changed the institutions of social welfare and will be a continuing source of change into the 1990s, require recognition.

1. *Cost control and change.* The social policy expenditures of provincial governments (education, welfare, corrections, health) now represent 70 per cent or more of total provincial spending and up to 100 per cent of current revenues. In other words, they have reached in total a practical limit of affordability at current levels of taxation.

However, the internal dynamics of the organizations are toward expansion to serve more people, solve more problems, and introduce improved technology. The result is increased conflict within organizations and between organizations in a win/lose form of competition. This differs from earlier stages when total revenues were growing and competition was reduced by win/win strategies. The challenge for administrators today is first to ensure cost control and then to find ways of changing the use of resources between different programs. Restraint may be necessary and has to be applied in a way that continues to provide opportunity for innovation and flexibility.

Human service organizations have "sunk" capital costs that inhibit this flexibility. Examples of such costs are buildings, systems, and the professional expertise of permanent staff. As these resources cannot be duplicated to provide for smooth transition from older programs to newer ones, it follows that there will be periods of deterioration for these sunk costs, followed by periods of major change and dislocation.

2. *Technology.* Human service organizations have extensive records and data management systems. Information, as a record of action, and in support of decisions is a major function in all human service organizations.

In earlier stages of development the records and flow of information were informal and unpatterned, but now consistency is required, not least to provide means of appeal to the consumer. Consequently, forms and procedural instruction proliferate. At the same time this detailed procedural control contributes to a steadily growing industrialization of practice.[24] This changes the nature of professional practice from a craft based on relationship to the client to an emphasis on assembling and processing information for the organization. Twenty years ago ten forms were needed to admit a child to care; now twenty are needed, and they are longer and more detailed: where once 20 per cent of social workers' time was spent on administration, it is now 40 per cent.

However, there is cause for optimism that these mechanistic changes need not in the end contribute to the dehumanizing of welfare institutions. The expansion of computer-based information systems is already under way, and this promises better management control and cost reductions through efficiency. These advantages to management are only a beginning. The real gains from advances in information technology will only come when the technology is seen as a tool for the use of the front-line practitioner, which can provide information and decision options directly to the social services worker and, hence, to the client.

One can go further and extend some aspects of this technology to the level of direct client-use systems. The process of cheque distribution is a good example of where direct client-user systems can be developed that provide all the necessary control features, protect client confidentiality, and reduce costs. At the same time the speed and certainty of this technology will have the effect of "tightening" the "loose coupling" that has been a source of flexibility and discretion in the present system.

3. *Labour relations and women's issues.* Personnel are the principal resource of human service organizations, and in major human service organizations people are organized into unions. This has increased the separation between the service domain and the management domain and provides a separate forum for negotiation and conflict. Formal public-sector disputes have become common as management has sought to respond to political directives or to make technological changes that displace staff (the closing of major

residential institutions for the mentally handicapped is an example). At the working level the same issues find expression in detailed grievance and appeal systems.

Most of the personnel of human service organizations at the working level are women. As we look toward the 1990s we should expect that women will become more influential in union organizations at the direct service level and will use this power base to obtain changes in services and working conditions that recognize such issues as flexibility of full-time/part-time statutes; day care; protection from violence or sexual harassment; adequate professional continuing education opportunity and working surroundings that are sensitive to both client and staff needs.

4. *Privatization.* Several factors contribute to the continued expansion of "privatized" forms of service delivery. The very size of human service organizations is seen by some to require control and reduction. Privatization provides for competitive processes around the award of service contracts – and hence the potential of better cost efficiency. Privatization institutionalizes "loose coupling" between parts of the social service system.

Whereas in the 1970s there was a tendency to place more of the direct management in the hands of government and to integrate services with major human service organizations, one can see an option for the 1990s whereby these organizations are broken up through privatization. Thus, the direct government functions would be reduced to policy, systems, finance, and audit.

5. *Organizational maturity and management.* Human service organizations are no longer in their formative stages; they are mature and settled institutions. As such, they have the strength of providing society with the security that comes from the consistent performance of significant social functions that meet both manifest and latent goals.

They also have major established and vested interests in their own right. The failure to obtain personal social services reorganization in the late 1970s should be ascribed principally to the obstacles that these vested interests placed in the path of change. The familiarity of known and established patterns of service and work (even if not effective or efficient) is preferred over the uncertainty and turmoil of change. Hasenfeld observes that "Human _rvice organizations seem to change only when under duress. . . . rare indeed are the instances when the organization has the foresight, the motivation, and the wherewithall to undertake innovation and change without external pressure."[25]

This is a major challenge for the management of human service organizations. It requires the development of theory and research on human service organizations through a practical combination of management and university expertise.

Notes

1. Y. Hasenfeld, *Human Service Organizations* (Englewood Cliffs, N.J.: Prentice Hall, 1983), p. 1.
2. James Kouzes and Paul Rico, "Domain Theory: An Introduction to Organizational Theory in Human Service Organizations," *American Journal of Behavioural Science.*
3. Adrian Webb, "Social Service Administration: A Typology for Research," *Public Administration* (Autumn, 1971), p. 326. (The examples used in this table have been adapted through use of Canadian rather than British programs.)
4. Lee Bolman and T. Deal, *Modern Approaches to Understanding and Managing Organizations* (San Francisco: Jossey Bass, 1987).
5. G. Westerlund and S. Sjostrand, *Organizational Myths* (New York: Harper Row, 1979).
6. Astrachan, Flynn, Geller, Harvey, "Systems Approach to Day Hospitalization," *Arch. Gen. Psychiatry*, 22 (June, 1970).
7. Mary Van Stolk, *The Battered Child in Canada* (Toronto: McClelland and Stewart, 1972), p. 15.
8. David Ross, "A Critical Look at Present and Future Social Security Policy in Canada," *The Social Worker*, 41, 4 (Winter, 1973), p. 260.
9. Hasenfeld, *Human Service Organizations.*
10. Lawrence Shulman, "The Dynamics of Child Welfare," in Ken Levitt and Brian Wharf, *Child Welfare* (Vancouver: University of British Columbia Press, 1985).
11. Noel Timms, *Philosophy in Social Work* (London: Routledge & Kegan Paul, 1978).
12. Bruce, *The Coming of the Welfare State*, p. 81.
13. Martin Rein, "Social Policy Analysis as the Interpretation of Beliefs," *Journal of the American Institute of Planners*, XXXVII, 5 (September, 1971).
14. For an introduction to the literature, see Harry Schatz, *Social Work Administration: A Resource Book* (New York: Council on Social Work Education, 1970).
15. Ajit K. Dasgupta and D.W. Pierce, *Cost-Benefit Analysis: Theory and Practice*

(London: Macmillan, 1972); A.J. Culyer, *The Economics of Social Policy* (London: Martin Robertson, 1973).

16. For an extended discussion, see Titmuss, *Commitment to Welfare*, Chapter 4.

17. R. Likert, *The Human Organization* (New York: McGraw Hill, 1967), distinguishes four styles of management: exploitive-authoritative; benevolent-authoritative; consultative; and participative.

18. Evelyn Shapiro, "Maximizing Client Participation: A New Direction in Agency Structure," *The Social Worker*, 40, 4 (December, 1972).

19. See, for example, the survey article by Helen Perlman, "Can Casework Work?" *Social Service Review* (December, 1968).

20. Neil Gilbert, "Dimensions of Social Welfare Policy: An Analytic Perspective" (Berkeley: School of Social Welfare, unpublished).

21. Walter Rudnicki, "Address to the School of Social Work, University of Manitoba" (Winnipeg, 1973).

22. Alberta, *Calgary Community Resource Index: Mental Health Services* (Edmonton: Department of Health and Social Development, 1973).

23. P.R. Kaim-Caudle, *Comparative Social Policy and Social Security: A Ten Country Study* (London: Martin Robertson, 1973), provides a useful source for comparing Canadian provisions to those available in other Western industrialized countries.

24. Michael Fabricant, "The Industrialization of Social Work Practice," *Social Work*, 30, 5 (September-October, 1985).

25. Hasenfeld, *Human Service Organizations*, p. 246.

Chapter 6

SERVICE DELIVERY:

INCOME SECURITY

Income security has been, and remains, a central feature of the social welfare institution. From a value perspective, income security is directly related to the important ideals of equality and social justice. From a definitional perspective, social welfare is defined in terms of a redistributive transfer of income or of services. From an operational perspective, income security programs – Old Age Security, the Canadian Pension Plan, Unemployment Insurance, the Canada Assistance Plan – form the largest arena of operations in terms of cost and in terms of the number of Canadian citizens who are direct beneficiaries.

Definition of what constitutes income security may at first sight appear obvious because major, familiar programs are included. However, these programs must be viewed as only part of a still larger whole, which gives recognition to four added elements: (1) the provision of goods and services rather than income; (2) the provision of assistance with social needs by tax and occupational benefits; (3) the relationship of income security to employment; and (4) programs of enforced dependency.

1. *Provision of goods and services rather than income.* Income is valued for what it permits the recipient to purchase. The provision of income is thus a means to an end. The recipient makes a choice about how he wishes to use his income and purchases the goods

and services that he or she needs. The direct provision of goods or services to recipients short circuits this chain of events in that the recipient, by gaining access to goods or services, has his need for income reduced.

The provision of housing to persons on welfare serves to illustrate the importance of this relationship. Those recipients fortunate enough to live in public housing pay no more than the "shelter" portion of their social assistance payment for rent. The difference between that amount and the full cost of the housing they occupy is provided as a second, hidden subsidy. Those who live in private-sector accommodation are denied this subsidy despite the fact that their shelter costs frequently exceed the "shelter" portion of their social assistance payment.[1]

This problem could be addressed through the development of a substantial program of subsidized, publicly owned housing (as exists in many European countries). To the extent that such a program was successful, the recipients of adequate housing would have a considerably decreased need for income.

Substantial government subsidies are already provided for medical care, education, transportation, and food costs. There are good arguments for expanding subsidies to day care to reduce costs to a level that women could afford to pay, thus helping them to avoid remaining on welfare to care for their children. These subsidies to producers reduce, and sometimes eliminate, the cost to consumers. Income alone is thus only a partial and incomplete measure of how a welfare need is met.

Debate as to whether need should be met by the provision of income or by the provision of goods and services has been dominated by concern, on the one hand, for the freedom of the recipient and, on the other, for the adequacy of the goods and services ultimately obtained. The provision of income rather than goods and services has been viewed as tending to increase the recipient's freedom. The recipient is free to choose less adequate housing in order to be better fed and clothed. The receipt of a welfare income is made similar to the receipt of income from any other source and the individual recipient can be held accountable for its use.

The provision of goods and services involves a decision as to what goods and services – and as to the standard of those goods and services. This form of subsidy decreases the consumer's freedom. These paternalistic and controlling decisions have been considered essential in the fields of primary and secondary education, social insurance, and medical care. Insofar as they apply to all, their visibility is less than is the case when such decisions are applied to individuals. At the individual level, such decisions are frequently made in social assistance programs by the provision of "discretionary" grants for such items as household repairs, winter clothing, and summer camps. Providing goods or services rather than income is inherently more efficient in terms of ensuring the ultimate receipt of the intended goods or services. Where costs are high, unpredictable, or unevenly distributed over the population, the provision of goods or services rather than income may be the only route to ensuring their ultimate receipt.

2. *Provision of tax and occupational benefits.* A second type of variant, affecting the individual's income, goods, and services (and thus relevant to the discussion of income services), acts on the original source of income. An individual's income is increased as effectively when the state waives a right to collect taxes as it is increased when the state decides to provide a specific grant. Thus the personal exemptions under the Income Tax Act increase the income enjoyed by earners with dependants. The effect is similar to that of a program like Family Allowance which involves direct grants for dependants.

In addition, an individual's control over goods and services is increased by the provision of occupational benefits. A sports club, an occupational health service, or subsidized meals are real benefits conveyed to their recipients. They may not be reckoned as part of a person's income, but they are part of the total package of compensation the person receives. Because occupational benefits are usually exempt from income tax they may be preferred types of compensation.

3. *Income security and employment.* A third influence on income security, and therefore a matter of relevance to income security policy, is the employment policies adopted by government. These are broadly of three types: policies designed to affect the quantity and distribution of employment; policies designed to affect the

rewards provided to employees; and policies designed to produce work incentives.

Policies designed to affect the quantity and distribution of employment are a product of the commitment of the Canadian government to pursue economic policies that "maintain a high rate of economic growth, full employment, reasonable price stability, an equitable distribution of rising income, and a reduction of regional economic disparities."[2] These policy objectives have not always been mutually compatible. For example, economic growth and high levels of employment have been found incompatible with price stability and an equitable distribution of rising income. In the 1960s, the commitment to full employment (variously defined as between 2 per cent and 6 per cent unemployment) was unambiguous. However in the 1970s economic policies encountered difficulty in obtaining either full employment or price stability, and the commitment to full employment was weakened. Now, in the 1980s, a 10 per cent national rate of unemployment and regional rates of 15 per cent are tolerated. These rates make it impossible for some people who want to work to find work.

There have also been programs designed to create employment by a system of government grants to organizations and groups of individuals (Opportunities for Youth and the Local Initiatives Program).

Minimum wage policies have been the principal means used to effect the rewards provided for employment. By itself, wage legislation has some deficiencies from an income security perspective, principally the lack of provision in wages for the extent of family dependencies the wage-earner has to support. This deficiency can be remedied by a combination of wage legislation and Family Allowances. Such a combination (a central feature of income security policy in France) illustrates the need to include minimum wages within a review of income security policy.

Finally, there has been much discussion in both government documents and in the media on the potential damages that could be done to the economy through a lack of co-ordination of employment and income security policy. To be specific, the vision of a large-scale exodus from employment (with consequent loss of production), and of large-scale application for income security benefits (with consequent increase in government expenditures), is frequently alluded to. To prevent such an occurrence, government policy is frequently directed at maintaining a system of positive incentives toward employment and negative sanctions on unemployment.

4. *Obligations to dependants.* A fourth residual area of influence on income security is the mechanisms of dependency enforcement. These used to be more extensive than they now are – during the 1930s, the extended family was viewed as a network to be used first by the unemployed, but today enforced dependencies are confined to adolescents and to women. Adolescents are often denied access to state income security programs and thereby forced to depend on their parents. Women with dependent children are denied access to state income security unless they agree to pursue the financial responsibility incurred by the children's father.

5. *The food banks.* Perhaps the most striking feature of the 1980s has been the role of the voluntary sector in the relief of poverty. In reality the voluntary sector never left this sector, but in the 1960s and 1970s its role was confined to desperate situations that were relieved by agencies like the Salvation Army. With the growth of unemployment and deterioration of benefit levels that have occurred in the 1980s, the voluntary sector has expanded, principally through the food banks.

The Canadian Social Security Net

The total Canadian income security system is composed of the following cash programs:

> Old Age Security
> Old Age Security – Guaranteed Income Supplement
> Family and Youth Allowances
> Child Tax Credit
> Canada Pension Plan
> Unemployment Insurance
> Workers' Compensation
> Veterans pensions
> Canada Assistance Plan (with Provincial Assistance Plans)

Assistance for native peoples.

The following goods or service programs are also part of the system:

Hospital insurance
Medicare
National Housing Act – low-income housing provisions
Provincial shelter aid and rental subsidies
Home maintenance and renovation programs
Vocational training programs
Legal Aid
Education.

In addition, the following employment related measures are included:

Full employment policies
Regional Economic Expansion Programs
Minimum Wage Legislation.

The income security system also includes the following enforced dependency measures.

Wives and children's maintenance acts
Unmarried Mothers Act.

The following fiscal measures are part of the package as well:

Personal exemptions
Tax credits
Retirement savings exemptions
Tuition free exemptions
Child-care expense exemptions
Medical and charitable expense exemptions.

Occupational welfare measures are generally employer-provided:

Sports and recreational facilities
Housing
Pension and insurance plans
Transport
Cars
Expense accounts

Tenured employment statuses (amounting to a guaranteed income).

Finally, there is the work of private agencies in food banks, shelters, and soup kitchens.

The Macdonald Commission focused its attention on social security programs and consequently did not include health, education, or employment programs; nor did it evaluate the costs of occupational welfare. Nevertheless, a total cost of $61.6 billion was recognized as a direct social security cost in 1984-85. (See Table 8.) There is no evidence that this substantial redistribution of income is being reduced. Indeed, the evidence is that this expenditure has increased at times of economic crisis and has been an effective instrument of social and political strategy.[3]

Objectives

The total system whereby the Canadian state recognizes need and acts to regulate the distribution of income – the income security system – affects the lives of all Canadians. No unified statement of objectives exists for this total system. Measures of occupational welfare are largely the subjects of employer-employee negotiation and of the design of executive compensation packages, and they are viewed as largely beyond the limits of government policy interest. The major question of government policy is whether or not these measures should be defined as income for income tax purposes. Part of the controversy raised by the Royal Commission on Taxation, the MacEachen budget (1981), and the Wilson budget (1987), resulted from the view that these measures should be considered as income. In response, there has been some change to include as income some of the more obvious occupational benefits (golf club dues, expense of maintaining a yacht, etc.). On the other hand, if a university, government department, or corporation chooses to maintain an unproductive employee on full salary, that is entirely their own private business.

Measures of fiscal welfare are part of government income tax policy. However, there is a marked tendency in government policy to deny, rather than affirm, their social policy effects. The Royal

TABLE 8: *Estimates of Government Social Security Programs in Canada, 1984-85*

| | Costs in billions $ | | |
Target Group	Federal	Provincial	No. of Persons ('000)
Poor			
Canada Assistance Plan	4.1	4.1	3,000
Provincial Tax Credits	—	1.6	107
Veterans' Allowance	0.5	—	—
Social Assistance to on-reserve Indians	0.2	—	—
Guaranteed Income Supplement & Spouses' Allowance	3.1	—	1,440
Child Tax Credit	1.1	—	5,000
Social Housing	1.1	—	—
Total	10.1	5.7	
Families			
Child Care Expense Deduction	0.1	0.0	3,700
Family Allowance	2.4	—	3,700
Child Tax Exemption	0.9	0.5	6,600
Married & Equivalent to Married	1.4	0.6	3,230
Total	4.8	1.1	
Employment Assistance			
Unemployment Insurance	11.6	—	3,200
Training Allowance	0.1	0.1	64
Worker's Compensation	—	1.6	620
Employment Expense Deduction	0.8	0.4	—
Total	12.5	2.1	
Elderly			
C/QPP	4.4(CPP)	1.6	2,330
OAS	8.3	—	2,700
Tax Assistance RRSP, RPP, C/QPP	4.7	2.3	—
Age Exemption	0.3	0.2	0
Pension deduction	0.1	—	903
Veterans' Pensions	0.7	—	655
Total	18.5	4.1	
Total income security	45.9	13.0	
Grand total	——61.6——		

SOURCE: Calculations supplied by Ministry of State for Social Development, based on 1984-85 estimates and Department of Finance figures; from *Report* of the Royal Commission on the Economic Union and Development Prospects for Canada, p. 772

Commission on Taxation accepted the need for arbitrariness in its discussion of basic exemptions:

> Income in the first bracket should be free of tax, partially to compensate for sales and property taxes, for which credit is not given against income tax liabilities, and partially because the first few hundred dollars of income are not available for discretionary use. The width of this zero rate bracket should not purport to exempt a minimum subsidized income from tax, nor should it vary with regional living costs.[4]

This tendency to arbitrariness is noted by commentators. Although there is reference in the literature to a subsistence standard "in principle," in practice "little or no attempt is made, or has ever been made, to relate the exemptions to the actual cost of living – itself an elusive concept."[5] The array of income tax exemptions constitutes an unintegrated and irrational aspect of income security policy.

The objectives of the employment-related group of programs are in a similar state of disorganization from a social policy perspective. One might think that minimum wages were designed to protect minimum standards of living. In practice, discussion is dominated by concern for the effects of adequate wages on low-income employers.

> An effective labour standards program should aim for a level of wages that is consistent with a defined minimum standard of living, and for regulation that protect workers from the hazards of long working hours. Minimum wages have rarely achieved levels considered necessary to provide for the necessities of life. Historically, it has been difficult for governments to meet their stated objectives for minimum wages because of fear that it would lead to widespread unemployment.[6]

The standard for evaluating minimum-wage levels is also changing. Whereas the standard was one of an adequate single income to support a small family, the standard is now often considered to be the adequacy of two incomes. Minimum-wage levels thus recognize that they are not set at a sufficient level to ensure that a family can live above the poverty line: rather, the test becomes whether two such incomes can ensure that a family lives close to the poverty line.

However, the concern that income security rates should not create incentives that would lead workers to opt for income security rather than low-wage employment remains. As a consequence, minimum-wage levels, which are set inadequately low, have a depressing effect on other income security policies, tending to hold them, as well, to inadequate levels of provision.

The goods or service programs include a diversity of provisions and objectives. On the one hand, the universal education and medical care programs have come to be expected from the government by all citizens. This universality of expectation results in a decrease in controversy and a tendency to overlook the effects of such programs on the field of income security. When international comparisons are made, the effects of the presence of additional programs in other countries (e.g., housing in Sweden) or the absence of programs in others (e.g., medicare in the United States) make apparent the income security relevance of universal goods or service transfers. In contrast, there are programs of a selective nature (e.g., public housing) that are inadequate in size or scope. This makes it impossible to treat such programs as reliable partners to income security policy as only a portion of the eligible population benefits.

Finally, the cash transfer group of income security programs has a unified statement of objectives only at the level of what is referred to in government documents as "guiding principles." These are so distant from the realities of provision that they fail to provide a substantial guide to provision. The Working Paper on Social Security in Canada (1973) asserts the following guiding principles:

> First, the social security system must assure to people who cannot work, the aged, the blind and the disabled, a compassionate and equitable guaranteed income.
>
> Second, the social security system as it applies to people who can work must contain incentives to work and a greater emphasis on the need to get people who are on social aid back to work.
>
> Third, a fair and just relationship must be maintained be-

tween the incomes of people who are working at, or near, the minimum wage, the guaranteed incomes assured to people who cannot work, and the allowances paid to those who can work but are unemployed.[7]

One looks in vain in statements of government policy for definitions of what is viewed as being "a compassionate and equitable guaranteed income," or "a fair and just relationship . . . between the incomes of people who are working . . . the guaranteed incomes, . . . and the allowances paid to those who . . . are unemployed." The Senate Committee on Poverty faced these issues and developed a series of poverty lines for Canada. The Committee then used these poverty lines as objectives for the income security system. The objectives declared were as follows:

TABLE 9: *Senate Committee Poverty Line, 1969 and 1985*

Family Size	1969	1985
1	$ 2,140	$ 8,850
2	3,570	14,750
3	4,290	17,700
4	5,000	20,650
5	5,710	23,600
6	6,430	26,550
7	7,140	29,500

SOURCE: Special Senate Committee on Poverty, "Poverty in Canada," Ottawa, 1973, p. 8; 1985 figures as published by Senate of Canada, "Poverty in Canada: Updated Poverty Lines 1985."

Having established these objectives, the Senate Committee's report recommended income security payments at a level that was considered "reasonable." This involved some compromises; allowances were proposed at 70 per cent of poverty lines, and non-Canadian citizens and single persons under forty were excluded from coverage.

The opinion of some commentators was that the 70 per cent goal was inadequate – "less than a first step toward ending poverty in Canada."[8] The Senate Committee's concept of "reasonable" appears to have been based on a net cost of $600 to $700 million dollars (1967), representing less than 1 per cent of Canada's Gross National Product in that year. From another viewpoint, the Senate Committee was thus proposing a redistribution of income of less than 1 per cent. The lowest 20 per cent of income-earners have received between 3.6 per cent and 4.4 per cent of total income in post-war years (see Table 10). A shift of 1 per cent would increase that share to around 5 per cent. The goal of the poorest 20 per cent of income-holders living at no less than half the average standard of living would be represented by a 10 per cent share of total income.

TABLE 10: *Distribution of Total Canadian Income by Quintiles*

	1st	2nd	3rd	4th	5th
1951	4.4	11.2	18.3	23.3	42.8
1961	4.2	11.9	18.0	24.5	41.1
1971	3.6	10.6	17.6	24.9	42.3
1979	4.2	10.6	17.6	25.3	42.3

SOURCE: Statistics Canada: Income Distributions by Size, 1979.

Nevertheless the objectives of the Senate Committee on Poverty were, and are, substantially in advance of government policies. The National Council of Welfare, the Canadian Council on Social Development, and Statistics Canada have maintained an annual series of poverty lines for Canada using a variety of methodologies. There has also been the patient documentation by David Ross of the level of income security payments and minimum wages.[10] In short, there has been no overall trend toward narrowing the gap between the poverty lines and the levels of social assistance payments or minimum wages available to low-income Canadians. Some gains were made during the 1970s, but holding on to them in the 1980s has been difficult. Some provinces froze assistance rates with the result that assistance declined relative to poverty lines. In reality Canada has two sets of poverty lines: one set is produced as "official" poverty lines by the Senate, Statistics Canada, and the Canadian Council on Social Development; the other is the poverty incomes determined by the provinces through their social assistance rates. The discrepancy is illustrated for British Columbia by Table 11.

The Present System

The present system (and it is stretching a point even to use such a term) fails to provide a statement of objectives from which its

TABLE 11: *Poverty Lines and Social Assistance Rates, B.C., 1984*

Family Size	Senate	Statistics Canada Rural	Statistics Canada Urban	Social Assistance Minimum	Social Assistance Maximum
1	8,850	7,276	9,839	3,780	5,160
2	14,750	9,510	12,981	6,840	8,100
3	17,700	12,734	17,365	9,240	9,660
4	20,650	14,270	20,010	10,440	10,860
5	23,600	17,117	23,318	11,280	11,800
6	26,550	18,687	25,468	12,120	12,540
7	29,500	20,590	28,032	12,960	13,380

SOURCE: Senator David Croll, "Poverty in Canada: Updated Poverty Lines, 1985." GAIN rates are as in effect in 1984; the variation is due to different benefits payable depending on the age, employability, and length of time on assistance of recipients.

performance can be viewed. As a consequence, the observer is forced either to construct his own statement or to adopt someone else's. In this review of the present income security system, the following criteria are used as a basis for judgement. (1) The Senate Committee's income objectives provide the standard for the benefits people should be assured of receiving. (2) Assurance should be comprehensive, in that no person is denied access to benefit because of marital status, age, employability, etc. In addition, all eligible persons should, in fact, receive benefits. (3) The means of providing benefits should contribute as little as possible to stigmatizing the recipient.

Based on these criteria, the beneficiaries, benefits, and effects of each part of the income security system can be briefly described.

1. *The occupational welfare system.* This is largely a product of the existence of governments and corporations and of the self-interest of the employees of both. Tacit recognition of occupational welfare is provided by its exclusion from the definition of "income" for tax purposes. The occupational welfare system would appear to be of greatest benefit to the upper fifth of the population, which already has 40 per cent of the total income at its disposal. No comprehensive studies exist in Canada of the form and value of occupational welfare programs. There is no stigma attached to the receipt of occupational welfare.

2. *The fiscal welfare system.* The fiscal welfare system is basically

a regressive system, giving maximum benefits to those whose incomes are highest. Studies of the incidence of taxes show that indirect taxes are borne most heavily by those whose income is lowest. The Senate Committee on Poverty indicated how the lowest group of family income-holders, those with incomes below $2,000 in 1961, paid 56.5 per cent of their income to government. This exceedingly high tax rate was composed principally of property taxes (16.3 per cent) passed on to them in the form of rents; federal and provincial sales and excise taxes (20.5 per cent); and corporate taxes (6.5 per cent passed on to them in the form of prices).[10] In contrast, those with incomes over $10,000 paid 37 to 38 per cent of their income in taxes.

The regressive nature of the fiscal welfare system is also illustrated by the effects on income of personal exemptions. These exemptions were valued at $9,190 for a family of four in 1985. The effects of this exemption are as follows:

> a. If the family had income of $9,190 they pay no tax; without the exemption they would have had to pay $2,058 in tax: the exemption is worth $2,058 to them.[11]
> b. If the family has an income of $20,650 (the Senate Committee poverty line) they pay tax of $2,689, reducing their income below the poverty line. Without the exemption they would have paid income tax of $5,495; the value of the exemption to them is $2,086.
> c. If the family had income of $40,000 they would pay tax of $8,842. Without the exemption they would have paid tax of $12,316; the value of the exemption to them is $3,574.

The total effect of the personal exemptions is thus to convey nearly twice the benefit to the family at the $40,000 income level as is conveyed to the family at the $9,000 income level.

Nor is this the end of the story. The higher the income the more exemptions from income tax can be claimed. For example, up to 20 per cent of earned income up to $3,500 can be exempted from tax through a registered retirement savings plan. However, to gain the exemption, the taxpayer has to have the money in the first place. Further, the value of this exemption increases with income in a manner similar to personal exemptions.

To these regressive features must be added the special treatments of income from capital gains, up to $100,000 of which are exempt from tax with the balance being treated at a reduced rate; of income from self-employment (from which business expenses may be deducted); and of dividends from taxable Canadian corporations (against which the "federal dividend tax credit" can be applied). All of these measures serve not to decrease income inequalities but to favour most those who already possess the highest incomes.

The receipt of benefit from the fiscal welfare system is viewed as being earned by its recipients. The Canadian Council on Social Development has argued that the entire structure of exemptions should be replaced by a program of tax credits. Such a program would specify a credit the size of which would be related to a poverty line (or other measure of minimum living standards). The credit would serve to exempt from tax all incomes below the total tax value of the credit. Beyond that value, the credit would have a single stable value and would not tend to increase in worth with rising income.[12]

The taxation proposals made by Finance Minister Michael Wilson in 1987 recognize the contribution to equity that tax credits (rather than deductions) can make. These changes will contribute to integrating the income tax and social security system in Canada.

3. *The employment relationship*. The failure of the post-war economic policies to produce a more equitable distribution of incomes has already been referred to. Despite a period of relatively full employment and considerable economic growth, the income distribution has remained constant. On analysis of the sources of income, it is found that, for families and individuals with the lowest 20 per cent of incomes, there has been a steady increase in the importance of transfer income (see Table 12).

Post-war economic policies would thus appear to have had the effect of reducing the importance of a variety of independent types of income and replacing them by an increasing reliance on transfer payments. The increase in government transfer payments has only served to prevent a fall in other types of income, leading to an increasingly unequal distribution of income.

During the early 1960s, the view taken of this problem, and of

TABLE 12: *Percentage Composition of Family Income: Lowest Income Quintile, 1951-81*

	Wages and Salaries	Self-Employment	Transfer Payments	Investment	Miscellaneous
1951	52.1	11.5	24.9	6.3	5.2
1961	46.5	9.7	34.9	4.6	4.4
1981	31.3	8.1	51.6	3.5	2.3

SOURCE: Dominion Bureau of Statistics, *Income Distributions 1961-1965* (Ottawa: Queen's Printer, 1969), p. 80; *Census of Canada*, 1981.

the relatively high unemployment rate then being experienced, was that it was caused by "structural" unemployment, that is, workers were not suitably trained for the jobs that an increasingly automated and technical society provided. The Department of Manpower and Immigration was created in 1965 to respond to this perceived problem. The Department's brief to the Senate Committee on Poverty stated:

> The primary goal of the Department is to contribute to the attainment of economic and social goals for Canada by optimizing the use, quality, and mobility of all manpower resources available to the country. Thus the policies and programs of the Department are essentially economic in character.[13]

The programs developed have served to screen the most qualified and educable workers, provide them with job opportunities and/or employment, and hence generally aid the operation of the labour market.

These are not unimportant functions but they inevitably constitute an institutional creaming function that tends to leave unserved those who are least competitive. The program serves to make the retraining of some more efficient at the price of reducing the opportunities available to those of lesser merit. There is additional evidence to the effect that even individuals who are singled out for employment (and/or training) are not necessarily the recipients of any increase in income. André Reynault, chairman of the Economic Council of Canada, explained in 1973 why an increase in the supply of skilled workers does not lead to any change in the income distribution:

Put simply, the explanation is that wages and salaries are fixed for given tasks, and the best workers get the jobs. Workers thus compete for *jobs*, not wages. From the point of view of the employer, the best workers are those who can be trained for the job at the minimum cost. If, for example, the supply of university graduates increases, they simply displace non-university graduates with no impact on the distribution of incomes.[14]

This view of the operation of the Department of Manpower and Immigration suggests that its placement and training programs[15] provide a subsidy to employers and industry rather than being relevant to the assurance of income security to individuals.

Finally, in regard to employment related income security programs, there are minimum wages, with a variety of levels in Canada. The federal government sets minimum wages for specified occupations within federal jurisdiction. For all other purposes, minimum-wage legislation is provincial. The legislation and programs contain a host of exceptions (agricultural works, trainees, piecework, etc.) and are difficult to enforce. An employee receiving less than the minimum wage has to complain, but his complaint can lead to dismissal; hence, few complaints are made. In addition, minimum wages vary widely by province and by industry. Nevertheless, in 1974 in British Columbia the $2.50 hourly minimum wage gave a total annual income, based on a forty-hour workweek, of $5,200. This income level was adequate (together with Family Allowances) to bring a wage-earner with two dependants to around the Senate Committee's poverty line.

Unfortunately, by 1985 there had been substantial deterioration. The 1985 rate in B.C. was $3.65/hour, which, based on a thirty-five-hour workweek, provided an annual income of $6,643, below the poverty line for a single person. Two such incomes plus Family Allowances and the family tax credit were, in 1985, insufficient to bring the low-income family in B.C. to the poverty line.

Thus, there are major deficiencies in the ways Canada has sought to ensure income security through employment. Other countries, notably France and Australia, have developed more substantial and more integrated programs. Further, David Ross considers that there are ideological reasons why an employment strategy toward income security should be pursued:

> To effect a fair distribution of income it will be necessary to create work and employment, and assign incomes to these employments so that people can have a proper income in the first place. It seems that any method of redistributing income that does not involve employment or making a contribution to society, will be construed simply as a transfer or a redistribution of incomes from those who work to those who do not work.[16]

The components of a policy to ensure "that people can have a proper income in the first place" have not yet been clearly defined. Indeed, despite much rhetorical endorsement of the value and importance of employment, the recent trend has been away from even the level of integration recognized in the 1960s and 1970s. Instead, in Canada, more energy has been expended on the alternative strategy of concealing and/or legitimating "a redistribution of incomes from those who work to those who do not work."In addition, there is increasing support for the idea of using transfer payments to subsidize the week-by-week incomes of the working poor. Cash payments from some form of guaranteed income would thereby subsidize employment incomes. This would continue the post-war trend to replace earned income by transfer income for persons in the lowest income quintile, and would increase the effect in the next highest quintile.

4. *Goods and/or service transfer programs.* One of the more effective ways of both concealing and legitimizing a redistribution is to link the transfer to a specified service and make it universal.[17] In essence, this is the approach Canada has adopted in the areas of primary and secondary education, hospitalization, and physicians' services. The approach is not entirely without flaw. The omission of such essentials as drugs and dental work from medical coverage is one such example. The tendency for both schools and medical services to best serve middle- and upper-income groups through an institutional creaming process is another. Nevertheless, in comparison to the state of much else in the income security field, these

programs stand out for the quality of service they provide (certainly well above "poverty-line quality"); the comprehensiveness of coverage; and the lack of stigma that accompanies use.

Canada has not developed a comprehensive public housing program, and those projects that have been built too often evidenced a "poverty" housing character. Attempts to correct this problem by strategies of dispersal and mixing also ran into opposition. In relation to dispersal, neighbourhood resistance is the problem, while mixing tenants of different incomes within a project results in substantial subsidies going to upper-income tenants or co-operative members. As a result, low-income families and individuals in Canada live principally in market housing where they frequently have no choice but to pay rents in excess of the maximum recognized by income security programs.

There are, of course, other Canadian housing programs — those in support of home ownership. These include the provision of mortgage insurance through the Canada Mortgage and Housing Corporation, the provision by provincial governments of home purchase grants, the provision of home ownership grants to defray local taxes, and the exclusion of capital gains on one's residence from the definition of income for tax purposes. These subsidies for home ownership are important social policy expenditures of government. Their deficiency is that they provide subsidies not to the poor but to middle-income groups, thus increasing the economic security of middle- and upper-income groups. They have failed to have any impact on the economic security of most low-income groups.

More generally, selective, means-tested goods and/or service programs have tended to provide low-quality goods or services, lack comprehensive coverage, and produce stigma in their recipients. The use of selective, as opposed to universal, programming for the delivery of goods and services does not appear to be a desirable income security technique.

5. *Cash transfer programs.* Cash transfers form the largest single group of income security programs. In its cash transfer programs, Canada uses six distinct income security techniques: demogrants, tax credits, income supplements, social insurance, compensation, and social assistance. The programs are also distributed between

the federal and provincial levels of government (see Table 13). The principle characteristics of each of the programs are as follows.

a. *Family Allowances and Child Tax Credit.* Family Allowances were introduced in 1945 partly as an economic measure designed to buttress spending power during the post-war period. However, since their introduction, these have been viewed primarily as an income security program. The program is operated by Health and Welfare Canada. In relation to the basic criteria outlined for the judgement of income security programs, family allowances present the following profile.

Levels of benefit under family allowances are allowed to vary by province. The average level in any province is $31/month/child (1985) and most provinces (Alberta and Quebec being the exceptions) simply pay this amount to the parents of the child.

Low-income families are also eligible to receive the child tax credit of $384/year, for a total federal payment per child under eighteen of approximately $750/year. This total payment does not meet the Senate Committee's standard, which indicates that the cost of maintaining a child at the poverty line is approximately $3,000/year. The federal government does not pretend the amount is adequate. Instead, the amount is referred to as a "contribution" designed to provide an adequate living standard "when combined with private or family earnings."[18] The level of payment is poorly

TABLE 13: *Income Programs*

Program	Technique	Government
Family Allowances	Demogrant	Federal*
Child Tax Credit	Tax Credit	Federal
Old Age Security	Demogrant	Federal
Guaranteed Income Supplement	Income supplement	Federal
Unemployment Insurance	Social Insurance	Federal
Canada Pension Plan	Social Insurance	Federal
Workers' Compensation	Compensation	Provincial
Social Assistance	Social Assistance	Provincial and Federal

* Quebec also operates its own Family Allowance program.

rationalized by such loose phrases. In recent years Family Allowance payments have also been criticized on the grounds that the
demogrant technique results in their being received by upper-
income-earners. Taxation of benefits has been the response to this
issue. Nevertheless, the need to reform Family Allowance payments, either to direct them fully to low-income-earners or to
abolish them as an expenditure saving, remains an issue at the
policy level. This uncertainty as to policy has also contributed to
periodic freezes, during which the value of Family Allowances has
not been adjusted to inflation. Family allowances are comprehensive in coverage. No person is denied benefit, so there is no
stigma attached to receipt.

In summary, the major deficiency in the Family Allowance program and the child tax credit is inadequate levels of payment. If
levels of payment were to be made adequate, they would represent
a most substantial and desirable approach to income security, providing a means of dealing with the problem of poor families without incurring stigma. Benefits to families with income above the
average could be fully recaptured by a redesigned tax system.

b. *Old Age Security*. Old Age Security was introduced in 1952.
The elderly were defined initially as persons over seventy; subsequently, the age level for receipt of benefit has been moved to
sixty-five. The program is administered by Health and Welfare
Canada. The level of benefit is now[19] set at $280/month. The value
of benefit is adjusted to inflation, the base figure of $100/month
having been established in 1973, but it is still inadequate to provide
a poverty-level living standard. The government of Canada recognizes this inadequacy and the Old Age Security – Guaranteed
Income Supplement program exists to correct this deficiency. The
base level of Old Age Security has been varied from time to time
in a similar manner to the value of Family Allowances.

Old Age Security is comprehensive in coverage. The only major
group not covered is persons with less than ten years' residence
in Canada. The recipients are not stigmatized by receipt of benefit.

In summary, Old Age Security is one of the most successful
income security programs. Its weakness is its benefit level, which
is partially offset by alternative government programming.

c. *Old Age Security – Guaranteed Income Supplement*. The Guaranteed Income Supplement program was introduced in 1966 as part of a comprehensive series of reforms affecting the income security of the elderly and is administered by Health and Welfare Canada. The reforms included revision of the age of eligibility and the benefit of Old Age Security, and the introduction of the Canada Pension Plan. The total effect of these revisions was intended to protect all elderly persons from poverty.

Benefit levels under GIS vary with the recipient's income. The maximum benefit level, paid to those with no income other than Old Age Security, is $332/month[20] for single persons and $217 per month for each member of a couple. The value of the maximum benefit is adjusted automatically to offset inflation. Additional income results in GIS payments being reduced by 50¢ for each $1 received. Assets are treated only to the extent that they produce income.

For the single person who is entirely dependent on Old Age Security and GIS the total annual benefit received is $7,356; for a couple the total benefit is $11,928. The total value of these minimum benefits is further behind poverty lines than it was in 1974 (Table 14).

Receipt of GIS appears to be broadly dispersed, the program is well advertised, and there are no substantial groups who are denied coverage. However, receipt of benefit does depend on application and completion of an income declaration. Receipt of GIS does not appear to incur a stigma. Although a selective program, the effects of selectivity would appear to be offset by wide public acceptance of the need to support the elderly.

d. *The Canada Pension Plan (Quebec Pension Plan).* The Canada Pension Plan and the associated Quebec Pension Plan were intro-

TABLE 14: *Federal Old Age Security and Guaranteed Income Supplement Benefits, Compared to Poverty Lines, 1974 and 1985*

		1974	1985
Single Person	Poverty Line	2,780	8,850
	OAS/GIS	2,247	7,356
Couple	Poverty Line	4,620	14,750
	OAS/GIS	4,288	11,298

duced in 1965. The two plans are compatible with respect to contributions and benefits. The Canada Pension Plan is administered by Health and Welfare Canada and the Quebec Pension Plan by the government of Quebec. Both are social insurance measures covering several types of long-term contingency; they are most widely known for their retirement pension provisions but they also provide benefits at death, widowhood (including orphan's benefit), and severe, prolonged disability. Benefits are adjusted automatically to preserve their value against inflation.

Benefit levels under the Canada Pension Plan are based on contribution level (for all categories of benefit) and on the number of years in which contributions were paid (for disability and retirement benefits). Contributions are based on earnings. The contributor pays 1.8 per cent of his annual earnings and his employer pays a similar amount. The ceiling (1985) on earnings for contribution purposes is $23,400. For the person who has made maximum contributions since the plan's introduction and who retired in 1985, the retirement pension was $435/month. A single person receiving such a pension would have a total government income (assuming no private income) as follows:

Old Age Security	$280
Canada Pension Plan	432
GIS ($332 less 50 per cent of $452)	116
Total	$828/month

The resulting annual income of $9,936 reaches the Senate Committee poverty line. Benefits for orphans are $87/month; benefits for widows approximate $250/month; benefits for the disabled are up to $414/month. These benefit levels are considerably below the Senate Committee's poverty lines.

The Canada Pension Plan covers all employed (including self-employed) persons, but the unemployed and the unemployable are excluded from coverage. Since 1978 there has been provision to split pension credits on marriage dissolution. This provides some equity to women, but housewives cannot contribute directly to the plan and hence are denied a benefit. Receipt of benefits is dependent on application. Thus the retired person may be eligible for three separate government payments, for each of which separate application must be made. Coverage of disability is restricted to disability that is "severe in the sense that he or she is incapable of pursuing any substantially gainful occupation; and prolonged in the sense that the disability is likely to be long continued and of indefinite duration, or is likely to result in death."[21]

Receipt of benefit under the Canada Pension Plan does not incur stigma. This would appear to be the result of the assumption that benefits are paid for by contributors. Actually this is not the case. Contribution levels are too low to cover benefits. Receipt of all retirement benefits was delayed for ten years after the plan's introduction, but this was an insufficient time period to fund full benefits. However, the demography of the Canadian population meant that in the first twenty years of the program there were many contributors and relatively few beneficiaries.

Total contributions and benefits under the Canada Pension Plan have been kept low on the assumption that private and occupational plans will provide a third level of pension benefit for Canadians. Government support for the third level of pension benefits is provided by RRSP deductions and registered pension plan deductions. The assumption is that this third level will close the gap between public plans that provide a "poverty-line" level of income, and the level of retirement income necessary to maintain the standard of living enjoyed during working years. The National Council of Welfare[22] notes many problems with this assumption. For example, more than half of the work force is not covered at all; workers frequently lose benefits through changing jobs; benefits are not indexed to inflation.

In summary, the Canada Pension Plan, in combination with other measures, does allow some retired people to escape from poverty. However, the assumption that private plans would provide the means for seniors to live in retirement with adequate incomes has not been fulfilled for many. In addition, the favourable demographic relationships between contributors and beneficiaries are beginning to reverse. Following the year 2000 this problem will become severe, forcing changes in contribution levels, general revenue subsidies, and/or reduced real benefit levels.

  e. *Unemployment Insurance*. Unemployment Insurance was in-

troduced in 1940 and has been revised several times. The major
revision of the Act in 1970 expanded unemployment insurance
to all wage- and salary-earners, increased benefit levels, increased
the period for which benefit could be obtained, decreased the
minimum period of employment that will qualify a wage-earner
for benefit, and included maternity and sickness benefits for the
first time. The intention of these changes was to increase the
income security of all wage- and salary-earners.[23] Unemployment
Insurance is administered by the Unemployment Insurance Commission, a self-independent body that reports to the federal Minister of Labour. Payments to the unemployed are provided from
the Unemployment Insurance Fund, created by contributions from
wage- and salary-earners, from employers, and from the federal
treasury. The federal treasury contribution has been essential to
the solvency of the fund in periods of recession. Wage-earners'
contributions have been raised to repay the treasury during periods of recovery.

Benefit levels from Unemployment Insurance are based on contributions, which rise with income up to a $460/week maximum
insured earnings (1985). Maximum benefits (as of July 1985) are
paid to a person whose income reaches or exceeds this ceiling for
twenty weeks and are paid at the level of 6 per cent of earnings
to a ceiling of $276/week.[23] The period during which benefits are
paid can range up to fifty-one weeks, depending on the unemployment rate and on the person's length of employment. The
benefit period for sickness and maternity coverage is fifteen weeks.
If a person's length of employment is less than eight weeks no
benefits are paid. Maximum benefits of $14,350/year are sufficient
to bring a wage-earner with one dependant to the poverty line.
This is a deterioration from the benefits available in 1974, when
maximum benefits were adequate to bring a wage-earner with
two dependants to the poverty line.

All employed persons contribute to the Unemployment Insurance Fund, but those with very short periods of earnings receive
no benefits and persons with periods of unemployment greater
than one year lose their benefits. The operational definition of
unemployment thus restricts coverage to those who are usually
employed and omits the longer-term unemployed.

Unemployment Insurance has been more controversial than the Canada Pension Plan, with beneficiaries being somewhat stigmatized. The controversy centres on the subject of work. To receive benefit, the applicant has to be unemployed and looking for work. It is assumed that some unemployment is sought (rather than involuntary), and that some beneficiaries' search for work is laggardly. A combination of employers' statements that they cannot get workers, public allegations of beneficiary "rip-offs," and administrative "cutting off" of benefits ensures that we periodically revisit this controversy.

Unemployment Insurance exhibits some of the limitations of a social insurance approach to income security. Beyond a certain point, the approach fails to conceal a transfer from one group of persons to another. The program then becomes controversial and begins to stigmatize its beneficiaries. In addition, this process begins at a point at which a considerable number of unemployed persons remain outside the plan either because of their marginal work histories or because of the length of their unemployment.

f. *Workers' Compensation.* Programs of workers' compensation were among the earliest forms of income security. The employer pays the premiums and the worker is assured some income protection but loses the right to sue the employer for damages. Such programs are typically administered by semi-independent commissions, reporting to the provincial Minister of Labour.

Levels of benefit under workers' compensation vary widely by province. A typical level of benefit is 75 per cent of salary up to a maximum. The maximum level of benefit varies widely by province, with an average of $24,000/year (1985). This brings a family of four to the poverty line, but many beneficiaries do not obtain maximum benefits. Benefits for widows and children are less adequate and, although these are now aided by the Canada Pension Plan, there are no provisions for integrating and co-ordinating the two.

Coverage under workers' compensation is required of all employers beyond minimum sizes. But there are gaps in coverage. The self-employed are one such gap. In addition, there are gaps at the individual level. The worker who undertakes duties not usually in his line of work, for example, the officer worker who assists with building renovations, may lose his protection. The process of determining eligibility, particularly in cases where the results of injury are not immediately apparent, can be lengthy and contentious. Benefits can be refused to the recipient who rejects medical advice and, say, refuses an operation that should increase his employability. Little if any stigma accompanies the receipt of workers' compensation benefits.

g. *Social Assistance.* Social assistance is the contemporary inheritor of the "poor law," "relief," "dole" tradition of income security. As such, it has a long history and no firm beginning point (unless we go back to the Elizabethan Poor Law of 1596). Recent Canadian programming has been affected since 1966 by cost-sharing between federal and provincial governments through the Canada Assistance Plan. The Canada Assistance Plan permits the federal government to enter into agreements with provincial governments whereby the provinces are reimbursed for 50 per cent of their social assistance expenditures. This reimbursement is conditional on a number of program criteria, of which the most important are: benefits must be based on need; residence cannot be a condition of benefit; provision for appeal must exist. The federal government offers consultative services to the provinces and will support services to needy persons "having as their object the lessening, removal or prevention of the cause and effects of poverty, child neglect or dependence on public assistance."[24] Benefit levels from social assistance vary by province.

Gathering accurate comparative information on benefit levels between provinces is difficult because of major variations in categories within each plan and substantial administrative discretion in meeting beneficiary needs. However, it would appear that when Family Allowances are added, benefit levels vary from approximately 50 to 70 per cent of the Senate Committee's poverty lines. Benefits from social assistance cannot usually be accumulated with any other form of income. If, for example, a beneficiary has a small disability pension, its value is simply deducted from the amount of social assistance for which the person is eligible. In addition, there are strict limits to the assets a person may have while obtaining social assistance. The differentials in levels of payment by province are more a product of different provincial ability or willingness to establish rates than of different living costs. The recognition of "need" accorded by provinces is uneven.

Table 15 provides an indication of this variation. Most provinces have made modest progress since 1974 but there are exceptions, B.C. being the most striking. In B.C. low-income people have lost ground substantially since 1974. In relation to the other provinces, B.C. went from being first to ninth in the degree to which its assistance payments ranked in relation to poverty lines.

Coverage of social assistance is broad but discretionary. It is broad in that there are no exclusions from coverage in the way that social insurance programs exclude persons who do not satisfy defined criteria. This leads to social assistance programs supporting all those persons whose need is not met by other income security programs (persons unemployed for more than one year, persons disabled but not severely disabled, elderly persons who are not yet sixty-five, etc.) Coverage is discretionary because no person is assured a right to a specific benefit level. Instead, his or her

TABLE 15: *Minimum Social Security Payments and Poverty Lines, 1973 and 1985*

	1973			1985			
Province	Payment	Poverty Line	%	Payment	Poverty Line	%	Change %
B.C.	3,840	5,740	66.8	8,561	14,750	58.0	− 8.8
Alberta	3,736	5,750	65.0	9,560	14,750	66.0	+ 1.0
Saskatchewan	3,696	5,740	64.3	9,504	14,750	64.4	+ 0.1
Manitoba	3,744	5.740	65.2	8,025	14,750	60.5	− 4.7
Ontario	3,896	5,740	67.8	9,949	14,750	67.4	− 0.4
Quebec	3,242	5,740	56.4	8,801	14,750	59.6	+ 3.2
New Brunswick	3,260	5,740	56.8	7,611	14,750	51.6	− 5.2
Nova Scotia	3,192	5,740	55.6	8,774	14,750	59.4	+ 3.8
P.E.I.	3,153	5,740	53.2	9,439	14,750	63.9	+10.7
Nfld.	2,880	5,740	50.1	9,239	14,750	62.6	+12.5

SOURCE: Senate Committee Report, adjusted for inflation to 1973 and updated in 1985. Social assistance rates for 1973 from "Working Paper on Social Security," 1973; Social assistance rates for 1984 from collected data. Minimum social security payments consist of social assistance rates, plus Family Allowances, plus child tax credit. Poverty lines and rates for 1973 are for a three-person unit; poverty lines and rates for 1985 are for a two-person unit.

circumstances are examined and assessed by the administering agency, which then makes a judgement as to whether "need" exists. Subject to limited rights of appeal,[25] the agency's judgement is final. This power is used to enforce a variety of types of dependency (e.g., upon a separated or divorced spouse), and is used to force the beneficiary to seek low-paid and unattractive work.

The stigma that accompanies receipt of social assistance is severe. The transfer is unconcealed by universality, insurance, or compensation. Surveys of public opinion indicate uniformly negative attitudes[26] and these show up in the form of the "welfare bum" stereotype. The effects on recipients are seen in their adoption of alienated attitudes and lifestyles. For most, these take the form of shame, concealment, or chronic depression. For some, they take the form of petty crime and remunerative deviancy (prostitution, shoplifting, delinquency).

Social assistance programming is a *bête noire* to social welfare critics because it visibly exhibits the failure to obtain the ideals of social welfare. Nevertheless, social assistance programming has proved very durable. Its durability is a product of its flexibility and of the lack of coverage by other programs of very common types of risk. The government of Canada recognizes these problems:

> . . . social assistance will probably remain the least acceptable type of income security payment. Because of this, income security policy should try to minimize the extent to which social assistance is used. Through the development of the guaranteed income, and social insurance programs, reliance on social assistance will be gradually reduced.[27]

This goal has not been fulfilled. As long-term unemployment levels have increased so has the number of Canadians who have no other choice but to use this last line of defence against lost income. In 1974 benefits were being received by approximately 1.2 million Canadians monthly. In 1985 benefits were being received by approximately 2 million Canadians.

6. *Enforced Dependency Programs.* Finally there is the "enforced dependency" group of income security programs. These operate in close relationship to the social assistance program. A person is considered not to be "in need" if he or she has an enforceable

dependency. Such programming affects two principal groups, youth and women with dependent children.

Youth, meaning persons between fourteen and eighteen years of age, can be held ineligible for social assistance on the grounds that their parents can, or should, support them. In practice, a considerable degree of administrative discretion is exercised. Refusing benefits, of course, does not immediately lead to the young person living with his parents. Instead, young people may subsist by panhandling, shoplifting, or prostitution.

Women with dependent children can usually assert a claim against the children's father, on the basis of either legal status (e.g., Wives and Children's Maintenance Act) or presumed natural paternity (e.g., various acts with respect to putative fathers). In either case, the woman has to lay a charge in Family Court. The charge is then pursued by a variety of collection agencies. Collection procedures have been gradually improved through reciprocal, interprovincial enforcement procedures and through automatic deduction-at-source policies. Nevertheless, this part of the income security system continues to have major problems, which include:

- Amount of support payments are inadequate even to public assistance levels. As the woman is supported in part by public assistance, the payment reduces the payment to her from public assistance. The woman gains nothing for her effort in pursuing collection.
- Payments are only collectable where the man is in stable employment. Hence, stability is penalized and moving from job to job encouraged.
- The man frequently enters into other family relationships and the effect of the payments can be to draw both families into poverty.

Some of these deficiencies could be corrected by more generous social assistance policies – permitting the mother to retain a portion of the payment so as to raise her total income.

7. *Food banks*. The food banks, located in all provinces except Newfoundland and Prince Edward Island but concentrated in Alberta and British Columbia, occupy a distinct symbolic position in the income redistribution system. They are symbols to three dis-

tinct interest groups: to conservationists they represent a means of making good use of surplus food that would otherwise be wasted; to neo-conservatives they confirm the hypothesis that voluntarism is alive and can fill gaps in the welfare system; to welfare state advocates the food banks are symbols of the failure of the state to provide adequate income security policies. To the embarrassment of the neo-conservatists the welfare banks primarily take the last of these views and are the source of continued criticism at the inadequacy of programs directed to the relief of poverty.

The primary users of the food banks are people on social assistance and Unemployment Insurance. As they serve an important function in conserving food one can expect food banks to continue and to evolve into a more integrated part of the income security system.[28]

Total System Features

Before leaving our discussion of the present income security system, the total system – a hierarchy of status and privilege – requires comment. For the upper and middle classes, there are the comfortable provisions derived from occupational welfare, fiscal welfare, and from the mortgage provisions of the National Housing Act. These provisions support standards of living well above poverty lines and the recipients are in no way stigmatized by the process of receipt. The "right" of beneficiaries is assumed to be beyond question. In addition, these groups participate in the universal service transfer programs, e.g., medicare and education, and, by a process of institutional creaming, receive the best of treatment from these systems. Despite periodic attempts to bring greater equity to the tax system the only discernible movement in the distribution of income is the increasing share enjoyed by the fourth income quintile and the lower shares enjoyed by the first, second, and third quintile.

Finally, the distinction between the "deserving" or "worthy" poor and the "undeserving" or "unworthy" poor, which has been made since Elizabethan times, remains with us. For specific categories of the deserving poor, e.g., the elderly and the temporary unemployed, poverty-line programs come in two basic forms, universal guaranteed income programs and social insurances. These programs do not totally avoid stigma and are patchy in their coverage, with some types of need being omitted. However, those persons who are covered are assured of a right to their benefits. The level of these benefits has been maintained through the 1970s and 1980s, but it has not improved.

Then there are the undeserving poor. Here the programs (social assistance, public housing, enforced dependencies, etc.) are definitely below the poverty line. The recipients are stigmatized and their benefits are subject to administrative discretion with only limited rights of appeal. In that the beneficiaries are covered by universal service transfer programs they tend to get the worst treatment – the poorest facilities, the least qualified professions, the inconvenience of long waiting periods. For this group the period since the Senate Committee on Poverty report has been very uneven. In some provinces they are now deeper in poverty than when the report was published. The effect of the lack of national standards is very apparent.

Proposed Reforms

A number of proposals bearing on the future of the Canadian income security system have been considered. The major proposals have been *Poverty in Canada*, the report of the Special Senate Committee on Poverty, (1971); *Working Paper on Social Security in Canada*, (1973); and *Report of the Royal Commission on the Economic Union and Development Prospects for Canada* (1985).

1. *Report of the Special Senate Committee on Poverty*. This report proposed the introduction of a new income assistance program for which eligiblity would be established on the basis of annual income as shown on the individual or family income tax returns. This program was referred to as a negative income tax program with the following features:

- Single persons under forty were excluded.
- Benefit levels were at 70 per cent of poverty lines.
- Earned income was recaptured at the rate of seventy cents on the dollar.

• Income tax exemptions were increased and integrated with the negative tax system.
• Old Age Security, GIS, and Family Allowances were abolished.

The proposed negative income tax program was viewed as additional to other income security programs rather than as an alternative. Social assistance would continue to exist for some categories of applicant and the Canada Pension Plan and Unemployment Insurance would be retained.

2. *Working Paper on Social Security in Canada*. Although this contained detailed proposals, for example, to increase at that time Family Allowances to $20/month, it was not comprehensive. It stated a variety of principles and five strategies:

• an employment strategy, including work incentives, government job-seeking, and a community employment program.
• a social insurance strategy, consisting of expansion of existing plans.
• an income supplement strategy, including Family Allowances, income supplements for the working poor, income guarantees for the unemployment, and a residual social assistance program.
• a social aid employment service strategy, including such services as training, counselling, and day care.
• a federal-provincial strategy designed to secure minimums while providing for provincial flexibility.

These were seen as the beginning point for federal-provincial negotiations leading to a new income security system for Canada – similar to that proposed by the Senate. However, lengthy negotiations did not produce federal-provincial agreement and the reform of income security was not achieved.

While federal-provincial discussions were proceeding, a major experiment in income security programming was undertaken in Manitoba to pre-test the effects of the proposed guaranteed annual income on work incentive. The test was concluded and its results supported the conclusion that the guaranteed income would not reduce work incentives.[29]

3. *Report of the Royal Commission on the Economic Union and De-*

velopment Prospects for Canada. The Macdonald Commission eloquently restated the case for major changes in the income security system. This case had been clearly made in the early 1970s, but by 1985 the weaknesses of the existing system were even more apparent:

- Many Canadians are still in poverty while payments go to many who are not.
- The system is too complex, with too many programs and too many people administering them.
- The system creates serious work disincentives; both Social Assistance and Unemployment Insurance having effective 100 per cent marginal reduction rates on benefits.
- The system is inequitable – tax benefits increase with income.

The Commission considered the case for partial reform but concluded that major changes were both possible and necessary to correct the weaknesses of the present system.

The principal proposal was for a "Universal Income Security Program" to replace the Guaranteed Income Supplement, Family Allowances, child tax credits, married exemptions, child exemptions, federal contributions to Social Assistance payments, and federal social housing programs. The central features of UISP would be a universal minimum guaranteed rate of income, federally funded and administered. Payments of UISP would be reduced with receipt of other income at a rate that would maintain work incentives and integrate with income tax rates. Although the Commission made specific proposals for guarantee and tax-back rates it also made it plain that these features should be flexible. The principal proposal was not specific rates but a fairer and simpler means of providing income security and work incentives than exists at present.

The reception to the Royal Commission's work has been divided and muted. Lack of enthusiasm can be ascribed to the following arguments:

- Although in total the present system is ineffective and contradictory, proposals to change large parts of it inevitably involve the withdrawal of benefits from those who are enjoying them at present: from a political perspective the chance of losing their support appears substantial.

• The proposed revision would still leave substantial numbers below poverty lines; thus, it was greeted without enthusiasm by those who would benefit.

• The proposals do not address fundamental issues of economic policy and equity; indeed, they are presented within an overall residual framework in which the major proposed change is the entry of Canada into a free trade union with the United States. The revised income security system is seen as a necessary mechanism to protect Canadians from the effects of some of the economic changes resulting from the union. This argument doesn't find support from those who reject the case for free trade in the first place.

• The agencies, both federal and provincial, that operate the present programs are committed to the status quo – their interests are vested in the present systems and administration. The view taken by them of the Commission is a mixture of astonishment and bemusement. The Commission is seen as being incredibly naive in its simplistic assumption that major changes in spending patterns could be achieved in the manner proposed.

Nevertheless, the Macdonald Commission has served as a reminder to us that the issues that made reform of income security a major issue in the 1970s remain unanswered.

Looking to the Future

As one looks to the future of income security and the distribution of Canadian income in the 1990s, three broad options appear to be open for public debate: (1) neo-conservative incremental retreat; (2) systems reform within its present fiscal boundaries; (3) systems reform and change in the income distribution in favour of the lower two income quintiles.

1. *Neo-conservative incremental retreat.* This option is based on a continuation of present conditions and policies into the 1990s. Social policy does not have to be a priority in this option, which is driven partly by concern for the budget deficit and partly by basic conservative values favouring economic freedom and min-

imum government. The hypothesis underlying this approach is that the welfare state has expanded benefits, thereby raising the threshold at which work is worthwhile and encouraging people to leave productive employment and live off benefits. Reducing benefits and making them more difficult to collect is thus necessary to restore work incentives.

Lipsky details various ways in which financial obligations in income security programs can be reduced "through largely obscure bureaucratic actions and inactions of public authorities."[30] These include:

- rationing access to benefits by increasing the cost and inconvenience to clients of applying;
- rationing benefits by setting aggregate dollar limits and adjusting administration within these limits;
- failing to adjust to inflation and other changes in need;
- decreasing worker discretion to meet "hardship";
- restricting access to system information to keep it away from the general public and critical inquirers,
- providing funding support to outside groups on a contract basis that restricts their freedom to criticize;
- contributing to the general perception that change will not occur so advocacy is useless.

The neo-conservative option is compatible with a major recession leading to restrictive policies, such as putting ceilings on expenditures and benefits. It could also be applied through an accelerated application of restrictive policies in a clear political initiative, as was undertaken by Premier Bennett in British Columbia in 1983.

Applied to people of working age, the approach leads to an increase in the gap between poverty lines and minimum income security rates. Indeed, one could expect to see poverty lines being either revised downward or, "better," abandoned. Why remind people of an objective set twenty years ago when there is no intent to pursue it? For the pension system this option leads to expansion of private pensions, aided by increased fiscal benefits. The Mulroney government has made a start there by raising RRSP deductions and not proceeding with Canada Pension Plan reform.

From the perspective of overall income distribution, one can expect that the combined effect of these changes will be to raise the total share of income enjoyed by the two highest income quintiles and reduce that held by the lowest two quintiles.

2. *Systems reform within present fiscal boundaries.* This option is essentially the one presented by the Macdonald Commission and, in a more limited way, by the Commission of Inquiry on Unemployment Insurance (1986). The problems of the present income security system are acknowledged within a fiscal framework that accepts that economic adjustment and growth are the priority issues. Furthermore, income security is seen as having a residual relationship to economic change and is intended to compensate for economic disadvantages resulting from changes in the economy.

The need to control budget deficits is accepted. Changes that can remain on the policy agenda within this framework include:

• retention of non-social security income and work incentives. This would ensure that income security recipients always retain a substantial portion of earned or unearned income. As a result, work would always be to the advantage of recipients and the working poor would receive equitable benefits.[31] Separated families and children could retain a higher portion of spousal maintenance. Investment income and savings could be retained by beneficiaries, rather than their being required to pauperize themselves as a condition of receipt of assistance.
• a broad program of subsidized day care.[32] A major problem of the present income security system is the difficulty of providing both adequate support to the one-parent family and a work opportunity to single parents. A comprehensive program of subsidized day care would resolve this problem and would be a major step toward making the income security system more equitable for women and children.
• political and administrative simplification. There is an excellent case for exclusive federal income security jurisdiction. Income security is a central aspect of citizenship, a companion to national economic policy, and a major means of ensuring interprovincial equity. The record of provincial action and

inaction causes no confidence that these objectives will be achieved on the basis of provincial initiative.

Major administrative advantages would also flow from exclusive federal jurisdiction. To the recipient this can and should mean "one-stop shopping" for income security. The recipient should be able to establish her or his full fiscal entitlement at one time in one place. In addition, administration and control would be improved through relation to the tax system.

• increase contributions and benefits through the Canada Pension Plan. The weaknesses of private pension plans are now clearly established. They cannot be relied on to provide retiring baby boomers (after the year 2000) with income replacement in old age. Now is the time to initiate substantial increases in both contributions and benefits.[33]

These changes require that income security be seen as a priority for policy attention at the national level. They could be introduced as a result of a major recession and the consequent need to look at income security comprehensively. However, as a recession would also increase income security costs, the fiscal boundaries of present expenditures would then have to be exceeded.

What cannot be accomplished within this approach to economic and social planning is a sufficiently large measure of income redistribution to ensure that low-income Canadians have a guarantee of incomes at established poverty-line levels.

3. *Reform and change in income distribution to favor the lower two income quintiles.* There have been major changes in the financial and fiscal situation since the early 1970s. At that time economic growth, accompanied by increased government revenues, was anticipated. Funding higher levels of benefit was then seen as a discussion about how to spend rising levels of total income. This period ended during the 1970s. In the 1980s economic growth is at best limited, while from a fiscal perspective the size of the deficit dominates government revenue/expenditure discussion.

This does not mean that all options to improve Canada's income distribution have been lost. But it does mean that the only option open is higher levels of taxation (both individual and corporate) on higher-income-earners in order to fund a better standard of living for low-income-earners. By international standards the proportion of Canadian income being redistributed through income security has remained at modest levels.[34] We could do more if we wanted to. Of the OECD countries, Canada's expenditure on pensions ranks twelfth, at 4.6 per cent of Gross Domestic Product. By way of comparison, Italy spends 13 per cent of Gross Domestic Product; Germany 12.5 per cent; Sweden 11.8 per cent; United Kingdom 7.4 per cent; U.S.A. 7.4 per cent. Clearly, we have not reached the limits of fiscal ability to make better public pension provisions.[35]

If more is to be done, it needs to be done in combination with the measures of systems reform discussed above: simply raising benefit levels in the present system will only increase contradictions and problems that have been thoroughly documented.

The relationship of work to income security also requires treatment within this perspective. Income security income is never completely free of stigmatizing consequences and is a secondary form of income in a society in which the primary forms are income from ownership or investment and income from employment. If the central objective of income security is a more equitable and stable income distribution, then income security payments on their own cannot be counted on to do the job. The first principle of such a system should be an employment strategy to ensure that all who want to work can work – and thereby provide a contribution to society for which they receive a reward. The basic strategy should be to expand employment income within the lower two income quintiles while maintaining the present levels of transfer income. This would reverse the post-war trend to replace employment income with transfer income. This will call for a more planned approach to the economy and work than that envisaged by the Macdonald Commission,[36] which adopted a traditional "liberal" position on the relationship between economic and social policy. The perspective taken in this view is reformist and socialist.

The second principle of such a system is that it should be contributory. The main significance of contributions is the contract they create between the contributor/beneficiary and the community. Contributions during employment have been a most satisfactory way of decreasing stigma and stabilizing welfare transfers. All the Western European states that have developed high levels of social expenditure have made social insurance a central part of their social security measures.

The Meech Lake Accord

At the time of writing it is difficult to assess the impact of the Meech Lake Accord on the future development of income security policy. The option that the Accord provides to provinces to opt out of new shared-cost programs and receive fiscal compensation would appear to make the initiation of such programs difficult. However, the provincial reception of federal day-care initiatives suggests that a positive response will occur where there is a joint advantage.

In the longer term, one could expect that the Meech Lake Accord will tend to strengthen the case for exclusive federal income security jurisdiction. Such a change would be consistent with clear national standards, rights, and benefits and would also be consistent with simplified administration and access for recipients.

Notes

1. Davis Neave, "Housing of Welfare Recipients in Calgary," *Canadian Welfare*, 49, 4 (July-August, 1973).
2. Canada, *Income Security for Canadians*, p. 11.
3. Keith Banting, "The Welfare State and Inequality in the 1980s," *Canadian Review of Sociology and Anthropology*, 24, 3 (1987).
4. Canada, *Report of the Royal Commission on Taxation* (Ottawa: Queen's Printer, 1966), Vol. 3, Part A, p. 35.
5. Gwyneth McGregor, "Personal Exemptions and Deductions," in *Canadian Tax Papers* (Toronto: Canadian Tax Foundation, 1962), p. 9.
6. Canada, "Task Force on Labour Relations," in *Canadian Industrial Relations* (Ottawa: Queen's Printer, 1969), p. 202.
7. Canada, *Working Paper on Social Security in Canada* (Ottawa: Queen's Printer, 1973), p. 17.
8. See Reuben Baetz and David Critchley, "Two Poverty Reports," *Canadian Welfare*, 48, 1 (January-February, 1972), p. 3.
9. J. Harp, and J. Hofley, *Structured Inequality in Canada*, (Toronto: Prentice-Hall, 1970), p. 25.

10. David Ross, *The Working Poor* (Ottawa: Canadian Institute for Economic Policy, 1981).

11. Tax rates used here are proportional to income. The actual figure for amount of tax payable is taken from the 1985 income tax guide for B.C.; amounts of provincial tax payable in other provinces vary slightly.

12. For a discussion of tax credits, see Canadian Welfare Council, *The Social Implications of Tax Reform* (Ottawa, 1970).

13. Department of Manpower and Immigration, "Brief presented to the Special Senate Committee on Poverty," First Session, No. 10, p. 372.

14. Andre Reynauld, "Income Distribution: Facts and Policies," speech to The Empire Club, Toronto, February 1, 1973.

15. In 1968-69 the Department operated 369 centres, employed 6,000 counsellors, and spent over $190 million to train 240,000 persons.

16. David Ross, "A Critical Look at Present and Future Social Security Policy in Canada," *The Social Worker*, 41, 4 (Winter, 1973), p. 271

17. For a discussion of transfer dynamics, see Chapter Two.

18. Canada, *Working Paper on Social Security in Canada*, p. 29.

19. Canada "Inventory of Income Security Programs," Ottawa, 1986.

20. *Ibid.*

21. Canada, *Disability Pensions and Benefits* (Ottawa: Department of Health and Welfare, 1972).

22. National Council of Welfare, *A Pension Primer in Pension Reform* (Ottawa, 1984).

23. Canadian Welfare Council, *Unemployment Insurance in the '70's* (Ottawa: Queen's Printer, 1970).

24. Canada, *Canada Assistance Plan* (Ottawa: Queen's Printer, 1966), Sec. 2(m).

25. For a discussion of appeal rights, see Walter Stewart, "Welfare and the Right to Appeal," *Canadian Welfare*, 46, 2 (1970).

26. See, for example, Alberta, *Public Attitudes Toward Public Assistance in Alberta* (Edmonton: Department of Health and Social Development, 1973).

27. Canada, *Income Security for Canadians*, p. 28.

28. For a fuller discussion of the role of foodbanks, see G. Riches, "Feeding Canada's Poor" in J. Ismael (ed.), *The Canadian Welfare State* (Edmonton: University of Alberta Press, 1987); G. Riches, *Food Banks and the Welfare Crisis* (Ottawa: Canadian Council on Social Development, 1986).

29. R. Splane, "Whatever Happened to the Guaranteed Annual Income?" *The Social Worker*, 48, 2 (Summer, 1980).

30. Michael Lipsky, "Bureaucratic Disentitlement in Social Welfare Programs," *Social Service Review*, 58, 1 (March, 1984).

31. National Council of Welfare, *The Working Poor: People and Programs* (Ottawa, 1981); Ross, *The Working Poor*.

32. Canada, *Report of the Task Force on Child Care, Status of Women* (Ottawa, 1986).

33. National Council of Welfare, *Pension Reform* (Ottawa, 1984).

34. See Table 2.

35. Keith Banting, "Institutional Conservatism: Federalism and Pension Reform," in J. Ismael, *Canadian Social Welfare Policy* (Montreal: McGill-Queen's University Press, 1987).

36. See, for example, Cy Gonick, *The Great Economic Debate* (Toronto: James Lorimer, 1987).

Chapter 7

SERVICE DELIVERY:

PERSONAL AND

COMMUNITY

SOCIAL SERVICES

Range of Services

The term "personal and community social services" is used to indicate a series of services with a number of common features, including: philosophy of service centres on the individual and is concerned that processes of socialization, mutual support, and adaptation be satisfying to the individual and to the community of which he is a part; the primary helping personnel are from social work or social work-related para-professions, e.g., child-care workers and probation officers; the auspices and resources of these services have come increasingly from the state, although some aspects of an earlier philanthropic stage of auspice and support remain; and the populations served are similar and overlap one another, causing problems in interconnection and relationship of services to each other. These common features provide the context for a series of differing patterns in which services have been integrated and related to local communities. In specific terms, the services to be considered include:

• social utility services:[1] day care, homemaker, information services, counselling, family planning, family life education, meals-on-wheels, transportation.

- social adaptation services: parental neglect and abuse, delinquency, mental illness, child welfare.
- institutional resource services: boarding homes, foster homes, nursing homes, children's institutions, institutes for the physically handicapped, institutions for the mentally retarded, etc.
- community adaptation services: social planning councils, community development services, community associations, etc.

The current auspices of these services include:

- entrepreneurial auspices: marriage counselling, psychiatry, some forms of day care.
- philanthropic auspices; family services agencies, Canadian Mental Health Association, social planning councils, etc.
- government departments of social welfare or social development: e.g., social assistance social services, child welfare services, children's institutions.
- government departments of health: mental health, family planning, etc.
- government departments of education: special education, alternative schools, etc.
- government justice departments: family court, probation, juvenile correctional institutions, etc.

Related service systems that share some features with those described above, but that differ in others, include:

- health services: private physician services, treatment hospitals, etc.
- schools.
- adult corrections: jails, penitentiaries, parole services.
- employment services; job placement, manpower training.
- income security: Family Allowances, Social Assistance, etc.
- physical planning.

Patterns of integration of these related service systems, vary widely, as shown in Table 16.

TABLE 16: *Provincial Child Welfare Service Systems*

Province	Ministry and Division Responsible for Child Welfare	Children's Service Integrated with This Ministry		Delivery System
		Juvenile Corrections	Health	
Nova Scotia	Department of Human Resources	X	—	13 Children's Aid Societies: 5 govt. offices
New Brunswick	Department of Social Services, Personal Social Services Division, Child and Family Services	—	—	Government offices changing to local resource boards and integrated system in 1985
Nfld.	Department of Social Services	X	—	Government offices
P.E.I.	Department of Health and Social Services, Social Services Branch	X	X	Government offices
N.W.T.	Department of Social Services, Family and Children's Services	X	—	Government offices
Yukon Territory	Department of Health and Human Resources	X	X	Government offices
B.C.	Ministry of Human Resources, Family and Children's Services	—	—	Government offices (formerly resource boards, similar to Quebec)

The Present System

The present array of personal and community social services was not designed as a total system. As a consequence they are dominated by a series of independent and competing service enterprises. Major characteristics of the whole of the system can be seen from this review of services relevant to family and children's service issues.

TABLE 16: *Provincial Child Welfare Service Systems*   (*Cont'd.*)

Province	Ministry and Division Responsible for Child Welfare	Children's Service Integrated with This Ministry		Delivery System
		Juvenile Corrections	Health	
Alberta	Department of Social Services and Community Health, Child Welfare Branch	X	X	Government offices
Sask.	Department of Social Services, Family and Community Services	X	—	Government offices
Manitoba	Department of Community Services and Corrections, Child and Family Services	X	—	Government offices 4 Children's Aid Societies; Native Children's Aid Societies
Ontario	Ministry of Community and Social Services, Children's Services Division	X	Mental Health	Over 50 Children's Aid Societies (Native Children's Aid Societies to be started in 1985)
Québec	Ministère des Affaires Sociales; Direction des Politiques du services sociaux, Services des politiques à l'enfance et à la famille	X	X	Local government social service centres with regional boards

SOURCE: Ken Levitt and Brian Wharf (eds.), *The Challenge of Child Welfare* (Vancouver: University of British Columbia Press, 1985).

1. *Social assistance social services.* Social assistance social services have been developed around the Social Assistance income security program and are administered by either municipal or provincial government departments. Expansion of such services was one of the major objectives of the Canada Assistance Plan. In contrast to earlier cost-sharing arrangements with the provinces, the Canada

Assistance Plan included provision for the federal government to provide 50 per cent of the costs of "welfare services." These were defined as including such services as casework, homemaker, day care, and community development.[2] As a result of joint federal and provincial actions the types and quantity of municipal and provincial social services were expanded.

The objectives of these services are broadly stated in the Canada Assistance Plan as being "the lessening, removal or prevention of the causes and effects of poverty, child neglect or dependence on public assistance." This desirable breadth of approach covers a variety of types of anti-poverty strategy including community development, designed to combat the culture of poverty. Homemaker and day-care services as well as individual and family counselling services are included.

Coverage of social assistance social services tends, for practical purposes, to be limited to income-earners below the poverty line. The intent of the Canada Assistance Plan was to provide services that would reach a rather larger population and thereby "prevent" some from falling into poverty. This is a difficult concept to apply. As a consequence, the primary criterion in access to such services is "need," which is decided by the application of "a test established by the provincial authority that takes into account the person's budgetary requirements and the income and resources available to him to meet such requirements." However, there is an additional reason why Canada Assistance Plan social services are limited to people living below the poverty line and to Social Assistance recipients. The services are "labelled," identified with Social Assistance payments. Since the services operate under the same stigma as the income program, people stay away to avoid being viewed as in "need" or "on welfare." Some provinces[3] have organized special independent preventative social service programs to overcome this problem.

The quantity and quality of social assistance services are also open to question. Government social assistance departments continue to exist with a public that views expansion of the extent and cost of the services they provide as inherently undesirable. Latterly, the test of service effectiveness has become the impact on recipients of assistance. The only way to get funding has been to argue the cost-benefit of the service in terms of public assistance expenditures, not the need of the families. The quality of the counselling has been low, principally because the size of the caseloads has been such that no counselling could be done. Caseloads in the hundreds are not uncommon. This in turn has made such counselling in public assistance unattractive to social workers and has led to the development of financial assistance workers: a subprofessional category dealing only with social assistance. This also served to reduce staff turnover. However, the agencies have rarely been able to develop the staff to provide the services they sought to offer.[4]

Evaluation of the effect of social services on the poor has not encouraged the ideal that such services offer an effective strategy to deal with poverty.[5] Even if services are adequate the result tends to be better served poor people; but they are still poor people.

As a consequence of these considerations there has been considerable interest in separating service and income programs. That is, the social services would be developed as services in their own right. The Senate Committee on Poverty advocated such a separation by removing all responsibility for income security to the federal level of government while leaving the provinces to provide social services, supported by a revised and expanded Canada Assistance Plan. Specifically, a service/income separation should have the effects of: (a) making services available to a wider public as the stigma of Social Assistance would not obstruct their use; (b) permitting services available to a wider public as the stigma to deal with poverty; (c) improving the quantity and quality of services by identifying them with positive aspects of the quality of community life; (d) removing the coercion that Social Assistance recipients feel in using services that are "recommended" to them by the same social worker who controls their income.

In some jurisdictions these arguments have been recognized, while in others social assistance social services remain as a special category of service – effectively limited to receivers of assistance and hence part of the overall poverty trap.

2. *Child welfare services.* Child welfare services were developed initially in urban centres by Children's Aid Societies, supported by organized philanthropy. In most provinces, this pattern has

been replaced by government services. The pattern in the sixties . and seventies was one of increasing government support to Children's Aid Societies (reaching up to 95 per cent of their budgets), followed by incorporation of their function into government social services. The government services are provided by provincial departments of social welfare and operate alongside – sometimes integrated with – the same department's social assistance programs, and are included under the cost-sharing provisions of the Canada Assistance Plan.

Although this "integration" was viewed favourably in the 1970s, experience has suggested that significant areas of conflict exist between the two services, with the result that: "In retrospect, many of the architects [of integration] would now do things differently . . . [and] would not integrate income assistance with child welfare."[6] The integration also served to avoid the administrative problems that some provinces would otherwise face in separating child welfare from social assistance costs. Health and Welfare Canada has not involved itself in the design and operation of provincial child welfare programs to any considerable extent.

The objectives of child welfare programming are primarily to correct a series of specific problems, including child abuse, child neglect, child behaviour problems, and unmarried motherhood. In order to provide resources for these purposes, child welfare authorities also operate foster homes, group-living homes, and more specialized institutional-type treatment homes. Child welfare agencies also provide adoption services. This residual, problem-oriented group of services can in no way be identified with any comprehensive view of the welfare of children. The position taken is that the welfare of children will be looked after by the family. In unusual circumstances, the family fails to perform expected functions and child welfare authorities intervene to make alternative arrangements for the children. Overlooked in such a view is the abundant evidence of difficulty experienced by *all* families in fulfilling their child-care functions in society. The development of a broad array of family supportive services – family life education, day care, homemakers, family counselling services – has not been viewed as a central function of child welfare authorities. Still less have child welfare authorities sought to play a social planning role in the development of a society that as a totality would show respect to children. For example, child welfare agencies have not developed programs to offset the effects of wide-spread child poverty.

The effects of the residual, problem-centred focus on child welfare services are seen, too, in the coverage and conditions of access to child welfare services. In relation to the most serious form of child-care problem, child abuse, child welfare services aim at comprehensive coverage. Data from a variety of services on the occurrence of physical child abuse tend to the conclusion that the majority of cases do come to the attention of child welfare authorities. This is not true for sexual abuse, where information from sociological studies suggests that as few as one in ten incidences of sexual abuse are ever brought before child welfare authorities.[7] Hence, the coverage of sexual abuse and of the more pervasive, and less clearly defined, "neglect" of children is both uneven and difficult to assess.

Neglect includes such conditions as leaving children unattended for long periods, and failure to obtain minimal standards of cleanliness, health care, and nutrition. These conditions are on a continuum with normal behaviours. The problem-centred approach to service development suggests that the continuum has to be cut at some point: but where? Any point seems arbitrary. In practice, considerable variation occurs depending on such factors as ethnicity, community norms, and individual worker variations. In contrast, a "social utility" approach to the subject of neglect would have defined the whole subject in terms of access to family supportive services. Coverage of unmarried mothers has similar features. The unmarried mother has to accept a "problem" definition of herself and deals with an agency that will tend to weigh her child-care abilities against those of a married couple who wish to adopt. Services for unmarried mothers that support a decision to keep a child are a recent development.

The quality of child welfare services, if measured by the extent of social work professional education, has been better than that of social assistance services. The development of Bachelor of Social Work degrees at the undergraduate level has been helpful here, with most provinces being able to require a BSW degree as the entry-level qualification. The availability and quality of resources, particularly foster homes, have been the cause of chronic concern. Foster parents are paid expenses and are now usually paid a fee for services based on the amount of supervision required. Gradually, increased numbers of people with formal child-care education have entered these roles, and the standards of professionalism are rising. These gradual changes remain to be formally professionalized through assertion of standards. They have also resulted in major increase in costs (particularly in urban areas) and the virtual disappearance of the older style of volunteer foster home.

This change to more professional child care has also been accompanied by shorter periods in care and an accent on permanency planning through adoption. A less desirable result of these changes is that they tend to see the child more in terms of "treatment" and "temporary care" than in terms of parenting. The result is seen in the records of children in care many of whom have lived in ten or more foster homes in a period of a few years. The result is also seen in the lives of children who grow up faced with a continuous pattern of rejection and no sense of relationship to others. Too often, social service instability has been the substitute provided for parental neglect.

Aware of the dangers involved in using foster homes and in the advantages of keeping a child with his or her natural parents, social workers have been reluctant to apprehend children and have stressed the need for preventive family services.

3. *Juvenile corrections.* The development of services for juvenile delinquents can be dated from the Juvenile Delinquents Act of 1908. The Act was revised several times and then in 1984 was replaced by the Young Offenders Act, which abolished the status of "delinquency" in favour of the more precise status of "offender." The Young Offenders Act is a federal statute, part of the Criminal Code of Canada, and provides, in effect, for a series of court procedures and court dispositions for persons between the ages of twelve and eighteen that are different from those applicable to adults. The Act also decriminalizes behaviour for children under twelve by withdrawing authority for criminal proceedings.

All aspects of the administration of the Young Offenders Act are provincial. Juvenile courts, probation services, and institutional facilities are all operated by the provinces. These services tend to fall across major established lines of provincial departmental bureaucracy, causing the development of a variety of administrative patterns. The Juvenile Court is usually administratively responsible to the provincial Attorney-General. On the other hand, some of the resources needed by a service to juveniles are obviously child welfare services (foster homes and children's institutions). The result is that while in some provinces the probation service is established within the Attorney-General's department, in other provinces it is established within the provincial Department of Social Welfare and in still others directly as a part of the Juvenile Court.

The objectives of juvenile correction services are even more clearly problem-focused than is the case with child welfare services. The central function of juvenile corrections has been to control and rehabilitate adolescents adjudged "offenders" by the courts. The implicit theory behind this function has the following features: the community cannot overlook (or tolerate) any form of criminal behaviour; if the offender can be caught, he should be punished and reformed, however, the punishments contained in the Criminal Code are too severe and overlook the importance of growth and change in young people's lives. Thus, flexibility is needed in the measures that can be taken, which include discharging offenders to parents, probation, and children's institutions. In addition, correctional authorities have increasingly recognized an obligation to work with families and communities to build both support and control at the community level.

The coverage of juvenile correction services has many similar characteristics to child welfare services. At the core of the phenomenon are a small number of brutal acts that endanger the life or health of other persons. These, indeed, cannot be overlooked, and most eventually appear before the court. They are surrounded by a much larger number of offences involving property (shoplifting, joy-riding in a "borrowed" car, etc.); disturbance of the peace (noise late at night); and the use of alcohol or drugs. This second group of offences merges into an array of normal adolescent behaviours. In fact, to have committed some, if not all, of the offences at some time or other can be considered sociologically normal behaviour.

To this view of the scope of juvenile correction services must be added the view derived from "labelling" theory, which suggests that the effects of any "label" are not neutral but tend to convey an identity that is subsequently acted out. Naming juveniles "offenders" is thus viewed as an act that, in and of itself, has the effect of increasing the chance of their becoming confirmed criminals in adult life. Thus, far from wanting to see juvenile correction services expanded to full coverage of all offences, it is desirable that the use of labels be as restricted as possible. That is not to say that the community should simply tolerate property damage or disturbance. It suggests that the point of intervention is not offences, but the structure of community facilities and services that makes community life worthwhile to adolescents, together with support to parents as a child welfare provision.

The extent of professionalism has been raised by the development of university programs of social work, criminology, and child care. In addition, juvenile correction services have usually maintained extensive in-service training programs for their staff. The result has been a separate sense of identity from the social work-dominated child welfare services. This separate identity has sometimes stood in the way of the integration of child welfare and juvenile corrections within a single ministry. The identity also served to link juvenile services to adult correctional services, confirming them in their labelling role. Nevertheless, in eight of the provinces and the two territories the case for integration has been recognized and juvenile corrections are now integrated with children's services. This pattern is not followed in British Columbia or New Brunswick, which maintain separate services despite the problems and increased expense.

4. *Family and children's mental health services.* Mental health services include a variety of major independent programs brought into association with each other in the 1960s and 1970s. They included the operation of the large mental hospitals that are the inheritors of the asylum tradition of mental illness segregation; the work of independent medical practitioners, psychiatrists, working in office-based practice and seeking to modify behaviour

by counselling and drugs; the community-based mental health clinics that had been developed from the earlier child guidance clinics; the pyschiatric wards within acute-care general hospitals; and the independent and largely volunteer-operated services provided by such organizations as the Canadian Mental Health Association. They may also include the work of specialized bodies dealing with the problems of drug and alcohol abuse. The clear trend within this complex of services is toward a greater degree of community rather than institutional care.[8] This trend would appear to result from the availability of new forms of drugs that allow behaviours to be controlled in the community; a professional preference for treatment in the community rather than institutionalization; and cost considerations. Mental health services have been organized under a number of governmental auspices, including Departments of Health, Departments of Mental Health, and Departments of Health and Social Welfare. These services are not covered by the Canada Assistance Plan, which tends to separate them administratively from child welfare and social services.

The objectives of this complex of services are not easily stated. As with the problem-oriented child welfare and juvenile correction services, there is a core phenomenon, severe mental illness, which requires a specific form of intervention. Beyond that core phenomenon, there is a much more diffuse arena in which behaviour can be labelled by using the terminology of mental illness (depression, anxiety, or character disorder), or it can be viewed as a by-product of the societal condition. If someone is destitute and alone it is not surprising to find that person also anxious and depressed. For the core phenomenon, the objectives of mental illness services are clear enough. For the more diffuse surrounding phenomena, the mental health objectives are not at all clear. As the definition of mental health is broadened to include all efforts to improve social life and deal with social problems, the name becomes increasingly inappropriate. Mental health, with its implications of a known or knowable set of ideal behaviours, is not an appropriate way of addressing the problems of political alignment, power, and change. Mental health services addressed to helping the poor cope with inequality can serve to sustain an unjust social order, an order in which the mental illnesses of the rich (greed, avarice, and delusions of wisdom) are untreated. Mental health, with its inevitable connection to the prestige and status of the medical profession, tends to lead to the devaluing of the contributions of lay persons and of other professions. Finally, mental health, with its tendency to organize reality on a health-to-illness continuum, has particular problems when used as a planning or developmental base.[9]

The trend toward community care has meant that considerable numbers of people who might have been hospitalized, or indeed who are hospitalized for short periods, are present in the community. Community mental health clinics with specialized nursing and social work programs have been developed to provide some community support to the mentally ill person. The "Lifeline" programs of the Canadian Mental Health Association serves a similar function. These services have expanded and continue to expand as community rather than institutional care objectives are pursued. However, it is questionable whether the expansion of mental health services is the desirable route to pursue. The supportive functions being developed under mental health auspices (visiting nurse, counselling, etc.) are the same functions that are needed as social utilities in their own right. If they are developed under mental health auspices, then it will be contingent on the recipients that they adopt a mental-illness label in order to obtain service. Although such a label is less stigmatizing than the corrections label, it has some of the same features of identity creation. The child who is referred from the school system to the child guidance clinic is likely to return with his records labelled in a way that causes him to be treated in future as an incipient problem child. It is better if the same advice on child behaviour in the classroom is conveyed to the teacher under a label that does not suggest the child is mentally ill.

One of the more encouraging trends has been the development of extensive "alternate" school programs by school systems. These adopt a social utility approach to providing educational service to all children, whether or not they have special needs or problem behaviours.

The mental health services are one of the more professionally staffed fields of personal and community social services. The central profession is psychiatry. However, psychiatrists are the direct treatment personnel in only limited parts of mental health services, principally private practice and acute treatment hospitals. In the rest of the mental health services, they serve primarily as consultants, treatment team leaders, and administrators. However, the dominance of psychiatry in the different mental health services is a major common feature. Working under psychiatric supervision has also been a source of attraction to casework-oriented social workers. The title psychiatric social worker has conveyed special status and higher financial rewards with the result that the social workers in the mental health service have viewed themselves as an elite group. More recently, with the development of community mental health centres, there has been conflict between psychiatry and social work as to which should be the co-ordinating discipline. Social workers have asserted claims to administrative and community liaison positions that psychiatrists had expected would be filled by members of their discipline. This may be an indicator that the dominance of psychiatry as a discipline in the mental health services is declining.

The mental health services are another potential part of the construction of personal and community social services. It is not always clear where the boundary between psychiatric case services and personal and community social services should be drawn. The need for links with local acute treatment facilities and the dominance in acute treatment parts of the system of psychiatry lie at one extreme. At the other extreme is the desirability of developing supportive family services, consultant services, day care, homemaker, visiting nurses, and the like as general-purpose social utilities rather than as treatment services for mental illness and related problems. In these parts of the system, the role of psychiatry is, at most, consultative and for large areas of service it has no role to play at all.

As with juvenile correction services, some provinces have integrated children's mental health services with both child welfare and juvenile corrections to overcome these problems. Where this is not done service rivalry, co-ordination problems, and gaps due to arguments about responsibility are inevitable – together with the additional unproductive expense that results.

Financial restraint has exacerbated these problems where services are provided by different ministries, as each ministry seeks
to restrict its costs by tightening and narrowing the definition of
its mandate and, hence, the services it accepts an obligation to
provide.

5. *Private contracted agencies.* Family service agencies were established in Canadian urban areas at an early point in the development of social services (e.g., Toronto Family Service Agency, 1914).
For most of their succeeding history, family service agencies have
been oriented principally to an individual and family counselling
role, and have been organized as part of "voluntary" sector social
service operations, governed by independent and largely self-perpetuating boards of trustees, and supported financially by United
Funds. Some other voluntary social service organizations provide
similar family counselling services. Neighbourhood houses, present in some metropolitan areas, provide such services. More recently there has been a trend toward government contractual
purchase of services from voluntary agencies, such as day-care
and homemaker services.

The development of major contracted community service agencies preceded the emphasis of the 1980s on restraint and privatization. However, these public policy objectives are in agreement
with increased use of service contracts with private agencies. As
a result there has been substantial growth in such contracting.
The former voluntary agency (i.e., the agency supported by local
community funding) has been replaced by the community-based
contract agency, exclusively or largely dependent for its funding
on government contracts.

With the increase in the number and value of contracts there
has also been a trend toward competitive tendering practices. Initially, the approach to government-community agency relationships was often in the form of a partnership. The contract terms
were loosely drawn with the expectation that flexibility and accommodation on both sides of the relationship would provide best
for the development of services to clients. However, the logic of
contracting has tended to take over: service specifications have
been clarified; cost savings have been sought; and privatization
has come increasingly to mean competitive practices.

Although the initial contracted agencies were usually community-based non-profit corporations, there has been increased entry into this field by entrepreneurial, profit-based companies. Such companies have often come into being as a direct result of government staffing cuts. Indeed, the effect of such cuts has often been softened by offering the staff being severed the opportunity to contract for services with government.

On the positive side, competitive contracting practices lead to increased clarity as to what service is being sought and a desirable search for economy in providing the service. Achieving these objectives without sacrificing service quality requires that attention be given to the credentials and experience of those providing direct service to clients: clear minimums must be stated in the tender documents. Attention must also be given in residential facilities to the expense parts of budgets necessary to provide for a healthful diet, recreation, etc.

6. *Community development and social planning agencies.* To this point, the agencies considered have been primarily case- and problem-oriented. Even the occasional reference to supportive services has basically been within a vision of stable social institutions that need outside resources, for example, day care, to perform their function. Community development and social planning agencies are directed to intervention at a different point in the symbiotic relationship between a community and its members. The community, not the members, is the target for intervention.

The early social planning councils were organized within the voluntary sector of social service activity. Their role was to identify need and suggest ways in which need might be served by agencies. These activities were seen as helpful to the fund-raising and allocating activities of Community Chests. In some centres, the social planning role was an integral part of the Community Chest or United Fund activities. In that the voluntary agencies were but part of a larger whole, it was inevitable that the studies of social planning councils increasingly dealt with the government sector of social service, if for no other purpose than to establish a frame of reference for the voluntary sector. The role of social planning councils was thus broadened. However, the lack of any mandate to plan for government services remained a major source of weakness. Research capacity was added to the larger councils, partly as a resource for the member agencies of United Funds and partly to improve the quality of the individual councils' evaluative and planning functions. The interest of social planning councils was expanded to include such activities as the development and submission of briefs dealing not only with such problems as poverty and social service affairs but also with such processes as physical development and urban renewal.

In recognition of the contribution to planning that was being made, some cities (Vancouver and Halifax) established their own social planning departments. Social planning councils were initially under the auspices of the United Fund agencies that sought their services. As the role of these councils was broadened, other groups, for example, poor people, sought participation. In some cases they gained representation; in others they were rebuffed. In still others, they effectively captured the social planning council only to find that they were left with a paper organization as the United Fund withdrew support. In the 1970s policy initiatives were undertaken to bring the benefits of community contract to bear directly on government services. In the more conservative 1980s these have been targets for cuts.

Community development services were introduced into Canada during the 1960s. Initial attention centred on such organizations as the Company of Young Canadians and such target groups as native persons and the poor. Work was largely initiated by government, although in some centres voluntary social agencies employed community development workers. The initial enthusiasm for community development was substantially dampened by a cyclical effect in which successful community work led to organized groups who expressed their own ideas as to what services they needed and were critical of the services they were getting. Threatened by such challenges to existing services, the funds for community development work were cut back or withdrawn. Nevertheless, it had been demonstrated that communities were able to take an interest in the services they were receiving. The democratic ethic of social welfare supported the idea that they should be heard and that services should be responsive. However, the established service agencies had shown themselves incapable of going this far.

Neither social planning councils nor community development activities have been large-scale developments in the sense of having substantial resources for their work. They did not have the resources for more than token attempts to assess, represent, and lead community decision-making. Their successes are a tribute to the professional skill of their staffs. The most important part of that success was the demonstration that a local planning and development capacity is both possible and useful in the development of social services. However, no means has been developed to provide a mandate and consistent funding for such a service.

7. *Federal services*. The development of personal and community social service has taken place primarily under provincial and voluntary auspices. However, the federal government has provided support to provincial governments through such cost-sharing arrangements as the Canada Assistance Plan. In addition, the federal government has developed some direct services of its own that impinge on the other social services and, it can be argued, should be considered part of personal and community social services. Important direct federal services include the operations of Employment and Immigration Canada, the Secretary of State, Indian and Northern Affairs Canada, the National Parole Board, and Canada Mortgage and Housing Corporation.

The most substantial federal social service, in terms of daily effect on people and on other social services, is Employment and Immigration Canada. This department views itself as having primarily an economic orientation, which is translated operationally into a primary interest in serving employers and industry and a secondary interest in serving people. However, the secondary interest is substantial. The direct services include employment counselling, job placement, and retraining. These interests lead to concern with the adequacy of such services as day care and family counselling. Such counselling services cannot be conducted without close and effective liaison with personal and community social services, a liaison that is not easily established with the present fragmented service structure.

The activities of Indian and Northern Affairs are another source of substantial federal activity. At one time, the activities of the department were principally rural and their social service component was poorly developed. More recently, the native peoples have been active in taking back responsibility for services and in asserting a right of self-government in this field. Movements toward integration – which is provided for in the Canada Assistance Plan – were impeded by the reluctance of Indians to give up their right (under the Indian Act) to be served by the federal government, and by the reluctance of provincial governments to provide service to an expanding and needy population. They have now been abandoned in favour of a strategy of self-government and separate development. The model mentioned favourably by native peoples on several occasions is the United States Indian Child Welfare Act (1978). This Act asserted federal jurisdiction over all native child welfare matters. A similar Act, or amendment to the Indian Act, would be needed in Canada to override the current provincial *de facto* jurisdiction.

8. *Minor services*. In addition to the services mentioned, hosts of minor social services are under voluntary, provincial, and federal auspices. These are addressed principally to specific sectional interests defined by problem, ethnicity, or geography and frequently represent the results of intensive lobbying. The family planning groups and the occasional family planning clinic are good examples of such services. To the tidy-minded, these numerous minor services are a source of irritation. However, the fact that they are minor makes their lack of logic much less serious. Change, the recognition of new needs, and the development of specific interests are indicators of lively interest in the social services. The search for comprehensive and substantial integration, which is important in the major parts of personal and community social service systems, should not be interpreted in such a way as to preclude the value of innovation outside the major delivery systems.

The existing complex of major social services delivery systems is not without substantial merits, the foremost of which is the developed ability of some of the separate parts to provide good services to their clients. In addition, the separate identities have provided clients with some choice of service; the client who did not like the services received from the child welfare agency might do better with the services received from a family service or mental health agency, and so on. The separate services have provided independent foci for growth and political support; hence the resources they have in total may be greater than could have been obtained by a unified approach. Finally, the independent services have provided the context for the development of specialized professional expertise.

Nevertheless, the existing array of major delivery systems has two major defects. The first is that none of the individual delivery systems provides the basis for comprehensive services. Each is built around particular sectional interest and most share a social problem/residual services approach to service design. The second type of defect is that the existence of a series of independent systems, serving overlapping populations, produces enormous inter-system boundary problems. These include such major problems as service interconnection, gaps, and co-ordination; they also include inter-system competition for resources, professional rivalry, and excessive administrative costs. In response, there has been a history of reorganization of the personal social services with the intent to find simpler and more economic means of service delivery.

Reorganization of Services

Signs of dissatisfaction with social service delivery were widely evident during the early 1960s. One major indicator was the continuous concern with the co-ordination of social services. Another was the design of experimental programs in which services from a number of agencies were integrated through one worker. These experiments were directed toward change in the "multi-problem family." Nevertheless, they also served to demonstrate the possibility of service integration in other areas.

In Britain these same issues were reviewed by the Seebohm Committee, which published its report in 1968.[10] Britain had already tried to operate a series of co-ordinating committees in order to relate its social services to each other. In effect, this approach was pronounced a failure. In addition, the whole idea of developing social services around such foci as problems, other institutions (hospitals and schools), age groups, or social units (the family) was also viewed as having failed. In the place of these service delivery patterns, a series of local social service departments were proposed. These departments would include all the services previously given but would be organized geographically rather than functionally. The front-line staff would be defined primarily by the population for whose social services it was responsible. Whether a family member was in hospital, in school, in the juvenile court, or suffering mental distress, the social worker would be the same. The local social service departments were made responsible to local county governments, which were to establish social service committees to provide a focus for policy development. The Seebohm recommendations were legislated in the Social Services Act of 1970, which came into effect in July, 1971. The ensuing changes in social service delivery filled the pages of journals and books published in the United Kingdom for several years.[11] The finer details of the British reorganization are less relevant to Canada than the demonstration that comprehensive reorganization of social service delivery is possible.

Two major approaches to the reorganization of social services in Canada have been pursued: co-ordination and integration.

1. *Co-ordination*. In a number of communities, local initiatives have produced combinations of services at the point of delivery. The extent of combination has varied from the type of "centre" created by a series of independent agencies sharing physical facilities to integration of such common elements between all agencies as reception, filing, community liaison, and development. The services themselves, and their staffing, remain under the control of the existing major service systems. The detail of relationships has increasingly been specified in protocol documents designed to ensure that reciprocal responsibilities are clearly defined and fulfilled.

Co-ordinative approaches do not overcome the fundamental design problems of the existing major systems. In addition, they are vulnerable to one system or another being unco-operative. However, co-ordinative approaches appear to be one of the few strategies that can be applied at the local level and with the co-operation of existing organizations. As they offer some improvements in social service delivery to the consumer, they should not be neglected. Co-ordination is essential, too, as there will always be some services that are necessarily managed separately but which have a contribution to make to the overall enterprise. Alternative schools provide a good example of an important social service that should be operated by one service – the school system, reflecting the primary objectives – but still needs to be managed in co-ordination with other social services to be effective.

The weaknesses of the co-ordinative approach are illustrated by the existence of service gaps, a problem that has become more severe as restraint in government expenditures has forced each ministry to examine priorities closely and, where possible, to narrow its mandate. Within Family and Child Services in one province in 1986 examples of gaps included:

• *Offences of children under age twelve.* The Young Offenders Act did not provide any route to prosecute a child under twelve for a criminal offence; implicit is the assumption that such children will be assisted as a child welfare matter. However, the provincial Family and Child Service Act was a "protection" statute and provided a clear mandate only where the child was being neglected, abused, or abandoned.

• *Juveniles under nineteen in need of financial assistance.* The provincial social assistance statute provided for aid to persons nineteen years of age or older. Implicitly, assistance to those under nineteen was a child welfare matter, but the young person under nineteen may not be in any "need of protection" – hence, no child welfare service was given.

• *Families needing homemaker service to assist them with developmentally handicapped children.* The provincial Ministry of Health had a limited budget for services to adults. The Ministry of Social Services had a limited budget for short-term service where the alternative is protection action. Neither had a mandate for the need identified.

• *Suicidal and severely emotionally disturbed adolescents.* The Ministry of Health had a mental health service oriented to adults. The Ministry of Social Services was only prepared to act where parental behaviour was abusive. Neither had resources for severely disturbed teenagers.

• *Preventative and support services on Indian reserves.* The provincial ministry provided a residual, apprehension and placement service where abuse or neglect was reported on reserve, which was paid for by Indian and Northern Affairs. But no agreement existed for the funding of preventative and support services, so the provincial Ministry did not provide them. Such services were available only to the extent that Indian bands organized them and paid for them with band funds.

This list could be extended. However, the intent here is limited to illustrating why there will always be specific types of gap between related services, which cannot be closed by co-ordination.

A second serious problem of co-ordination is the extent to which professional, financial, and systems resources are duplicated and consumed in providing for effective co-ordination. Instead of a social worker and supervisor being able to decide the direction to be followed in a case, they are rendered incapable of decision until they have consulted and co-ordinated with related services. Decisions, or non-decisions, are made in committee and require the attendance of large numbers of professionals. This is all professional service time that is not available for direct client contact. In addition, each social service maintains separate intake functions for its own work: assessment, rather than helping, becomes the primary enterprise. From the perspective of the client, he or she has to repeat a personal story time after time . . . only to find that the result is a further referral and request to repeat it again.

The B.C. Inter-Ministry Child Abuse Handbook (107 pages) is a model of both the strengths and weaknesses of the co-ordinative approach. The strength is in the specific and detailed attention the Handbook gives to clarifying relationships between four ministries whose roles all bear on child abuse. The weaknesses are (a) that detailed attention is necessitated in the first place by having four ministries involved rather than one; (b) that the detailed interfaces are costly to maintain, each requiring at least two professionals to discuss the situation before acting; and (c) that observing the detail becomes the test of good service rather than the exercise of professional judgement.

2. *Integration.* Quebec's Bill 65,[12] passed in 1972, was a major

attempt in Canada to create a Seebohm-type comprehensive re-organization of social service. The reformed pattern of social service delivery was based on the following types of delivery and governing units.

The local community service centre (LCSC) was the first level of service delivery. Its emphasis was on preventing and support, related to both health and social needs. For intensive services, the personnel in the LCSC made referrals to the other service units of the system, the hospital centre, the social service centre, and the reception centre.

Each LCSC was seen as serving a designated geographic area. The intention was that services should be readily accessible; hence, an upper limit of a thirty-minute travel time to an LCSC was sought. In population terms, urban LCSCs served a minimum population of 30,000, while rural LCSCs served a minimum population of 10,000.

The LCSC was governed by a board made up of: five persons, residents of the area, elected at an annual meeting; two persons, residents of the area, appointed by the Lieutenant-Governor (a measure to ensure that socio-economic minorities are represented on the Board); one person elected by the professionals practising in the centre; one person elected by the non-professional staff of the centre; one person from the associated hospital centre; one person from the associated service centre; and the general manager of the centre (advisory capacity only). The function of the board was to identify needs, oversee services, and serve as a focus for community action.

After the opening of approximately forty LCSCs in 1975, this march toward community control and service integration was halted because of professional and bureaucratic opposition – and the conflict and disruption such opposition occasioned.

Control and direction were reasserted centrally through a budget and administrative process that distributed services to centrally defined target groups. The service philosophy changed to that of "complementarity" between the LCSCs and other existing services. Now, in the late 1980s, Quebec is re-examining the lessons that have been learned on social service organization, relating them to the political, funding, and administrative context of the current decade. The theme of decentralization is being re-evaluated as a means of dealing with issues of excessive centralization, regulation, bureaucratization, and cost. Lesemann has an optimistic view of the future:

> There is, in our opinion, no doubt that decentralization will be a basic issue at the centre of debate on the crisis of the Welfare State. Around this issue will be negotiated the new consensus necessary to reposition a less directly interventionist State, one which guarantees the fundamental principles of equality and social justice.[13]

The Quebec integrated service pattern contrasted sharply with the "local co-ordinative approach." Reorganization of service delivery (in the Quebec case including both health and social services) was intended to be fundamental rather than superficial. An entirely new pattern of services and accountability was aimed for, and, although not fully achieved in the 1970s, a model for service delivery was created that can be used in the 1990s. Development in Quebec will be watched closely by other provinces.

The B.C. Community Resource Board Act (1973)[14] was intended to apply integrative principles to the reorganization of social service in British Columbia. Similar principles were espoused by the *Report of the Royal Commission on Family and Children's Law* (1976).[15] The view taken of the future of personal social services, and particularly of family and children's services, was that the key feature of access to service should be through recognition of children's and families' rights to community-based support services. In other words, an "institutional" view was taken of the future of personal social services. It was thought that such services would result in fewer children having to be served by the residual child welfare, juvenile correction, and mental health services. Furthermore these support services would be based in the local community and thus able to reflect differing community needs.

This vision was not fulfilled. Reasons included a change of government, with the new government receiving support from some interest groups who were opposed to some of the concepts in the Community Resource Board Act, such as local elected boards. The individual ministries also lacked clear policy direction (following the change of government) and agreed among themselves on a co-ordinative approach. Increased funding, which appeared necessary to fund the social utility services properly, was not available, and after 1981 the financial agenda was dominated by issues of restraint, not new expenditure. Lastly, there were professional doubts as to the extent to which social utility services would reduce the need for residual services. Social utility services were desirable but the residual services, which faced new problems (for example, more reporting of sexual abuse), often had the clearer case to argue for what limited funding was available.

The result was a failed reform. The Community Resource Boards were wound up and the ministries went to a direct segmented service form that was more tightly drawn than that which existed earlier, lacking some of the community-based intermediary bodies, such as Children's Aid Societies, which had been terminated when the Community Resource Boards were introduced.[16]

Issues for the Personal Social Services

Seven major issues are affecting the future of the personal social services.

1. *The residual/institutional issue.* The personal social services have been developed principally on a residual basis, responding to severe problem conditions that can be justified to a court as warranting the intervention of the state: to protect children; to ensure correction of juveniles; to suspend personal rights in the name of mental health. These narrow, problem-oriented services are needed, but their operations occasion many problems. They result in authoritative intrusion into areas of privacy; they result in serious labelling problems, stigma, and other secondary consequences; and they often do not provide any long-term solution to the problems faced by families and children.

In contrast, the institutional services – day care, alternative schools, community-based counselling services – offer a non-stigmatizing and supportive service to families that ask. However, these services are rarely available in sufficient quantity to meet predictable needs. For example, in British Columbia there are 800,000 children; it would be reasonable to expect that 5 per cent, or 40,000 children, would require substantial family support because of handicaps or emotional problems. In practice, services are available for approximately 10,000 children annually. In addition, many of the families and children that require residual-level intervention will not ask for service, even where available. There are few grounds to think that the serious child-abuser will be stopped – apart from through the role played by the investigative residual service.

The residual/institutional issue is thus not an either/or debate but an issue of informed choice and balance for both levels of intervention. From the perspective of effectiveness both levels face a common problem. Their effectiveness is determined by the ability (a) to identify a client who has the potential of being helped, and (b) to identify the form of intervention that will be helpful. The interaction between these elements permits four possibilities:

TABLE 17: *Service Effectiveness and Client Identification*

Client Identification		Successful	Unsuccessful
Intervention	Effective	1. Client can be helped and is helped.	2. Client did not need help – service wasted.
Effectiveness	Ineffective	3. Client needs help but is not helped.	4. Client did not need help nor could service be helpful.

Success for both types of service is achieved only in cell 1 of the 4-cell matrix. For institutional services a major form of lost effectiveness occurs in offering effective services to people who did not need them, or who need them but do not ask for help (cell 2). For residual services, cell 3 is a major form of lost effectiveness – clients with serious problems are identified but help cannot be given. For both forms of service, cell 4 is a complete loss.

In achieving a realistic balance between the two levels of service, and the most efficient use of available staff and dollar resources, research on service effectiveness is a priority. Such research will move the debate from arguments about values and principles to arguments based on fact.

2. *Principles of service organization.* Experiments with social service reorganization and integration have made it apparent that one cannot simplistically place all forms of personal social service into a single service arena and hope for the best. The issues that divided services into separate organizational units simply recur as internal issues to the new organization. Hence, it is important to recognize that there will be important divisions within the personal social services, and it is desirable to make a deliberate and informed choice of where these are to occur.

There are two major bases for personal social service organization: client age and function. Organization by function — e.g., corrections, mental health, rehabilitation — is the principal mode of personal social service organization and provides a case-specific basis for serving adults. However, this base is not so readily applicable to either children or the elderly. Both children and the elderly require integrated services that can relate to the whole of their condition and do not result in stigmatizing labels.

It would follow that personal social services should be organized using both bases of organization. In essence, there would be integrated services for children and youth through one organization, functional services for adults, and integrated services again for the elderly. The major issue to be decided is one of boundary lines. Is the limit for the children's service to be twelve, sixteen, or eighteen years of age? Is the age limit for the gerontological service set at sixty-five, or does it rely on an assessment based on individual aging factors?

3. *The role of the community.* The personal social services are part of community functioning. Their role is to provide social support, social adaptation, and social control within the context of community life. The personal social services need community understanding for their effectiveness, and the community needs to establish limits of integration, support, and tolerance.

It is difficult to see how these close community functions can be performed successfully over time without some channels for formal recognition. Formal bodies, based on interest in the social services, exist, for example, in the Children's Aid Society and similar local community boards. There has also been experience with appointed boards and with locally elected boards. There are arguments for and against all of these possible routes; however, any one of them is preferable over the bureaucratic isolation that results when there are no formal ties to the local community.

4. *The federal role.* The federal role in personal social services has taken the form of a few specifically federal personal social services, e.g., manpower services, and a series of cost-sharing or financial-support relationships to provincial services. The federal manpower service can be clearly tied to the federal full employment and economic security role and hence not considered a subject for integration at the provincial level. The development of federal jurisdiction so as to provide native peoples with the opportunity to apply self-government to their personal social services will be a more contentious subject but one worthy of public discussion and negotiation with native peoples.

The effect of federal cost-sharing provisions is hidden but pervasive and tends to support the continuation of the present segregated service structures. Difference in approaches to recognizing provincial costs among health, social service, and correctional programs creates program requirements at the provincial level that are directed toward maximizing the provincial return through cost-sharing.

These pressures result in substantial administrative costs and divert attention from the significant question of how best to organize services to meet client needs. In 1977 the federal government introduced a federal Social Services Act that was intended to provide a federal basis for broad participation in the social utility level of service. However, faith was lacking that the provinces would consistently apply the proposed block funding to expand their social utilities, and it was feared that the provinces might take the opportunity to reduce their funding levels. As a result, the bill was opposed by the National Council of Welfare and others and was withdrawn.

This left the federal role in its current segregated and poorly rationalized state. For the future the issue of federal-provincial relationships affecting the personal social services remains to be settled. Discussion is needed as to whether the federal role should be concluded – possibly as part of a round of negotiations in which the federal government fully assumes the income security responsibility. Alternatively, should the federal role be asserted in a rational way involving defined national standards for service and a single basis for cost-sharing.

The Meech Lake Accord would seem to make the first of these constitutional possibilities more likely. We may have no long-term option but to end this debate and settle personal social service issues at the provincial level.

5. *Changes in information technology*. The personal social services are information-based organizations. They perform their service-giving and status-changing roles on the basis of information concerning clients, reviewed and assembled to legitimate action by professionals. They maintain long-term records of these actions and use the records as a source for maintaining consistency of decision-making and continuity of status ascriptions. For the most part, these have been paper-based systems of enormous size, containing millions of files, with each file permitting daily entries.

Technological change is altering these systems in major ways. The transformation from paper to electronic system is not a simple matter of substituting one for another. The electronic system has characteristics of its own, particularly in its ability to transmit, sort, and assemble data, functions that were impossible in the paper-based systems.

The electronic system was introduced first to facilitate critical functions, such as record checks and file indexes; then to process essential transactions, such as payments on behalf of children in care; then to develop management information in the form of reports on client and staff activity and normative patterns. This, however, is but the beginning.

The real potential of the electronic system will only be realized as it becomes a direct tool of the front-line worker – the alternative to the files the worker now keeps "at hand"; the entry point for new data that at present has to be recorded manually by clerical staff; and the production system that provides the worker with the paper needed to do the job – notifications, standard letters, medical forms, court documents, etc. At present, professional staffs tend to regard the computer systems as alien from them, imposed on them by management as part of the regimen of industrialization and control. This attitude will change as the systems become "hands-on" and "user-friendly."

The development of these systems and their enormous processing capacities are additional reasons for concern at the varied conceptual and organizational bases of the personal social services. It will be inefficient if each ministry has its own system, incompatible with the work of others; if compatible systems are developed, exchange of data and integration of service responses will be facilitated.

The change to electronic-based systems is taking place despite restraint – partly because there are true efficiency gains to be achieved and partly because the new technology is so clearly superior to the old. The negative side is the "Big Brother is watching you" undertone that the new technology inevitably creates. The personal social service organizations, and the people who work in them, are being empowered by their technological change and the services they provide, and the nature of their work will change in manners we cannot yet foresee. Certainly, in the major social services agencies the future social worker or probation officer will work with a keyboard and terminal rather than with a pen and paper.

6. *"Trust" responsibilities: liability and advocacy.* The personal social services are in a trust relationship to their clients: that is, they empower their staff in relation to clients with authority and information, while the client is rendered vulnerable by a lack of information and a decrease in status. This trust relationship can be abused.

Sometimes abuse is deliberate and flagrant. With the increase in the reporting of sexual abuse have come reports of present and past abusive relationships that were carried on within the trust relationship established between the personal social services agency and client. The client rendered vulnerable by the relationship to the agency was then exploited by a staff member. The personal social services are taking action to make such events less likely. These include criminal record checks, careful reference checking, and clear internal review procedures. Where such relationships are abused, future opportunity has to be denied to the abuser to ensure the safety of vulnerable people.

Sometimes the abuse is the result of negligence or incompetence, as when the agency empowered with the trust relationship fails to act. Such failure may be the result of systems failure; it may be the result of inadequate staffing; or it may be the result of the unprofessional behaviour of individual staff members. Dissecting the specific causes of failure requires internal audit and review policies and the staff to carry them out.

The first responsibility to control internal abuse and ensure a diligent provision of service must rest with the social service agency. However, legal liability and external review also have significant roles to play. Lawsuits conducted against social service agencies because of damaging actions carried out under the auspices of the agency are becoming more common.

In other situations the role of external review and inquiry is carried out by an ombudsman or someone else in a similar public position. In Alberta this role is performed for children's services and for wards by the Children's Guardian.

Earlier assumptions about the benign nature of the trust relationships established by the personal social services have proved to be faulty. As a consequence both internal review and external advocacy and inquiry mechanisms are being strengthened. Public reporting of their activities is also necessary. The trust relationship must not only be upheld, it must be seen to be upheld. In the financial field the role of external public auditors and their responsibility to report publicly is understood. Similar public reporting is needed in the personal social services to provide assurance that the services are conducted with integrity and in accord with the public policy intent on which they are founded. Confidentiality was introduced initially to preserve the integrity of the client-worker relationship. This veil of confidentiality must now be pierced by external scrutiny to ensure that the client is being properly treated behind the veil.

7. *Privatization.* The personal social services offer many opportunities for privatization, and a few activities could be completely privatized where fees can be charged directly to clients. Examples

include international and infant adoptions and adoption reunion registries. The government role in these situations could be one of regulation and review only.

For most of the social services, privatization takes the form of contracting for professional services rather than providing them directly by government employees. Contracting has several advantages over direct operation. The process of tendering for services causes the contracting agency to define clearly what service it needs, while a competitive process between contractors causes each to seek efficiency. Contracted services can also be more flexible, avoiding the fixed costs associated with government establishment levels, unions, employee relocation costs, and so on. These advantages have to be weighed in specific situations against some disadvantages of contracting, such as the costs and uncertainties of tendering, the problems of quality control, and the problems for clients, particularly for children, where a contract is ended. These issues must be considered if services are to be contracted. The contracting agency has to have the capacity to manage, review, and evaluate, and if necessary, replace its contractors.

Options for the 1990s

As with income security services, there appear to be three broad options for change in personal social services, during the next decade.

1. *Confirmation of a residualist approach.* This approach does not require that personal social service issues be priorities for government at either the provincial or federal level. It is fully compatible with the vested interests of major existing social service organizations. It is not incompatible with the broad government objectives of financial restraint and privatization. Nor is it incompatible with change in information technology and the strengthening of trust relationships.

The consequences of this approach will include a gradual narrowing of mandate and service definitions, partly to limit definitions of need to the resources that are available, but also to support the increased administrative costs resulting from the coordination and assessment functions occasioned by the narrowing definitions. In total, fewer people will be served at higher cost and the list of service gaps will grow larger.

Occasionally there will be specific sweeping cuts made and whole service categories deleted in the name of restraint, as occurred in British Columbia in 1983 when family support workers, child-abuse teams, and preventative services were removed. However, for the most part the changes will be incremental and largely invisible – except in the aggregate trend data, which will show fewer people being served and unit service costs rising.

2. *Reform within existing fiscal parameters.* This perspective accepts the broad government objective of fiscal restraint and seeks a mandate to establish an informed community and professional view as to how to make the most effective use of existing resources. This requires that the personal social services be treated as a priority on government agendas. It is not fully compatible with existing vested organizational interests, for the effectiveness and efficiency of existing practice will be closely questioned. It will also precipitate internal reorganization. It is compatible with an increase in privatization. This approach could be assisted by a federal willingness to look at the logic and effect of existing cost-sharing mechanisms – and a readiness to simplify them – but the principal initiative can only come from the provinces. Within this framework changes that are possible include the following.

(a) Integrated services for both children and seniors. There is no reason why major simplification of service structures could not be achieved, bringing with it an increase in accountability to both client and community. The key to such integration is to ensure a single case contact between senior or child and the social service, rather than the multiple contacts that exist at present.

(b) An information-driven review of the effectiveness of both the residual and institutional service levels. For both levels there are legitimate concerns that existing resources are not being applied in a manner that makes best use of available dollars.

(c) A policy emphasis on decision-making that responds to client needs rather than organizational issues. The introduction of a Children's Guardian in Alberta provides one model, which recognizes that the human service organizations that have been established cannot be relied on to subordinate internal interests to the child's welfare. An external and authoritative monitor and critical deci-sion-maker is needed.

(d) A reassertion and strengthening of the role of local com-munities in providing channels of communication between the social services and the communities of which they are a part.

(e) An increased use of family support to the parents of hand-icapped, emotionally disturbed, and neglected children. This is an effective, less costly alternative to present priorities that provide support to children only where the role of parents is assumed by the state and the child is placed outside the parents' home. In addition, this approach will require clarification of organizational structures to assist in the change to electronic-based information systems.

3. *Reform with expanded fiscal resources.* The fiscal limits of reform recognized above stand in the way of developing a broad social utility service base as was envisaged during the 1970s. Unlike the costs of raising minimum incomes to the poverty line, the costs of supporting a comprehensive series of personal social services are comparatively low. The issue is not one of absolute cost but of relative priority within the total health, education, social service, and correctional expenditures of provincial governments. Any one of these sectors can make a strong case for improved levels of service at increased cost. In total, their expenditures dominate provincial budgets to the point where there appears to be no fiscal leeway for general increases; indeed, the fiscal pressure is for a general reduction to permit provincial governments to attain a balance between current expenditures and revenues. It is doubtful that a convincing special case can be made that the personal social services be exempt from these general arguments.

As a result, major expansion of social utility expenditure will be difficult to achieve in the 1990s. It is also true that, if expansion is to occur at all, convincing and factual reasons will be needed.

Notes

1. "Social utility" is a term developed by A. Kahn (*Theory and Practice of Social Planning*, pp. 176ff). The term indicates "a resource designed to meet a generally experienced need in living." Although entitled social

utilities, many of the services indicated as examples are so poorly developed as to lack general availability.

2. Canada, *Canada Assistance Plan* (Ottawa: Queen's Printer, 1965), Sec. 2(m).

3. See Alberta, Preventive Social Service Act, 1967.

4. In the Ministry of Social Service and Housing (B.C.) in 1986, 30 per cent of social workers had been in their jobs two years or less and 60 per cent had no formal education in social work.

5. United Community Services, *The Area Development Project*, Research Monographs I, II, III, (Vancouver, 1969).

6. Michael Clague and Brian Wharf (eds.), *Reforming Human Services* (Vancouver: University of British Columbia Press, 1984).

7. See Canada, *Sexual Offences against Children*, (Ottawa: Queen's Printer, 1984).

8. For discussion of those features and a set of recommendations based on them, see W.R. Blair, *Mental Health in Alberta* (Calgary: University of Calgary Press, 1969).

9. See, for example, Canadian Council on Social Development, *Case Studies in Social Planning*, Chapter 2; *Field Unit, McMaster University: A demonstration project in community health* (Ottawa: 1971).

10. United Kingdom, *Report of the Committee on Local Authority and Allied Personal Social Services* (London: H.M.S.O., 1968).

11. For an introduction to the issues, see Kathleen Jones, *The Year Book of Social Policy in Britain 1971* (London: Routledge and Kegan Paul, 1972).

12. Quebec, Bill 65, An Act to Organize Health and Social Services, 2nd Session, 29th Legislature, 1971 (reprint version).

13. Frédérick Lesemann, "Social Welfare Policy in Quebec," in Yelaja (ed.), *Canadian Social Policy*, revised edition (Waterloo: Wilfrid Laurier University Press, 1987), Chapter 16.

14. British Columbia, Community Resources Board Act, 1974.

15. British Columbia, *Report of the Royal Commission on Family and Children's Law* (Victoria, 1976).

16. Brian Wharf and John Cossom, "Citizen Participation and Social Welfare Policy," in Yelaja (ed.), *Canadian Social Policy*, Chapter 12.

Chapter 8

SOCIAL WELFARE

RESEARCH

Richard Titmuss is said to have pointed out, during one of his last visits to Canada, that one of the greatest problems of our times is that no way has been found to build the faculty of genuine self-criticism into our institutions. Such a role is often conceived to be served by research. The researcher is of most use when he is not only an analyst but also a sceptic who looks for facts before acknowledging accomplishments. Yet the products of research dealing with social welfare often fail to support such a conception.

Research can be defined narrowly or broadly. This chapter takes the broad view, including within the definition of research the gathering of book data, evaluation, forecasting, logical analysis, and ethical analysis.[1]

Descriptive Data

The preponderance of data relevant to issues of social policy is basically descriptive. Extensive demographic data, problem-oriented data, and "service output" data exist.

The Canadian census provides a typical major source of descriptive demographic data on population, age distribution, location, migration, income, housing, land use, employment, etc. The census is supplemented by extensive survey data developed by Statistics Canada and by provincial departments of vital statistics covering such continuing subjects as births, marriages, divorces, deaths, and epidemiological illness patterns. Furthermore, the meaning of these data are explored through monographs that indicate historical trends and provide comparisons between provinces and countries.[2] The reasons for selecting some subjects for information gathering while neglecting others are principally historical, influenced by specific requests and policy initiatives. The influence of a research and statistical establishment is also evident in the attention typically given in such data to issues of historical comparability. Data from these sources represent an essential beginning point for the analysis of quantitative aspects of social welfare but are typically insufficient in detail to be of immediate utility in assessing social welfare programs or institutions.

Based in part on this general demographic data, Canada has developed ongoing data series that are essentially descriptive of particular social problems. The social problems chosen for the development of such series are usually those that have been of social policy interest. Typical examples of such series are poverty lines, unemployment rates, crime and delinquency rates, and the consumer price index. These "social problem" series differ from general demographic data in that they are developed around some basic set of government policies and thus tend to have a normative thrust. For example, governments since World War II have had various degrees of commitment to the goal of full employment (variously defined as between 2 and 10 per cent unemployment, and rising with each successive wave of recession). Unemployment statistics provide criteria for the success or failure of employment-related public policies.

The development of such series has important implications for social policy, affecting the degree of attention given the particular types of social problems. Although such data are used to judge government performance, it remains essentially descriptive. The data are not evaluative of the means used to obtain the particular performance but are confined to describing a social phenomenon. The description of the phenomenon through an ongoing data series tends to confirm the social definition of the phenomenon, which has led to the development of the series. Thus the phenomenon of unemployment is defined in terms of people who state they are searching for work; the consumer price index is constructed around the cost of purchasing a "standard" assort- ment of items; poverty is defined in terms of size of household and income. These standards, or social definitions, serve the in- terests of those who deal with the problem in the way that the standards define them to exist. They permit such organizations to develop the case for their services on the basis of external "ob- jective" data; they tend to deflect attention from alternative def- initions of the particular phenomenon. For example, poverty lines have been constructed by a variety of techniques,[3] but in each case the critical judgements have been professional; no major research has been directed toward discovering how the poor define the adequacy of their situation.

The third type of descriptive data, available in voluminous quan- tity, is service output and service resource data. The accessibility of this data has grown enormously with the introduction of elec- tronic data-processing. However, the detail is usually not available for external analysis. Public data are usually restricted to annual reports that describe, in general terms, the type and quantity of the services. Thus, a day-care service will report so many "child- days" of day care; a counselling service will indicate the total number of clients seen and the average number of appointments; and a prison will indicate the number of persons admitted, in- carcerated, and discharged. Such annual reports may describe the cost of such services, the personnel by whom they were rendered, and the physical resources used. But the detail of geographic dis- tribution and cross-referencing between age, income, ethnicity, etc. is restricted.

Demographic social problem data are aggregated in relation to people, but these data are aggregated in relation to services, and there is an understandable tendency for each service unit to de- velop its own distinct set of measures for data collection. The result is that there is little certainty as to whether the "individual coun- selling services" provided by one agency are, in fact, similar ser- vices to the "individual counselling services" provided by another. The units used in counting are often different. Hence, it is im- possible to get a measure of the aggregate output of a series of social agencies, let alone relate that information to an aggregate population or problem being served. Descriptive service output and service resource data have their primary use in the internal affairs of the social welfare organizations that produce them.

Furthermore, this information is incomplete and unco-ordinated. The larger the organization, the greater the ability to afford research and to produce informative data. Since there are a great number of small programs at the neighbourhood and local community level (and this includes most that are of the self-help type), meaningful inquiry about their experiences is so fragmented that, for practical purposes, no useful information is available. Complete listings of such programs and of those conducted by such local institutions as churches and fraternal organizations do not exist. There is also a serious problem due to the lack of data co-ordination between major agencies, making it impossible to discern whether different agencies are serving the same or different client populations. As the "inter-ministry" co-ordination approach to service delivery involves several ministries having records on the same client, there is a substantial overlap. Thus, the available descriptive data are at the same time both incomplete and duplicative, making it impossible to determine the real level of client contact and service delivery without data co-ordination and analysis. The heterogeneous, unrelated, and incomplete character of these basic types of descriptive data has been a cause of dissatisfaction to social scientists and policy analysts.

The data that already exist and the continuing efforts to improve their quality result in descriptive information on social phenomena as they are seen as relevant to the issues of governance in Canada. The basic character of such data, given the fundamentally residual character of social problems and social welfare institutions, is conservative. These descriptive data provide extensive documentation of issues, problems, and services as they are viewed from the perspective of traditional legitimated institutions. Despite a general but vague sense of the inevitability of change, the operating assumption is continuity – of the present socio-economic structure, of existing patterns of interpersonal relationship, of the presence of a great multiplicity of social problems, and of strategies for maintaining order (to contend with problems).

The point of this characterization is not that such descriptive data are unimportant or that their gathering should be discontinued; rather, such data basically are by-products of the bureaucratic/professional social welfare establishment. When viewed in this way, such data can be seen as important, indeed essential, to the operation of existing social welfare institutions. In contrast, such data are not oriented to rational overall priority analysis (they basically assume the priorities that have shaped their own development); they are not a good source of criticism of the institutions that produce them (the data basically serve the interests of the producing institutions and do not recognize the views of service consumers); and they present a unified view of the social reality based on one point of observation.

Attempts in the 1970s to use this data base to establish a series of social indicators failed due to the inability to establish a common conceptual framework and agreements between users.[4] Today this data could be a rich source for a deeper understanding of services and trends – but this will require a policy commitment by government to data analysis, and a willingness to permit independent researchers to examine government data bases. Those who benefit from such independent examination will be the general public and political leaders. Present practices of restricting data access and analysis principally benefit bureaucratic interests as they permit the bureaucracy to maintain complete control over the information that informs public debate and political decision-making.

Evaluative Data

Some research is directed toward the evaluation of social welfare institutions. Evaluative analysis requires the assertion of a standard of judgement and is concerned with the relationship between means and ends in social welfare. Thus, evaluative research has more extensive terms of reference than descriptive research, terms of reference that pose both conceptual and methodological problems.

Evaluative research dealing with social welfare began in the 1960s. The Area Development Project (Vancouver, 1964)[5] in which integrated family services were made available to an experimental

group of multi-problem families – matched with a control group
– was among the first of such experiments. Since the early 1960s,
the volume and the methodological sophistication of evaluative
research have increased considerably. Nevertheless, the total social
investment in such research is much less than that devoted to
descriptive studies. Evaluative research is dominated by specific
studies of specific situations rather than by any overall commitment to evaluation. Further, although for each study there is a
developed rationale, there is no overall sense of priority as to
where such research should be conducted. There is not even a
body in existence in Canada with responsibility to assess the overall need for evaluative research.

The emerging field of evaluative social welfare research may be
divided into three substantial areas: the study of specific interventions, such as casework and community development; the
study of the impact on the society of social programs; and the
study of costs and their allocation, for example, cost-benefit analysis. These three separate areas of evaluative research each have
their own characteristics.

Specific interventions have been the subjects of professional
research for some time. Early work done in this field relied on
systematic case-study techniques and was, in essence, an extension of the case recording practised by social workers and social
agencies. The development of the profession of social work has
shown a preoccupation with issues of methodology, primarily because the claim to professionalism has been developed on the basis
of methodological expertise. The issue for experimental evaluative
research is thus whether such methodologies have their intended
effects.

The early case-study approaches to research lacked any sense
of statistical rigour. Positive change was typically reported, but the
sceptic asked whether the change might not have been a result
of chance or of the way that the investigator concentrated his
attention on certain clients. The application of experimental designs[6]
introduced disciplined observation and statistical rigour to this
field. The designs were applicable basically to case-oriented practice in which it was possible: (1) to establish a group of clients

who would receive the service, matched by relevant characteristics with a group who would not receive the service, and (2) to specify what the service was that was being provided.

A good example of this research is provided by Shulman's major study of child welfare practice in British Columbia.[7] This study employs a model of the total child welfare system as its basis, which permits observation of patterns of relationship among policies, courts, workers, clients, socio-economic change, etc. By chance, the time period of Shulman's analysis straddled the British Columbia "restraint" program. Publication of the full results of Shulman's work will increase our understanding of the effects of change in this period. In addition, Shulman's methodology provides a way for continuing to track the effects in terms of client service of major changes in both government activities and the external environment.

Shulman's work assists our understanding of earlier studies that tended to show that change in individuals as a result of case practice variables was difficult to detect by showing how the effects of an individual's technique are lost in the effects of the social conditions under which consumers live. Differences in casework technique are too weak an independent variable to be detected. The focus of study should not be the techniques of individual social workers but the effects of social programs – in gross terms, the effects of their presence or absence.

The central questions for such research are those of program effects and program efficiency. Novia Carter and Brian Wharf provide an excellent introduction to such research.[8] Their introduction included consideration of the following major elements of such research.

1. *Purposes.* The purposes of such research were initially divided into two major groups – the organization-oriented, which were related to the development of the program being evaluated, for example, to demonstrate to others that the program was worthwhile or to justify past or projected expenditures; and the personally oriented, which were related to the satisfaction and interests of key personnel. The two groups were not independent. The effects of organizational motivation were related to a "success cult" in evaluation studies. The success cult was geared to find

ways of convincing others of a program's accomplishments and relied on the results of evaluation to "pass" the program.[9]

Such objectives were not compatible with critical analysis and tended to lead sponsors of research to seek control of the distribution and release of results so that an unfavourable finding could be suppressed.

2. *Intended and unintended consequences.* Social welfare programs have both intended and unintended consequences. An exclusive occupation with intended consequences biases an evaluation toward favourable conclusions. At best, the intentions have been achieved; at worst, they have not. Attention to unintended consequences allows exploration of negative effects, such as a stigmatized and problem-oriented group of consumers. Furthermore, critical analysis forces the evaluator to look at the total system effect of intervention – without filtering the intended from the unintended. The distinction between these categories appears increasingly arbitrary to the researcher, for the so-called "unintended" consequences are seen as having a functional and systematic relationship both to the society and to the human-processing function of human service organizations.

3. *Goal-versus-system models of evaluation.* A goal model of evaluation concentrates attention on program purpose and means and a system model focuses on the organization that provides the program. For both, the program is viewed as one component of the organization's behaviour, other components including other programs, integration with the society, and internal survival needs. The systems model is more expensive, more demanding, but much more critical and revealing.

4. *Feasibility.* There are several sub-components of the feasibility of program evaluative research. (a) Such research requires a substantial program to be worthwhile. The scattered "cottage industry" aspects of much social service delivery results in a multiplicity of programs, none of which has a sufficient substantial impact on the society to be worth evaluating. (b) Provision for evaluation needs to be built into the program design. This allows discipline to be applied throughout the process of data-gathering. Records developed without such a disciplined perspective rarely have any research utility. Post-facto studies of interventions are not a sat-

isfactory approach. (c) The continuing program must be monitored from an evaluative research perspective. Changes in program may prevent the attribution of program results to a known source. This is a frequent cause of conflict between evaluators and program administrators. (d) Adequate resources in terms of personnel and time are expensive. The costs of evaluation may be a substantial fraction of the cost of the program being evaluated.

5. *Cost-analytic techniques.* The introduction of an efficiency orientation to such program evaluation – generally indicated by the use of cost-analytic techniques such as cost-benefit analysis, cost-outcome analysis, and planned program budget systems (PPBS)[10] – adds a further dimension to such research.

Despite the existence of these substantial qualifications on the emerging field of social program research, an increasing volume of such research is undertaken in Canada. The most impressive single experiment was the negative taxation experiment in Manitoba, modelled on the United States experiments conducted in New Jersey, Seattle, Denver, and Gary, Indiana.[11] The central question for the experiments was whether expanded welfare programs, particularly programs more available to the working poor, resulted in a decreased work effort. This question was significant, related as it was to one of the central objections to welfare expenditures – that they undercut the work ethic.

On the other hand, the results of research revealed some of its limitations in contributing to social policy. The research program took three to five years to complete. The conclusion that work effort was not decreased by a guaranteed income was significant in relation to the original objectives of research, but it was not significant vis-à-vis a decision to introduce a guaranteed annual income. By the time the results were known, social policy issues had lost priority on the agenda of governments and a decision not to proceed had already been reached on political and financial grounds. The results of research became a footnote to history rather than an important event.[12]

Forecasting

If evaluative research relevant to social welfare is in its infancy, forecasting, as a quantitative research exercise, remains in an early state of gestation. Some of the foundations for social welfare fore-casting exist; the best developed is in demography. Within defin-able limits, and with decreasing accuracy as the future is perceived as more, rather than less, distant, the future population of Canada can be forecast. Immigration remains less predictable and the in-ternal distribution of the population also contains areas of uncer-tainty, but a beginning on forecasting is possible.

To this demographic data it is possible to add some economic data. The establishment of the Economic Council of Canada (1963) represented a commitment to develop economic planning within a medium-term perspective (five to ten years). In its *Fifth Annual Review*, in 1968, the Council commented:

> Under today's conditions of rapid and complex change, and of great uncertainties about the future, we feel that this em-phasis is more important than ever. Focusing on the imme-diate, short-term problems, to the neglect of the wider horizon, may easily result in missed opportunities and, in all likelihood, increased difficulty in coping eventually with problems that might be averted by timely action.[13]

Subsequently, the Economic Council of Canada devoted consid-erable resources to the development of computer models of the Canadian economy with the general objective of outlining future patterns of economic growth compatible with low unemployment and acceptable cost and price stability.[14]

Urban growth and housing are two related fields that have been the subjects of serious attempts to develop research forecasts. Both lead to conclusions respecting the social problems Canada will face. H. Lithwick develops the relationship between urbanism and pov-erty,[15] and there has been a continued commitment to forecasting Canadian housing requirements.[16]

The field of social welfare in Canada lacks a central agency with forecasting and planning responsibility. There is, as yet, no parallel to the Economic Council of Canada. Canadian social welfare in-stitutions lack the sense of a planning horizon that the develop-ment in Britain of ten-year plans for health and welfare services produced.[17]

In the 1970s there was a general vision of the major lines of welfare development that professionals saw as desirable, such as the wish for a guaranteed income. However, this general vision was not related to critical demographic or economic analysis. In the 1980s even this sense of future vision was lost as it was realized that government resources (or the lack of them) were the principal reality faced by social policy. A challenge for the 1990s is to return to the subject of forecasting – using the much more detailed descriptive data bases now available – and developing an objective and critical methodology for forecasting.[18]

Auditing

Auditing has been applied systematically to the financial functions of government for a generation. Since the 1960s the role of the public auditor, with a statutory responsibility to report to the legislature on the fiscal management of government, has been accepted as essential.

In the social service field the performance of essential trust functions, for example, the guardianship of children, calls for a similar process of critical examination and public reporting. One of the major problems of social service organizations is that they conduct their affairs confidentially and secretly. The problems this can lead to when trust relations are violated have been referred to in Chapter Seven. These violations, though, are but specific examples of a more general problem – the need to assure the public that the social service agencies are in fact fulfilling their critical functions in the manner required in legislation.

Auditing, as a type of formal systematic internal inquiry, can fulfil this requirement, provided that statutory authority exists to undertake inquiries and to report results to the public.

Logical and Ethical Analysis

Discussion of social welfare research is incomplete without reference to non-quantitative forms of inquiry. Logical and ethical analysis examines policy and programs for internal consistency, conflicting objectives, conflicts of interest, and legality.

These have been principal forms of inquiry into social policy, and have been used to probe the fine detail of how social policy functions.[19]

Auspices and Control of Research

Social welfare research, even in its present poorly developed state, is a complex and technical exercise. The resources needed in terms of money, manpower, and access to information make research dependent on the establishments that dominate the social welfare enterprise. The same basic technology could be used by non-establishment or anti-establishment interests, but the need for these resources results in research becoming an establishment instrument.

Further, the researchers themselves represent a sub-group within the bureaucratic/professional establishment. Researchers beget more researchers; research stimulates more research; the analysis of existing data identifies data uncertainty and data inadequacy. The researcher, more than others, is convinced as to the essentiality of inquiry. The very existence of research competence impels the use of professionals who, in turn, as they are used in program design and evaluation, demand the greater use of research planning and built-in evaluation for special programs. There is hardly a research report today that does not include a section deploring the neglect of competent assessment or recommending improvement of the research components. In some cases, the position is taken that the sanctioning of programs must await preparatory survey and/or design analysis, or that programs ought not to be undertaken if they lack a means of competent analysis.[20]

Professionalization acts in other ways to support this development. One fundamental thrust is the advance of knowledge, as in the improvement and diffusion of practice theory and technique and the increased use of sophisticated systems of inquiry. Another is the development of a critical competence that motivates concern for accuracy in the conduct of research activity and begins to produce critical assessment of the adequacy and scope of researched knowledge.

As social welfare research is installed in the structural system, not only is it consolidated in the decision-making structure as a familiar component, it acts on it to influence its perspectives. The importance here is not only in the reinforcement of the efficiency but in the communication of professional values. The key conceptions are that policy and practice consequences (to be determined) should test the validity of policy and practice.

Leslie Pal provides an analysis of the policy research industry, one branch of which deals with the examination of social welfare policy.[21] Table 18 details the principal auspices of research that exist in Canada, most of which undertake some social policy research.

The National Welfare Council and the Status of Women Council have been major sources of well-informed social policy analysis. These bodies have brought an analytic and critical dimension to the examination of current programs and proposed policy. Both councils have maintained excellent reputations for the quality of the work undertaken and for their willingness to question the effects of current programs. Their work makes an important contribution to informed public debate.

A major aspect of the conduct of research is that government ministry research is largely a hidden, secret process. This research contains no state secrets, nor does it contain indications of future legislation that might be viewed as infringing on the rights of Parliament or provincial legislatures. The reason for the confidential and restricted circulation of research documents is largely to protect the programs and bureaucracies with which they deal. Research reports can be unfavourable to programs, and the bureaucracy that sponsors or commissions a report asserts its right to suppress or censor the product. Such reports are useful in the process of interdepartmental and intergovernment politics and competition, and use of the report requires attention to the status of those who are expected to be influenced and to timing. Finally, the tendency to place restrictions on such reports is sufficiently advanced that the process has prestige elements. A "restricted" or "confidential" document has a superior status to an unrestricted one. The report, it is thought, will have more influence on its readers because of the restrictions on access. Thus, from an organizational perspective, secrecy and concealment of such studies are understandable. From any other perspective, it is a pathology to be deplored.

Secrecy is, on occasion, breached. The frustrated individual report

TABLE 18: *Policy Research Sectors in Canada*

State Sector		Private Sector		
Government	*Quasi-Government*	*Profit*	*Non-Profit*	*University*
• central agencies - Privy Council Office - Prime Minister's Office • ministerial staff • departmental policy advisory groups	• advisory councils - Status of Women - National Welfare Council - Economic Council of Canada • regulatory agencies - Canadian Radio-television and Telecommunications Commission - Energy Resources Conservation Board • royal commissions and task forces • parliamentary committees	• consultants - Public Affairs International - DPA Group • pollsters - CROP - Decima - Goldfarb	• institutes and centres - C.D. Howe Institute - IRPP - Canadian Institute of International Affairs - Fraser Institute - Canadian Centre for Policy Alternatives - Canada West Foundation	• institutes and centres

NOTE: The examples are only illustrative, not exhaustive.

SOURCE: Leslie Pal, *Public Policy Analysis* (Toronto: Methuen, 1987), p. 75.

writer, when he sees that his work is being ignored, suppressed, or distorted, may seek alternate means of reaching the public. The formal penalties for breaching departmental secrecy can include investigation by the RCMP, criminal charges, and imprisonment. Although these penalties are not usually enforced, they are threatened. Dismissal, or in the case of an external contract, the lack of any future contracts or research grants, can be expected.

Beyond the boundaries of government, organizations with sufficient independent resources to conduct their own analyses of social welfare institutions are few, but a growing number of entrepreneurial organizations are in existence. These possess the capability for independent research but are, in practice, so dependent on government contracts for their continued existence that they are not a source of public information. Indeed, their dependency makes them even less likely to "leak" information and reports than is the case with internal government research.

The universities represent a potential site for independent research, but they are only now developing the type of institutional structures that will permit interdisciplinary research. Initiatives to develop research centres at McGill University, the University of Manitoba, the University of Saskatchewan, Carleton University, and the University of Victoria show the potential of establishing an effective Canadian network. However, a full development of these promising beginnings requires the development of relationships with government. Only through such relationships can a collective research capability of sufficient size be efficient and stable.

The non-governmental sector of social welfare activities represents a third potential site for research. At the local level, social planning councils, supported by United Funds, have performed independent research roles in a number of communities. However, they lack sufficient resources for the larger research and evaluative tasks. At the national level the Canadian Council on Social Development, in Ottawa, has been a major source of research, study, and criticism. Reports of the Canadian Council on Social Development are a major source of independent analysis of Canadian social welfare. Nevertheless, even the CCSD is not independent of government. It depends heavily on government for its annual budget while lacking the legislative sanction for an independent role like that held by such bodies as the Economic Council of Canada. The ability of the CCSD to act as an independent critic is a tribute principally to the skill of a succession of executive directors who have established a record of independence, technical ability, and political sagacity.

The Nature of Social Welfare Knowledge

The characterization of social welfare research developed in this chapter has given considerable attention to the purposes for which research is conducted. What has become of the allegedly "pure" scientific concern with knowledge *per se*? The realm of pure scientific knowledge, free of considerations of value and politics, would appear to be not only unknown to social welfare research but also unknowable. In social welfare, the nature of knowledge is always related to the values of which it is perceived rather than to the purity of the methodology by which it is produced. There is no such thing as value-free social welfare research. Given that social welfare values are themselves in contention, it is not surprising to find that social welfare research is an element in a contentious and political process.

The impact of research on social welfare policy and practice is uncertain. One would be naive to assume research is only undertaken to establish facts and to evaluate programs. Research can be undertaken for a variety of reasons: to "contain" social problems by diverting attention from immediate reform proposals and establishing a distance, in time, before reform is again on the public agenda; as a symbolic gesture, recognizing political alliances, past commitments, and good wishes; to establish social control over an opponent by examining their weaknesses and harassing them in the process of inquiry;[22] to establish a veneer of objectivity disguising conclusions already established on ideological premises. In all cases it is important to probe the auspices of research as well as the methodology before reviewing the results.

Research reports, even if accessible, are fundamentally produced by an elite for an elite. More frequently than not, information is couched in technical language and contributes thereby to a condition of social mystification. Findings may be inadequately translated into their meaning for application. The ordinary participant, whether consumer, member of the public, or elected official, operates from direct impressions and belief (affected in obscure ways by past inquiry).

Conversely, those who operate in the elite realm of research have no monopoly on knowledge. The methodology of inquiry not only brings precision, it also inevitably distorts the varied state of human affairs by emphasizing patterns of similarity and consistency at the expense of individual variations and uniqueness.

At its best, research contributes to the understanding of what exists and what has been created. The genuinely new and creative is beyond the scope of research.

Notes

1. Throughout this chapter, the author is indebted to the late Professor A. Comanor, School of Social Welfare, University of Calgary, with whom he worked on a paper on Canadian research and social development prepared for the International Conference on Social Welfare, November, 1974.

2. For examples of such work, see: Jenny R. Podoluk, "Incomes of Canadians," *1961 Census Monograph* (Ottawa: Dominion Bureau of Statistics, 1968), Larry I. Bell, *Metropolitan Vancouver: An Overview for Social Planners* (Research Development, Community Chest and Councils of the Greater Vancouver Area, 1965).

3. See Canada, *The Measurement of Poverty* (Ottawa: Department of National Health and Welfare, 1970).

4. See, for example, Raymond Bauer, *Social Indicators*, (Cambridge: MIT Press, 1966); Kenneth Land, "On the Definition of Social Indicators," *The American Sociologist*, 6, 4 (November, 1971); Bertram Gross (ed.), "Social Goals and Indicators for American Society," *The Annals*, 371 (May, 1967); American Academy of Political and Social Science, Dorothy Walter, "Social Intelligence and Social Policy," in *Social Indicators* (Ottawa: Canadian Council on Social Development, 1972), pp. 7-8, 11-12; Douglas Harland, "Social Indicators: A Framework for Measuring Regional Social Disparities" (Ottawa: Department of Regional Economic Expansion, 1971, unpublished and restricted).

5. Larry I. Bell, and Beverly Ayres, "The Area Development Project," *Research Monograph* (Vancouver: United Community Services, 1968).

6. Alfred Kahn, "The Design of Research," in Norman Polansky (ed.), *Social Work Research* (Chicago: University of Chicago Press, 1960), p. 58. Kahn distinguishes four principal levels of research: random observa-

tion; formulative-exploratory (case study); diagnostic-descriptive; and experimental.

7. Lawrence Shulman, "The Dynamics of Child Welfare," in Levitt and Wharf (eds.), *Child Welfare*.

8. Novia Carter and Brian Wharf, *Evaluating Social Development Programs* (Ottawa: Canadian Council on Social Development, 1973).

9. *Ibid.*, p. 17.

10. See, for example, Roger Patillo, *Vancouver Planning Program Budgeting Systems Project: Progress Report* (Vancouver: United Community Services, 1973).

11. See Arnold Katz, "Income Maintenance Experiments: Progress Towards a New American National Policy," *Social and Economic Administration*, 7, 2 (May, 1973).

12. Richard Splane, "Whatever happened to the G.A.I.?" *The Social Worker*, 48, 2 (Summer, 1980).

13. Economic Council of Canada, *Fifth Annual Review*, 1968, p. 2.

14. André Reynauld, Chairman, Economic Council of Canada, "Address to Ministers of Finance," Ottawa, January 19, 1973.

15. Lithwick, *Urban Canada*.

16. Andrew Armitage and Michael Audain, *Housing Requirements: A Review of Recent Canadian Research* (Ottawa: Canadian Council on Social Development, 1972).

17. Philip Hepworth, "Personal Social Services in England and Wales," *Canadian Welfare*, 49, 4 (July-August, 1973), p. 6.

18. See, for example, H. Dyck, *Social Futures, Alberta 1970-2005* (Edmonton: Human Resources Research Council, 1970).

19. See, for example, Richard Titmuss, *The Gift Relationship* (London: George Allen and Unwin, 1968).

20. See Kelly Maurice, "The Faith of the Evaluator," in Yelaja, *Canadian Social Policy*.

21. Leslie Pal, *Public Policy Analysis* (Toronto: Methuen, 1987).

22. Martin Rein, *From Policy to Practice* (New York: Sharpe, 1983), Chapter 11.

Chapter 9

THE FUTURE OF

SOCIAL WELFARE

This book began with an outline of the values that have characterized the aspirations of the political leaders and professionals who, between them, have asserted the leadership in the development of Canadian social welfare policy and programs. Since the first edition of this book was published in 1975 there has been substantial growth in the critical analysis of Canadian social welfare. In 1975 most writing was undertaken from an historical perspective, with an underlying assumption that further growth was expected. Another assumption appeared to be that expansion, more social workers, more programs, more resources would lead in the course of time to a society in which the values that characterize social welfare would be fulfilled: that we would, through steady growth, move toward a more just and compassionate society.

In 1975 the perspective taken by this book was that of embracing the value base but submitting the accomplishments, programs, and organizations to critical analysis. Serious internal contradictions were seen then and have tended to be confirmed by the failure to obtain basic reforms in either personal social services or income security. These contradictions have been confirmed, as well, by the major increase in administrative costs and bureaucratization that has occurred. The incremental path has extended some accomplishments but the shortcomings have become more apparent – providing ammunition to both the neo-conservative critics on the right and the Marxist critics on the left.

The future of social welfare is discussed here from six broadly drawn perspectives, each of which has an internal validity of its own, and which together, and in unpredictable combination with each other, continue to shape our expectations of the 1990s.

Reform Perspective

The reform perspective of the 1970s remains a part of the total vision in the late 1980s. However, the time frame necessary to accomplish major goals – ensuring that no Canadian lives below the poverty line; developing a comprehensive and available framework of social utility services (day care, homemakers, etc.); incorporating social security rights into citizenship – has had to be extended. In the early 1970s these were objectives for the decade. In the late 1980s they are distant objectives without a time frame.

The strength of the neo-conservative reaction, the reduction in economic growth and government revenues, and the displacement of social policy issues from government agendas have all had a combined effect. An indefinite pause has taken place on the path to utopia. New events, or political change, are seen as necessary to reshaping the policy agenda of government. There is even some tendency to look forward to the next major recession or other social policy crisis as the means of restoring the unfinished business of welfare program development to the policy agenda.

This perspective can overlook deeper causes of criticism. The objectives of social welfare were formed as moral reactions to aspects of the social condition rather than from a comprehensive view of future possibilities. Of particular importance in that social condition were the commitments to economic growth, affluence, and the ideology of a "free" marketplace. Social welfare values were expressed in the form of reactions to this ideology, reactions, however, that confirmed the centrality of the phenomena against which they were reactive. Hence, they indirectly supported its continued major role. In addition, the concept of community had an influence on welfare ideals, tending to cause those ideals to be expressed as attempts to achieve the goal of an integrated and meaningful local community in the face of massive urban expansion and increasingly functional (rather than personal) relationships between people. This conservative thrust appears particularly strongly in the attachment to the concept of "social problem" as the organizing principle for the development of social welfare programs.

The institutions established as a result of these purposes have been bureaucratic and professional, the power of which is based on technical expertise, official independence, anonymity, and avoidance of partisan politics. These characteristics have been seen as desirable for social welfare institutions. However, a less desirable set of consequences must be acknowledged. These include bureaucratic secrecy, administrative arbitrariness, inter-professional rivalries, and tension between service providers and consumers. The capacity for self-criticism was not built into our social welfare institutions and evaluations are often self-serving.

These criticisms have particular validity where the development of social welfare is seen in terms of expansion of what already exists. Dealing with these criticisms must be treated as an intrinsic part of the unfinished business of building a compassionate society.

As resources are not available to support new programs or raise minimum incomes to poverty lines, now is the time, it can be argued, to deal with known internal problems – making the best use of existing resources. The reform agendas for income security and personal social services, *within current fiscal boundaries*, discussed in Chapter Six and Seven fall within this perspective, while the more expansive objectives calling for more resources aim at the full agenda of the 1970s.

Neo-Conservative Perspective

The neo-conservative perspective draws attention to the problems, both internal and external, of the welfare state. The internal problems include the ways in which a supposedly benign and supportive institution can readily become an intrusive one: interfering in family and community life without having a policy mandate from government. The external problems include the growth in the costs of this enterprise and the need to restrict all government costs in the name of personal economic choice, incentive, and initiative.

It is too easy to think that the neo-conservative position is based only on the perceived need to restrict spending on social services. In fact, even if there is an economic limit to social expenditure levels, Canada is much further from it than most Western European countries. The neo-conservative position is based on a long-established view of the public welfare that draws its strength from values shared with social welfare. The values of concern for the individual – faith in man and faith in democracy – are shared. However, these values are set in a context that also values personal freedom over social justice and incentive over equality, and it seeks to limit, rather than expand, the compulsory, collective welfare transfer.

Although these values are held by many business leaders, they derive their strength from the meaning they give to common experiences of all people:

> The strength of Thatcherism is its ability to ventriloquize the genuine anxieties of working-class experience. The declining economy and reduced living standards are explained by the expensive burden of public services as the economics of the State are reduced to the accountancy of the kitchen."[1]

This effect was certainly at work in the 1983 British Columbia provincial election. Working people might have liked to think that the province could back off from restraint and spend its way out of recession, but they could not bring themselves to believe it. It seemed that the only thing to do was to cut back services that were costing more than could be afforded. On the positive side: "The ringing appeal to freedom has displaced any lingering enthusiasm for the musty attractions of social democracy, so readily identified with an enervating Statism."[2] Privacy is valued over the intrusion of social workers; risk and entrepreneurship are valued over the privilege of either union tenure or civil service security; selectivity, keeping intervention and costs as limited as possible, is valued over universalism; residual programs that stigmatize and punish the deviant are preferred over universal ones. This view gains added strength from the impression that social programs often cannot change people. Changing people, if it is to happen at all, requires an authoritative approach, clear sanctions, and willingness in the end to put the protection of the victim's freedom over the rehabilitation of the deviant.

The neo-conservative critique also has a perspective on the relationship of Canada to the world. Can we afford more generous social programs than our major trading partner, the United States? Generous social programs may protect us too well from the need to make major changes in our economy and enterprises, and this protection could result in too low a financial incentive to encourage the entrepreneurial risk involved.

Whether or not these arguments have a factual base can be argued at length, but it is abundantly clear that they have a major political base in all developed Western countries. The neo-conservative perspective on the welfare state leads toward specific actions of the following types.

1. *Dismantlement.* Major programs are the subject of searching re-examination, e.g., perhaps the Family Allowances program could be withdrawn in total; perhaps support to families is unnecessary and child welfare can rely on a simplified residual policing function.

2. *Incremental restrictions.* Major characteristics of incremental restriction were identified in Chapter Six. The perspective is one of progressive marginal erosion, reversing the process of incremental marginal growth that was used to build many current social welfare programs.

3. *Deunionization and privatization.* Another way to cut costs and reduce the established power base of social welfare organizations is to break them up – and then require that the pieces compete with each other in an entrepreneurial manner.

A beginning was made in Chapters Six and Seven in exploring the future of neo-conservative measures, but as Richard Splane says, "The full consequences of this trend have not been systematically examined and the quest for effective strategies to combat it have proved elusive."[3] The need for systematic examination is urgent because a continuation of these trends seems probable. Theoretical clarification is also required. A statement of conservative principle, similar to the historic 1834 principle of less eligibility,[4] needs to be asserted in a form broad enough to cover the full range of social expenditure. This would clarify the political choice that neo-conservatism represents.

Planning and Technological Perspective

The planning and technological perspective takes an internal view, of human service organizations. Major aspects of this view were introduced in Chapter Five. Max Weber's examination of bureaucracy provides a conceptual base for understanding an organization's tendency to drift further and further into internal preoccupation with detail. The end is reached when the organization's resources are used almost exclusively on internal processes, while the external output in terms of specific services, grants, and so on is slight. These tendencies need to be dealt with through internal reform and reorganization to ensure that the resources our society can devote to welfare services reach their intended beneficiaries rather than being used by intermediaries and lost to organizational and inter-organizational confusion.

Etzioni characterizes capitalist industrial society as "drifting" and argues for the development of social units able to shape the future through active intervention.[5] The development of such institutions would be a corrective to the unmanageable anarchy of the social welfare enterprise that has been established in the incremental "drifting" process. The individual delivery system units would have broader and more comprehensive mandates, the consumers of service would have less difficulty locating relevant services, and, finally, services would be more efficient.

The elaboration of research technology applied to social welfare is a central aspect of this view of the future. Included are development of better data bases; elaboration of social science models of social change; evaluation of the effectiveness of simulated interventions; cost-benefit analyses; and the capacity to produce forecasts. The reaction to this view of the future takes the form of concern with its Orwellian undertones. As Gail Stewart wrote in 1972:

> What is even more important in my view, and also is not yet clear, is whether the path of change in Canada will lead us

along routes which tend to enslave us and give us less personal responsibility for the condition of our lives and the quality of our living. Will we continue to build our society in the image of a vast productive machine to which we as people relate predominantly as human resource inputs and consumers of its output? Or will we build our society in such a way that it allows for and nurtures a broader image of what it is to be human – to be a person in a community with other persons living on that part of the earth's surface currently designated as Canada?[6]

The social welfare ideals of humanism could be denied by a technocratic approach to their accomplishment. The system could be supreme in the name of the people but the individual could be lost.

The technocratic model has elitist aspects. Only a few have the knowledge, skill, and access to data that will be required of the planners. Elites usually identify the public interest with their own and there is no reason to expect that a technocratic welfare elite will be any different. Similarly, the technocratic view is implicitly totalitarian. It does not provide for irreconcilable differences, nor does it provide for challenge and reversal of its own view of what is good. Such a challenge would tend to be viewed as irrational and illegitimate. Further, the technocratic view is implicitly centralist. Choices tend to be classified between the important and significant, which are the subjects of central decision-making, and the less important or irrelevant, which can safely be left in local hands.

Despite these causes for concern, the trend to planning and technocracy is firmly established. At all levels of government, and particularly at the federal level, the 1970s and 1980s are characterized by an expansion of research and planning enterprises designed to shape the future of social welfare. Ideally, a better planned approach to social welfare offers the opportunity to be less meddlesome, less intrusive, and more responsive. The technocratic planning process need not be monopolized by those who are already established. Just as the International Development Research Centre funds research carried on, in, and by developing countries, social welfare funding agencies support sophisticated technocratic research on behalf of the disadvantaged through bodies like the National Council for Welfare and the Council on the Status of Women. All classes should have equal access to the technocracy whereby the future is modeled. By such means choice becomes possible and democratic.

Marxist Perspective

The Marxist perspective directs attention to the society of which social welfare is a part and explains the operation of the welfare state within a functional relationship to capitalist society. The underlying values are again humanistic, recognizing the dignity and worth of individuals, but in this perspective seeing capitalism and the capitalist wage economy as the major causes of the dislocation and human suffering with which social welfare deals.

Social welfare is conceived as an institution of social control, necessary to maintain social stability in face of the contradictions and inequalities of capitalist society. At the same time, social welfare is also a product of the struggle of workers faced by these conditions and is maintained by resources derived from capitalism.[7]

This analysis provides an explanation for the present process of neo-conservative erosion. Capitalism, with its unequal distribution of power, is viewed as inherently concentrating resources in the hands of the powerful and removing them from the powerless. As long as there is no strong alliance among workers, unions, professionals, and other supporters of social welfare, erosion will continue. Eventually the process may be arrested, but only when it has reached the point that the consequences include a loss of social control, thus threatening the social stability the capitalist society needs. Even then there is a choice, between expansion of social welfare to obtain social control and police repression as in Chile and South Africa. Piven and Cloward express this view as follows:

> The key to an understanding of relief giving is in the function it serves for the larger economic and political order, for relief is a secondary and supportive institution. . . . In other words,

relief policies are cyclical, liberal or restrictive depending on the problems of regulation in the larger society with which government must contend.[8]

The Marxist perspective is effective in deepening our understanding of welfare in relation to society and dispelling a naiveté that can proceed from thinking that the humanistic values of social welfare are so self-evidently good that implementation is only a question of time. The perspective is also of assistance in understanding specific changes that are occurring, such as privatization and deunionization. The future it points to is one of continued struggle to resist the expansion of inequality, always with an awareness that a truly equal society is not possible within capitalism:

> talk of the "elimination of poverty" is no more than illusion or a deception. Something can be done by even a modestly reforming government. But the truth – and it is a bitter truth – is that the abolition of poverty will have to wait until the abolition of the system which breeds it comes onto the agenda, and this is a question which far transcends the issue of poverty itself.[9]

Occasionally under a "modestly reforming government" there is the opportunity to enact progressive changes and to reverse, for a time, the underlying trend.

This perspective also leads to a specific interest in the issues, alliances, and power of disadvantaged groups who are working for social change in the 1980s. Two of these require special mention.

1. *Native peoples*. The Indians, Inuit, and Métis are not satisfied with the Canadian social welfare state at all. They reject it not only because of the inadequacy of benefits it provides to them, nor because they have been the subjects of deliberate measures intended to assert control and to force assimilation, such as the residential schools. The rejection proceeds from their demand that they be recognized as separate national peoples within the larger Canadian society.

Land claims and self-government are the leading issues for aboriginal peoples, followed by child welfare. Child welfare is seen primarily from a family and cultural perspective. The children are the future of the people, and the values and culture of the people are transmitted through the family, band, and nation. Thus, native peoples must provide for their own children to secure their own future.

This view leads to conflict with some of the ways welfare values have been incorporated into social programs. The policy principle of "the best interests of the child" frequently used in child welfare can be asserted in a manner that attempts to disregard cultural and racial origins – or at least sees these considerations as only one factor among many requiring consideration. Native peoples, with growing recognition from professionals and policy-makers, are asserting an alternative view, that they are able to provide for the best interests of the child through his or her people.

2. *Feminism.* Feminism directs attention to gender differences and to male dominance. With specific reference to social policy and social welfare, Brandwein distinguishes three levels of analysis:

> The first and most obvious is to examine those policies that deal with what are inherently "women's issues." The second level is to analyze all policy issues from a feminist perspective and the third is to examine how a feminist approach affects not only policy outcomes but also the process of policy-making itself.[10]

The Canadian Council on the Status of Women maintains a program for studies the key watchword of which for the 1990s is vigilance:

> vigilance in recognizing new threats to the social, economic and legal status of women; vigilance in identifying emerging sources and division or discrimination; vigilance in protecting loved ones and community and social institutions; and vigilance in ensuring a climate of fairness and harmony in society.[11]

Social welfare concerns itself with issues in which women and children are disproportionately represented. At one level, analysis is directed at bringing these facts to public attention; at a second level, analysis probes the reasons why women and children remain in disproportionate number the clients of social welfare.

There is also a challenge here to establish organizational forms and the roles they create.

> Women administrators have generally had to adapt to male-defined positions, rather than having the opportunity to change the positions' requirements and characteristics. . . . In effect the basic message to women managers is "Think like a man, dress like a doll, work like a horse."[12]

The challenge is to think again about how society and social welfare are organized and examine the extent to which male values of contest, hierarchy, and management have been incorporated into our institutions at the expense of female values of collaboration, collectivity, and facilitation.

The "Withered" State and Citizen Participation

A fifth, more utopian view of the future of the welfare state serves to expand our vision beyond the limiting horizons derived from the historical situation.

Almost forty years ago, the view was proposed that "planning should normally imply simplification and rationalization," and hence reduce "direct and detailed state regulation." The welfare state that has been built is viewed as an excessively meddlesome institution. In every field we should be attentive to situations in which the state can withdraw from detailed engagement with individuals. The "welfare state" should give way to a "welfare culture" in which

> we could achieve a gradual diminution of direct state intervention by activating the people to take care of their own interests within the rules laid down by the democratic state. . . . We should not make peace with bureaucracy. I view as short-sighted those would-be reformers, both in the United States and in other Western countries, who, in their urge to improve society, place an almost exclusive trust in continual extension of state regulations.

The author recognized that such a move would not correspond to bureaucratic self-interest.

Now as always, bureaucracy has its own will to survive. To give up autocratic patterns, to give up administrative controls and to dismiss personnel employed in managing them, and generally to withdraw willingly from intervening when it is no longer necessary, are steps which do not correspond to the inner urgings of a functioning bureaucracy.[13]

Part of the attraction of reformed patterns of income programming is that they should result in the withdrawal of the state from the continuous and meddlesome engagement in people's lives that is characteristic of social assistance. Such a goal corresponds to an emphasis on preventative and educational programming rather than on remedial and case-oriented interventions. It also encourages universalist and social utility service delivery designs instead of selective and social problem-oriented service delivery. Finally, such a goal supports the board dispersal of helping skills rather than the restriction of such skills to a registered professional elite.

In both the health and welfare fields, changes have been made, and are proposed, that reduce the amount of detailed intrusion that government makes into people's lives. This objective deserves greater prominence than it has achieved. It provides a distinct perspective for viewing neo-conservatism, technological change, and the uncertain future of citizen participation.

A major problem for social welfare is that its institutions have become isolated from the general public. The isolation is shown by two related phenomena: complaints that needs are not being met; and hostility to what is being done and its cost. Social welfare institutions are principally government institutions. As such, they are politically accountable. On the other hand, formal political accountability has not given citizens a sense of control over social welfare institutions. This can be traced to the technical and personal nature of the services provided, to the organization of service within the context of an apolitical civil service, and to the reluctance to have welfare institutions so involved in partisan politics that a change of government results in changes of philosophy, legislation, and personnel. If the concern to avoid partisan politics is understandable, the unintended consequence has been the development of welfare institutions that are isolated from democratic political processes and that deny in their day-to-day behaviour the democratic ideals they claim to hold.

Citizen participation is directed toward the establishment of more open relationships between welfare institutions and the communities of people they serve. Demand for such representation increased considerably during the 1960s. The establishment of the Company of Young Canadians and the general concern of the War on Poverty with the alienated and powerless state of the poor were early indicators of community demand for participation. In the larger Canadian urban areas, politically active neighbourhood groups were developed, for example, the Riverdale Community Organization in Toronto, the Point St. Charles community group in Montreal, and local area councils in Vancouver. These groups sought a means of obtaining the social services they perceived to be needed in their community.

As discussed in Chapter Seven, this vision of local responsibility and autonomy was largely lost in the later 1970s and 1980s when initial attempts to introduce effective community structures failed. The 1990s may provide an opportunity to revisit this agenda.

Privatization can lead to the reduction of the power of established social welfare institutions and to the establishment of many smaller contracted, but community-based, social agencies. Technological change, which in its initial stages has favoured centralized systems and management dominance, may in the end be equally compatible with autonomous decentralized systems and community and professional control. The opportunity remains to bring welfare institutions, particularly the personal social services, closer to the people they serve.

Social Development and Personal/Private Solutions

Finally, there is a view of social development that entails a fundamental rejection of the roles of government, bureaucracy, and professionals as they have been carried out in social welfare. The means of these three groups to achieve humanistic values are viewed as fatally and irreparably faulty. The only route that offers any means toward these values is the essentially personal route that depends on the individual and his or her immediate primary relationships. The self-governing and self-contained commune is viewed as having more chance of obtaining the ideals of social welfare than any government mechanism. Such an approach may not be applicable to all, but that is no reason why individuals, groups, or families should not assert it for themselves. Such an approach can also make a distinct and independent contribution to the reconstruction of present society and its welfare institutions.

Conclusion

The institution of social welfare as a major commitment of Western industrialized society remains secure, but knowledge of its internal contradictions and shortcomings grows. We are now aware of serious obstacles to fulfilling the vision of a just and compassionate society in keeping with the major values of individual respect, faith in man, democracy, equality, social justice, and community. The immediate challenge is to establish the agenda for the internal reform of social welfare that recognizes concerns the community has expressed. The longer-term challenge is to build a society incorporating these values as its foundation principles rather than as a reaction to the many social problems that have resulted from economic growth, industrialism, and the inequalities that have been justified as necessary to that growth.

The purpose of this book is fulfilled if it has made a contribution to these objectives by encouraging critical analysis of the present and a vision of the future.

Notes

1. David Bull and Paul Wilding (eds.), *Thatcherism and the Poor*, Poverty Pamphlet 59 (London: Child Poverty Action Group, April, 1983), p. 10.
2. *Ibid.*, p. 11.
3. Richard Splane, "Further Reflections 1975-1986," in Shankav, *Canadian Social Policy*.
4. Bruce, *The Coming of the Welfare State*, p. 81.
5. Amitai Etzioni, "The Active Society," in Sara Jane Heidt and Amitai Etzioni (eds.), *Societal Guidance: A New Approach to Social Problems* (New York: Crowell, 1969).

6. Gail Stewart, "On Looking Before Leaping," in Novia Carter (ed.), *Social Indicators* (Ottawa: Canadian Council on Social Development, 1972), p. 24.

7. D.W. Djao, *Inequality and Social Policy* (Toronto: John Wiley, 1983), especially Chapters 5 and 13.

8. Frances Fox Piven and Richard Cloward, *Regulating the Poor* (New York: Random House, 1971), p. xiii.

9. V. George and Paul Wilding, *Ideology and Social Welfare* (London: Routledge and Kegan Paul, 1976), p. 104, quoting Miliband.

10. Ruth Brandwein, "A feminist approach to social policy," in Nan VanderBerg and Lynn B. Cooper (eds.), *Feminist Visions for Social Work* (New York: National Association of Social Workers, 1986), p. 252.

11. Canadian Advisory Council on the Status of Women, *Fine Balances: Equal Status for Women in Canada in the 1990s* (Ottawa, 1987), p. 5.

12. Nancy R. Hooyman and Rosemary Cunningham, "An alternative administrative style," in VanderBerg and Cooper (eds.), *Feminist Visions*, p. 165.

13. Myrdal, *Beyond the Welfare State*, pp. 61-74.

GLOSSARY

The field of social welfare has an extensive terminology that is frequently confusing to the student. The source of confusion derives in part from the overlapping definitions of terms and in part because the meaning of terms is defined in two spheres – ideology and programs. Thus, a term can be used to indicate an idea. However, when the same term is used to refer to a program, the program is often only a partial fulfilment of the idea. The term's meaning is thus changed and, quite often, a new term will be coined in order to reassert the idea.

The purpose of this glossary is not to provide a definitive discussion of social welfare terminology (such a task would be a subject for a book itself); the purpose is more modest. The first objective is to indicate the meaning of terms as used in this book; the second is to indicate major meanings that the student may find in source materials; and the third is to indicate where terms have been used in Canada to describe operational programs – and the meaning of the term in such contexts.

Child welfare: Child welfare is a specific field of practice inclusive of a series of case-oriented measures designed to protect children. The primary services included are protection, unmarried motherhood, adoption, foster care of children, and treatment for psycho-social problems (including residence treatment).

The term is used in modified form as in the title Children's Aid Society. It is also used in some provinces as part of the title of a senior administrator in the provincial department of social welfare, as in Superintendent of Child Welfare.

Community development: Community development refers primarily to a community self-help methodology.[1] The term is also used to refer to a program designed to apply the methodology in specified communities, as in the "community development program" of ____.

In some literature, the term is used to indicate the product rather than the methodology, that is to say, the development of the community. Such uses can only be found through inspection of the context.

Corrections: Corrections is a field of practice inclusive of a series of measures designed to protect society from criminal behaviour and to rehabilitate those judged criminal. Corrections includes probation and parole programs.

Demogrant: A demogrant is a cash payment to an individual or family based solely on their demographic characteristics (usually age). No recognition is given of differential needs. Family Allowances and Old Age Security are demogrants.

Field of practice: Field of practice refers to a subdivision of the totality of social work practice. Thus child welfare, corrections, mental health, etc., are fields of practice.

Guaranteed income: Guaranteed income is a term that has had wide use and several different meanings. The primary use is to indicate a social objective, the provision of a guarantee of minimum income for individuals and families.

However, the term is also used to indicate the means for obtaining this objective. As there are several different means available, and as each of these may be referred to as a guaranteed income program, there is confusion in meanings. The different means include social insurance, social assistance, negative income taxes, and demogrants. Which method of income guarantee is intended by a particular author can usually be discerned from the context.

Human service organization: A human service organization is one having a mandate to protect, maintain, or enhance the personal

well-being of its clients by "shaping" them through information, status changes, grants, medical technology, or coercion.
Examples include schools, welfare agencies, mental health services, and correctional facilities.

Income security: Income security refers primarily to all programs
in which a cash payment is made to beneficiaries. In some uses,
as in this book, the term has an expanded meaning, including
all those measures whereby government seeks to ensure material well-being.

Negative income tax: Negative income tax refers to a proposed
program of payments to individuals and families in which the
amount of payment would be determined on the basis of an
income declaration. The paying agency might be the relevant
income tax department rather than a traditional welfare agency.
The precise form of program envisaged by a particular author
can usually be discerned from the context.

Social administration: Social administration is used to refer to
the planning and management of all aspects of social welfare.
It is an activity engaged in by "social administrators," who are
usually identified as being the senior officials of social welfare
organizations.

In the British literature, "social administration" is used to
indicate a field of studies. In turn, university departments are
sometimes entitled Schools of Social Administration.

Social assistance: Social assistance refers to income security programs that utilize a "means" or "needs" test to determine eligibility for benefits. These programs are also referred to as *social
allowance* programs. In the American literature, they may be
referred to as *public assistance* programs. The term is also used
as the title of specific income security programs. Thus, some
provinces have a Social Assistance Act.

Social development: Social development is used to indicate the
entire field of social welfare, with particular emphasis on change
and on the future. The term has been used in a number of
recent books and has had a variety of meanings. What a particular writer means, beyond a future orientation, has to be
discovered from the context.

The term has also been used by a number of government

departments, as in the Department of Health and Social Development; it also forms part of the title of the former Canadian Welfare Council, now the Canadian Council on Social Development. These uses may, or may not, indicate change in the functions of the organizations concerned. That, too, can only be discovered by studying what they did and what they do. Changes in name are easier to accomplish than changes in substance.

Social indicators: Social indicators are a proposed set of time series statistics which, in total, would provide a representation of the social affairs of the society. Some social indicators already exist, for example, unemployment rate, but a comprehensive system of social indicators is not yet available.

Social insurance: Social insurance refers to income security programs in which eligibility for benefits is determined on the basis of a record of contribution and on the occurrence of a foreseen social contingency, be it unemployment, retirement, injury, or widowhood.

Social planning: Social planning refers to a professional activity carried out as part of social administration. The activity centres on the design and evaluation of social programs. In the American literature, particularly the writing of Alfred Kahn, the term social planning is used very broadly. In such use, it encompasses all parts of the process whereby social programs are introduced.

The term is also used in the title of a number of local bodies, such as the social planning councils. These are typically voluntary social welfare organizations that engage in studies of social needs and programs.

Social policy: Social policy is a broad term encompassing not only social welfare but other activities of government affecting social life. Marriage and divorce legislation and support to culture and the arts are examples of social policy that lie beyond the field of social welfare. The term is also linked with "economic policy." In this sense, it usually contrasts a concern for people with a concern for economic issues and growth. Shankar Yelaja identifies four key assumptions implicit in social policy. (1) The government has responsibility to meet the needs of the less fortunate members of society. (2) The state has a right to in-

tervene in areas of individual freedom and economic liberty.
(3) Governmental and/or public intervention is necessary when
existing social institutions fail to fulfil their obligations. (4) Public policies create social impacts, the consequences of which
become the moral obligation of some group to act upon.[2]

Social security: Social security is a term used to refer to programs.
It has had a number of uses and some inspection of the context
is usually necessary to understand the writer's meaning. In
United Nations and most Canadian writings, the term refers to
income programs plus social services. Thus, the total of both is
referred to as "social security."

The existence in the United States of a major government
department and a number of programs using social security as
parts of their title further affects the term's meaning. These
programs are all income programs and most use a social insurance technique. Thus the Social Security Act indicates a program of retirement benefits. As a consequence, "social security"
in American writing frequently has the reduced meaning of
income security and may have the even narrower meaning of
"social insurance."

Social service: Social service is a broad term used to indicate the
provision of services, other than income support. Thus adoption, day care, protection, and probation are all social services.

Social service worker: Social service worker is a term that has
received increased usage as the social work profession has sought
to restrict "social worker" to its own members. Social service
worker has been used to cover not only professional social workers
but all those who perform similar functions, for example, case
aides and probation officers. The term indicates an occupational
class.

Social utilities: Social utilities is a term introduced into wide usage
through the writings of Alfred Kahn. The term refers to "a social
invention, a resource, or facility, designed to meet a generally
experienced need in social living."[3]

Social welfare: Social welfare is the term used in this book, and
elsewhere, to describe the totality of the enterprise under study.
There is a tendency to use it to describe the present rather than
the future, hence the connection in meaning to the more fu-

ture-oriented term "social development." There is also a tendency to use the term to indicate both intended and unintended consequences. Social welfare is what has been produced, warts and all. In earlier writing, social welfare has rather more of a future orientation than it has in contemporary use. The term is also used as part of the title of government departments, as in the Department of Social Welfare.

Social work: Social work refers to a professional skill used principally in social welfare. The skill can be applied to both individual and small-group activities, to communities, and to social administration.

Social work is also the name of a profession. Indeed, to some, the profession is the principal determinant of the term's meaning. Social work means that which professionals calling themselves social workers do. On the other hand, there is a tendency for social programs to provide job descriptions that define employees as "social workers" even though they do not have professional credentials. Thus, every "social worker" is not eligible for professional membership. In such usage, the term has to be defined by reference to the job description and qualifications.

Voluntary agency: A voluntary agency is one in which the sponsorship is not government. The term is used to refer to at least three types of non-governmental organizations:

a. *The quasi-non-governmental agency*: privately incorporated but depending almost, if not entirely, on government support. Children's Aid Societies and children's treatment institutions are typical examples.

b. *The private-service agency*: which may be answerable not to a membership but to itself, that is, to a paid professional staff and a self-perpetuating board of trustees. It is legitimized by the utility of its program rather than by its status as the representative organ of defined bodies of citizenry. A family service agency and the YMCA are typical examples.

c. *The truly voluntary association*: resulting from action taken by private citizens on their own volition, not for profit, and outside the initiative and authority of government. A self-help organization for alcoholics and a community recreational association would be typical examples.[4]

Welfare state: The welfare state is used to indicate a state in which there is a commitment to use resources primarily for the collective welfare. Originally, the "welfare state" was contrasted with the fascist "warfare state." In the immediate post-war period it was used to indicate that totality of legislation whereby social security (in its broad sense) was obtained, plus the commitment to maintain a focus on welfare into the future. In recent writing there has been less of a tendency to use the term welfare state. Perhaps this is related to the fact that the earlier welfare states, primarily Britain, but also Sweden, have tended to be viewed in North America as overly bureaucratized and stagnant. This is far from the truth, but the term has taken on these pejorative undertones in some literature.

Notes

1. See W. and L. Biddle, *The Community Development Process* (New York: Holt, Rinehart and Winston, 1965).
2. Yelaja, *Canadian Social Policy*, p. 1.
3. A. Kahn, *Theory and Practice of Social Planning* (New York: Russell Sage Foundation, 1969), p. 178.
4. Based on definitions in United Community Services, "Supplementary Bill on Social Service Organization in Vancouver" (Vancouver, 1973).

CANADIAN SOCIAL
WELFARE (1900-1988):
CHRONOLOGY

This annotated chronology is intended to provide the student with an overview of the sequence of development of legislation and institutions. It is not intended to provide a history of the development of Canadian social welfare institutions; that is a subject for another book. However, within this book, dates and events are referred to. This chronology is designed to provide a framework to which those dates can be related.

Major sources used in the development of the chronology are the articles by Bellamy and Willard in the *Encyclopedia of Social Work*,[1] and Dennis Guest's *The Emergence of Social Security in Canada*.

Pre-1900

The development of Canadian social welfare provision is principally a twentieth-century phenomenon.[2] Pre-1900 programming included the following major features:

a. Limited municipal responsibility for the poor and indigent – responsibility assumed *only* for the sick, elderly, young, and women with dependent children; *only* after all the family financial resources have been exhausted: and *only* where local residence was clearly established.

b. Custodial institutions for the mentally ill and mentally retarded.

c. Custodial institutions for criminals, with some provision for the segregation of young offenders into reformatories.

d. Beginnings of major voluntary welfare organizations, principally in Toronto: Toronto Children's Aid Society (1891); Red Cross (1896); Victorian Order of Nurses (1897).[3]

e. Early forms of workmen's compensation legislation (1886).

f. Separate authority for services to native peoples based on treaty obligations incurred by the Crown and, subsequently, on the Indian Act.

1900-1920

During this period, there was a continuation of the pattern of programming noted for the pre-1900 period with some expansion and modification. These changes include:

a. Growth of major voluntary welfare organizations. Children's Aid Societies were formed to serve other urban areas; the Toronto Family Service Agency was founded in 1914, the Canadian Mental Health Association (1918), the Canadian National Institute for the Blind (1918), the Canadian Council on Social Development (1920), etc.[4]

b. Segregation of juveniles in criminal proceedings was increased. The Juvenile Delinquents Act (1908) provided for juveniles to be charged as delinquent rather than as offenders, and provided for a broad range of court dispositions.

c. A mothers' allowance program was introduced in Manitoba in 1916, providing for payments by the province to morally upright women with dependent children. Character references were required for eligibility. The program removed one category of destitute persons from dependence on municipal relief. Subsequently, many other categories were added (veterans, unemployed, elderly, etc.) and the whole relief function has been progressively transferred to provincial and federal governments.

1920-1930

During this period, there was the first substantial involvement by the federal government in the field of income security. The federal involvement was a product not only of high regard for veterans but also of social unrest, including the Winnipeg General Strike. Returning veterans were not assured work and found a marked contrast between the society's rhetoric and their destitute circumstances. Principal events during this period included:

a. Various acts affecting World War I veterans. These included Returned Soldiers Insurance (1920), an act that provided for veterans to purchase private retirement annuities to a value of $5,000; Soldiers Settlement Act (1927); and War Veterans Allowances (1930), allowances being payable to veterans, widows, or orphans who by age or incapacity were unable to earn an income and had insufficient means. These federal programs were introduced on the basis of the federal responsibility for the armed services.

b. The Old Age Assistance Act (1927) was the first federal-provincial shared-cost program. An allowance was paid to the elderly on the basis of a means test. The provinces administered the program but were able to obtain 40 per cent of their costs from the federal government.

c. The Canadian Association of Social Workers was founded in 1928.

1930-1940

This period was dominated by the Great Depression. Millions of Canadians were rendered unemployed and, on the Prairies, a period of drought destroyed farms and farm income. The results included many persons turning to their municipalities for relief. However, the municipalities' source of income was principally the local property tax and the same circumstances that caused the need for relief payments also caused much tax delinquency. The result was municipal bankruptcy or near bankruptcy. Provincial governments were the guarantors of municipal bonds indebtedness. As a result, the provinces had increasingly to assume responsibilities, including the "relief" responsibility from municipalities.

However, some provinces, notably Saskatchewan, had the same problems in supporting relief payments as had been faced by municipalities: they lacked a sufficient income to cover their responsibilities as governments. In response, the federal government was increasingly involved in payments to the unemployed. As in the case of veterans' payments, the federal role was also a response to serious disorder. In Regina, workers on their way to Ottawa to protest inadequate programs were met with force by the RCMP. Principal actions by government included:

a. A series of unemployment relief measures enacted by the federal government. Between 1930 and 1935 these took the form of *ad hoc*, short-term acts, allowing federal funds to be used to provide relief. The emphasis was on work projects for the unemployed, including the establishment of labour camps. In southern Saskatchewan, the federal government took over the entire relief function through the establishment of the Saskatchewan Relief Commission.

b. In 1935, the federal government passed the Employment and Social Insurance Act, which was intended to institutionalize the federal unemployment role. The Act was challenged in the courts by Ontario and was eventually ruled *ultra vires* by the Privy Council in 1937.

c. In 1937 the federal government appointed the Royal Commission on Dominion-Provincial Relations (the Rowell-Sirois Commission). The Commission was charged with responsibility for "a re-examination of the financial and economic basis of Confederation and of the distribution of legislative powers in the light of the economic and social developments of the last 70 years" (since Confederation).

1940-1950

During the period 1940-1950 the foundations of the modern structure of Canadian social welfare institutions were created. This was done, in part, through the reports of a series of inquiries related to the structure of social welfare in Canada. Principal inquiries that were reported during this period included the following.

a. The Royal Commission on Dominion-Provincial Relations reported in 1940. A central conclusion was that "Not only national duty and decency, if Canada is to be a nation at all, but equity and national self-interest demand that the residents of these (impoverished) regions be given average services and equal opportunities . . . ."[5] The Commission proposed a federal unemployment program and a system of equalizing grants to the poorer provinces, but that the general responsibility for welfare should remain provincial.

b. The Committee on Health Insurance (Heagerty Committee) was appointed in 1942. The Committee proposed a reorganization of health services, including a full range of medical benefits: physician, dental, pharmaceutical, hospital, nursing, etc. Coverage was to be provided on payment of an annual $12 registration fee with financing from provincial and federal governments.

c. The House of Commons Advisory Committee on Post-War Reconstruction reported in 1943 (the Marsh Report). The Marsh Report suggested a twofold classification of income security risks: universal risks such as medical care and pensions; and employment risks, unemployment, disability, etc. Marsh's report shared ideas with the British report on "Social Insurance and Allied Services," 1942 (the Beveridge Report). A comprehensive set of income security proposals designed to protect national minimums was proposed.

d. The Dominion-Provincial Conference on Reconstruction, Proposals of the Government of Canada, 1945 (the Green Book proposals) presented formal proposals of the federal government "for establishing the general conditions of high employment and income policies, and for the support of national minimum standards of social services."

The results of these inquiries were twofold. General objectives for Canadian social welfare policy were established. In addition, some specific legislation was passed.

a. The Unemployment Insurance Act, 1940. The provinces

agreed to a constitutional amendment giving power to the federal government for unemployment insurance.

b. The National Employment Service (the forerunner of the Department of Manpower) was established in 1941.

c. The universal Family Allowances program was legislated in 1944 and introduced in 1945.

d. The National Housing Act was legislated in 1944, and the Central Mortgage and Housing Corporation was established in 1946.

e. Although there were no federal health insurance acts, some provinces began to provide specific types of health insurance, for example, hospital insurance acts in Saskatchewan (1947) and British Columbia (1949).

1950-1960

The decade 1950-1960 was a period of incremental extension in Canadian social welfare legislation. Important measures enacted included the following.

a. Income security provisions for the elderly and incapacitated was substantially revised. These revisions included universal Old Age Security payments (1951) beginning at age 70; and a revised Old Age Assistance Act (1951) for persons aged 65-70. A Blind Persons Act (1951) similar in its provisions to the Old Age Assistance Act was also legislated. In 1955, those federal cost-shared, means-tested programs were extended to the permanently disabled through the Disabled Persons Act.

b. In 1956, the Unemployment Assistance Act was passed whereby the federal government agreed to furnish 50 per cent of the costs of provincial Social Assistance payments.

c. In 1956, a federal Hospital Insurance Act was passed whereby the federal government agreed to share in the costs of provincial hospital insurance programs.

1960-1970

The decade 1960-1970 was a period of more substantial action than the preceding decade. During this period, there was action taken to develop the social welfare institutions that had been foreseen during the 1940s. By the end of the decade, the only major fields in which the objectives of the 1940s had not been legislated were housing, particularly housing for low-income persons, and maternity allowances. In addition, new action was begun, centring on the subject of poverty. Finally, the issue of responsibility for social welfare was reopened during the series of federal-provincial conferences that followed Quebec's Quiet Revolution.

a. In 1961, the Royal Commission on Health Services (the Hall Commission) was appointed. In 1962, Saskatchewan enacted the first universal government medical care insurance program in North America. Despite a doctors' strike on its introduction, the program was generally regarded as successful. In 1964-65, the Hall Commission reported, advocating a universal medical insurance plan. In 1968, the federal Medical Services Act came into effect, whereby the federal government agreed to share in the cost of provincial programs of medical insurance. Despite initial provincial opposition, all provinces had enacted medical insurance legislation within three years.

b. In 1962, the Royal Commission on Taxation (the Carter Commission) was appointed. The subject of government payment programs to individuals (income security) was outside the terms of reference of the Commission. When it reported in 1966, the Commission asserted a principle of equity in the treatment of income, regardless of source. The Commission's proposals were the subject of a government White Paper, "Proposals for Tax Reform," 1969 (the Benson proposals). Revised income tax legislation, incorporating some but not all of the Carter commission's proposals, was introduced in 1971 and came into effect in 1972.

c. There was substantial revision in provision for the elderly and incapacitated. The Canada Pension Plan, covering retirement, widowhood, disability, etc. through social insurance was introduced in 1966. A companion plan, the Quebec Pension Plan, provided similar coverage in that province. In addition, the Old Age Security-Guaranteed Income Supplement program (1966) was introduced. This program supplemented Old Age Security payments, ensuring that no elderly person's monthly income fell below a prescribed level.

d. The Canada Assistance Plan (1966) extended federal cost-sharing in provincial social welfare programs. The plan provided for a consolidation of previous cost-sharing programs, unemployment assistance, old age assistance, blind and disabled persons assistance; the inclusion of child welfare measures and the inclusion of administrative costs.

e. The War on Poverty, begun in the United States in 1964, had an effect on Canadian social welfare programs. The objectives of the Company of Young Canadians (1965) showed similarities to those of the American Office of Economic Opportunity community action programs. The objectives of the Canada Assistance Plan, "the prevention and removal of the causes of poverty," are similar to the early War on Poverty declarations. In addition, careful study of poverty in Canada was begun. In 1968, the *Fifth Annual Review* of the Economic Council of Canada indicated that one in five Canadians lived in poverty. Also in 1968, the Special Senate Committee on Poverty (the Croll Committee) was appointed.

f. In 1968, the federal-provincial constitutional conference agreed to undertake a complete review of the constitution of Canada. Federal proposals on income security and social services were presented at a meeting in 1969. It was apparent, during the meeting, that the federal proposals (which basically affirmed the status quo) did not provide Quebec with the increased social policy responsibility that the province sought.

1970-1980

The 1970s, in particular the first five years of the decade, were a period of major change and development in welfare programs. The future foreseen was characterized by expanded social welfare measures and restructuring of existing programs.

a. The process of constitutional review continued and proposals were presented to a federal-provincial conference on the constitution in Victoria (1971) that increased provincial jurisdiction over welfare. However, the increased authority was not adequate to satisfy Quebec and the proposals were rejected.

b. The Unemployment Insurance Act was amended in 1971, extending coverage to groups not previously covered, e.g., fishermen, and expanding coverage to include sickness and maternity leave. These changes, along with the previously enacted Canada Pension Plan, provided Canada a full range of social insurance coverage for the major insurable life contingencies foreseen by Marsh and Beveridge in the 1940s.

c. The concern with poverty continued with the publication of the Report of the Special Senate Committee on Poverty (1971). Concern with poverty was institutionalized at the federal level with the establishment of the National Council on Welfare and the publication by Statistics Canada of regular data on poverty.

d. The major federal initiative aimed at the design of a guaranteed income was initiated in 1971 with the federal proposal *Income Security for Canadians*. A two-level system was foreseen, one level for unemployable people and a second level, integrated with working income through wage supplementation, for unemployed but employable people. These proposals were published in 1973 in the *Working Paper on Social Security in Canada* but no basic changes were enacted for both technical and financial reasons.

e. The personal social services were substantially expanded at the provincial level and major initiatives were undertaken to improve their integration and co-ordination. These initiatives took the form of an expanded provincial jurisdiction in relation to services previously provided by local government and private societies. There were also changes in interministry jurisdiction to integrate services more closely and the introduction of new structures for the accountability of services to the local community. In most jurisdictions child welfare legislation was revised to reflect rights and due process. These changes were influenced by the British Seebohm

Report (1968). However, they were not always consolidated, and legislation, such as British Columbia's Community Resource Board Act (1974), was both introduced and withdrawn again by the end of the decade.

f. The Canadian Council on the Status of Women was established in 1973, following a recommendation from the Royal Commission on the Status of Women.

1980s

The 1980s began with much uncertainty. (1) The federal income security review failed to produce a guaranteed income plan, and most provinces (Quebec is an exception) failed to reform personal social services in the manner foreseen. (2) The welfare state was under fresh attack in both the United States and Britain on both ideological and financial grounds. (3) There was a reduction in economic growth and uncertainty as to future economic prospects. These trends evidenced themselves in the following ways.

a. *Restraint and cutbacks.* Expenditure levels in all the social services have been subject to intense and continuing scrutiny, with sudden major reductions being enacted, as in B.C. (1983) and Saskatchewan (1987), and a continuing annual process of erosion — budget adjustments fall behind changes in real costs.

b. *Obsolescence.* Social and economic changes, not foreseen when the Canadian welfare state was legislated, have begun to show (e.g., long-term unemployment), resulting in reliance on the most residual measures of assistance in both the income security and personal social service fields.

c. *Erosion of political support.* The ideological initiative moved to the advocates of neo-conservatism, who looked for ways to liberate the individual from the bonds (as they see it) of regulation and collective security. Measures repealed include rent controls, land-use controls, union protections, etc.; and program changes aimed at reduction in pension indexing and permitting the erosion of health coverage were introduced incrementally.

d. *Divisions within the welfare constituency.* The primary strategy of the advocates of the welfare state has been a defensive incrementalism, buttressed on occasion by the use of legislation to protect major objectives from erosion. This latter strategy was seen in the enactment (1984) of the Canada Health Act to arrest the deterioration of universal medical coverage through the growth of provincial fee-for-service practices. However, there are also welfare state advocates who are prepared to recognize that some of the criticisms of the neo-conservatives have validity, e.g., their concerns with cost, bureaucratization, and intrusion on personal freedom. Recognition of these criticisms suggests a reform process that the defensive incrementalists fear because it may open the door too far to neo-conservative attack.

e. *Emergence of new vocal constituencies.* Women, native peoples, and new immigrants have become more prominent and it has been recognized that these groups constitute the great majority of the receivers of benefits and services; each of them had suffered from disenfranchisement and, in consequence, a lack of recognition of their issues when services are discussed.

f. *Constitutional accord.* Authority to amend the Canadian constitution was established in Canada in 1981. The constitutional documents included the Charter of Rights and Freedoms, incorporating fundamental civil rights into the constitution. However, Quebec was not a signatory due to concerns about the amending formula and federal spending power as these impacted on provincial jurisdiction for language and social policy. The principles on which Quebec's full agreement could be obtained were mutually agreed in the Meech Lake Accord (1987), wherein the federal government agreed to permit provinces to exclude themselves from federal-provincial shared-cost social programs in areas of exclusive provincial jurisdiction and receive financial compensation if they undertake initiatives compatible with the national objective. The Accord thus strengthens the provincial authority for social policy and programs in all provinces.

g. *Macdonald Commission (1985).* The Report of the Royal Commission on the Economic Union and Development Prospects for Canada refocused attention on the unfinished business of income security reform, arguing that a better system was needed to assist in the process of economic adjustment that would follow from a free trade agreement with the United States.

Notes

1. D. Bellamy, "Social Welfare in Canada," and J. Willard, "Canadian Welfare Programs," in *Encyclopedia of Social Work* (New York: National Association of Social Workers, 1965).
2. For an account of pre-1900 social welfare provision, see R. Splane, *Social Welfare in Ontario 1791-1893* (Toronto: University of Toronto Press, 1965); T. Copp, *The Anatomy of Poverty: The Condition of the Working Class in Montreal 1897-1929* (Toronto: McClelland and Stewart, 1974).
3. Some of the organizations have changed their names. The current name is used here, even though the organization may have been founded under another name.
4. See note 3 above.
5. *Report of the Royal Commission on Dominion-Provincial Relations* (Ottawa: King's Printer, 1940), Book II, p. 128

BIBLIOGRAPHY

Abel-Smith, Brian, and Elizabeth Titmuss, eds. *Social Policy: An Introduction.*
London: George Allen and Unwin, 1974.

Adams, Ian, William Cameron, Brian Hill, and Peter Penz. *The Real Poverty
Report.* Edmonton: Hurtig, 1971.

Alberta. *Public Attitudes Toward Public Assistance in Alberta.* Edmonton:
Department of Health and Social Development, 1973.

Apostle, Jim. "A Question of Autonomy," *Canadian Welfare*, 48, 4 (1972).

Austin, David, and Yeheskel Hasenfeld. "A Prefatory Essay on the Future
Administration of Human Services," *Journal of Applied Behavioural Science*,
21, 4 (1955).

Baetz, Reuben C., and David Critchley. "Two Poverty Reports," *Canadian
Welfare*, 48, 1 (1972).

Banting, Keith. *The Welfare State and Canadian Federalism.* Montreal: McGill-
Queen's University Press, 1984.

Banting, Keith. "The Welfare State and Inequality in the 1980s," *Canadian
Review of Anthropology and Sociology*, 24, 3 (1987).

Bauer, Raymond. *Social Indicators.* Cambridge: M.I.T. Press, 1966.

Bella, Leslie. "Social Welfare and Social Credit: The Administrative
Contribution to Alberta's Provincial Welfare State," *Canadian Social Work
Review* (1986).

Bellamy, Donald. "Social Welfare in Canada," *Encyclopedia of Social Work.*
New York: National Association of Social Workers, 1965.

Beveridge, William. *Social Insurance and Allied Service.* New York: Macmillan,
1942.

Blair, W.R. *Mental Health in Alberta.* Calgary: University of Calgary Press,
1969.

Block, Walter. "The Case for Selectivity," *Canadian Social Work Review* (1983).

Bolman, Lee, and Terrence E. Deal. *Modern Approaches to Understanding and Managing Organizations.* San Francisco: Jossey Bass, 1986.

Bottomore, T.B. *Critics of Society: Radical Thought in North America.* New York: Random House, 1969.

Boulding, Kenneth. "The Boundaries of Social Policy," *Social Work*, v, 12 (1967).

Brager, G., and S. Holloway. *Changing Human Service Organizations.* New York: Free Press, 1978.

British Columbia, Office of Ombudsman. *The Use of Criminal Record Checks to Screen Individuals working with Vulnerable People.* Victoria, 1987.

British Columbia. *Report of the Royal Commission on Family and Children's Law.* Vancouver, 1976.

British Columbia. *Interministry Child Abuse Handbook*, 2nd Edition. Victoria, 1985.

Brown, Gordon. *The Multi-Problem Dilemma.* San Francisco: Scarecrow Press, 1968.

Bruce, Maurice. *The Coming of the Welfare State.* London: Batsford, 1961.

Cameron, Gary. "Social Work Research Centres," *Canadian Social Work Review*, 5 (1988).

Caldwell, George. *Indian Residential Schools.* Ottawa: Canadian Welfare Council, 1967.

Caldwell, George, Jean Goodwill, Joanne Hoople, and Joseph Katz. "The Emerging Indian Crisis," *Canadian Welfare*, 43, 4 (1967).

Callahan, Marilyn, and Brian Wharf. *Demystifying the Policy Process: A Case Study in the Development of Child Welfare Legislation in B.C.* Victoria: School of Social Work, University of Victoria, 1982.

Campbell, J., G. Riches, and G. Temowelsky. *Unavoidable Dates with Intervention.* Regina: Social Administration Research Unit, 1985.

Canada. *The Community Health Centre in Canada.* Ottawa: Queen's Printer, 1972.

Canada. *Inventory of Income Security Programs in Canada.* Ottawa: Queen's Printer, 1985.

Canada. *The Measurement of Poverty.* Ottawa: Queen's Printer, 1970.

Canada. *Report of the Commission of Inquiry on Unemployment Insurance.* Ottawa: Queen's Printer, 1986.

Canada. *Report of the Task Force on Child Care.* Ottawa: Queen's Printer, 1986.

Canada: *Report of the Royal Commission on Dominion-Provincial Relations.* Ottawa: King's Printer, 1940.

Canada. *Report of the Royal Commission on the Economic Union and Development Prospects for Canada.* Ottawa: Queen's Printer, 1985.

Canada. *Report of the Royal Commission on the Status of Women in Canada.* Ottawa: Queen's Printer, 1970.

Canada. *Report of the Royal Commission on Taxation.* Ottawa: Queen's Printer, 1966.

Canada. *Sexual Offences Against Children,* vols. I and II. Ottawa: Queen's Printer, 1984.

Canada. *Statement of the Government of Canada on Indian Policy.* Ottawa: Queen's Printer, 1969.

Canada, Special Senate Committee on Poverty. *Poverty in Canada.* Ottawa: Queen's Printer, 1971.

Canadian Corrections Association. *Indians and the Law.* Ottawa: Canadian Welfare Council, 1967.

Canadian Council on Children and Youth. *Admittance Restricted: The Child as a Citizen of Canada.* Ottawa, 1978.

Canadian Council on Social Development. *Case Studies in Social Planning: The Winnipeg Audit.* Ottawa, 1971.

Canadian Hospitals Association. *Introduction to Nursing Management.* Ottawa, 1985.

Carniol, Ben. *Case Critical.* Toronto: Between the Lines, 1987.

Carter, Novia, ed. *Social Indicators: Proceedings of a Seminar.* Ottawa: Canadian Council on Social Development, 1972.

Carter, Novia, and Brian Wharf. *Evaluating Social Development Programs.* Ottawa: Canadian Council on Social Development, 1973.

Cassidy, Harry M. *Public Health and Welfare Organization in Canada.* Toronto: Ryerson, 1945.

Cassidy, Harry M. *Social Security and Reconstruction in Canada.* Toronto: Ryerson, 1945.

Clague, Michael, Robert Dill, Roop Seebaren, and Brian Wharf. *Reforming Human Services: The Experience of the Community Resource Boards in British Columbia.* Vancouver: University of British Columbia Press, 1984.

Culyer, A.J. *The Economics of Social Policy.* London: Martin Robertson, 1973.

Currie, J., and F. Pishalski, *Loosening the Fabric: The Termination of the Family Support Program in British Columbia.* Vancouver: B.C. Association of Social Workers, 1983.

Denholm, Carey, Roy Ferguson, and Allan Pence. *Professional Child and Youth Care.* Vancouver: University of British Columbia Press, 1987.

Dennis, Michael, and Susan Fish. *Programs in Search of a Policy: Low Income Housing in Canada.* Toronto: Hakkert, 1972.

Djao, Angela. *Inequality and Social Policy.* Toronto: John Wiley & Sons, 1983.

Dobell, A.R., and S.H. Mansbridge. *The Benevolent State.* Toronto: Paramont Press, 1987.

Draper, James. ed. *Citizen Participation in Canada.* Toronto: New Press, 1971.

Drover, Glen. "Beyond the Welfare State: CASW Brief to the Royal Commission on the Economic Union and Development Prospects for Canada," *The Social Worker,* 51, 4 (1983).

Drover, Glen, and Alan Muscovitch. *Inequality: Essay on the Political Economy of Social Welfare.* Toronto: University of Toronto Press, 1981.

Economic Council of Canada. *Fifth Annual Review, 1968*. Ottawa: Queen's Printer, 1968.

Etzioni, Amitai. *Modern Organizations*. Englewood Cliffs, N.J.: Prentice Hall, 1964.

Fabricant, Michael. "The Industrialization of Social Work Practice," *Social Work: Journal of the National Association of Social Workers*, 30, 5 (1985).

Ferguson, Evelyn B. "Liberal and Socialist Feminist Perspectives on Child Care," *Canadian Social Work Review*, 5 (1988).

Galbraith, Kenneth. *The Affluent Society*. London: Penguin, 1958.

Galper, Jeffrey. *The Politics of Social Services*. Englewood Cliffs, N.J.: Prentice Hall, 1975.

George, Vic, and Paul Wilding. *Ideology and Social Welfare*. London: Routledge and Kegan Paul, 1976.

Gilbert, Neil. *Dimension of Social Welfare Policy: An Analytic Perspective*. Berkeley: School of Social Welfare, 1971.

Gonick, Cy. *The Great Economic Debate*. Toronto: James Lorimer, 1987.

Green, Christopher. *Negative Taxes and the Poverty Problems*. Washington: The Brookings Institute, 1967.

Gross, Bertram, ed. "Social Goals and Indicators for American Society," *The Annals*, 371 (1967).

Guest, Dennis. *The Emergence of Social Security in Canada*, 2nd Edition. Vancouver: University of British Columbia Press, 1986.

Halmos, Paul. *Personal Service Society*. London: Constable, 1970.

Halmos, Paul. *The Personal and Political: Social Work and Political Action*. London: Hutchinson, 1978.

Harland, Douglas. "The Measurement of How Things Are," *Canadian Welfare*, 48, 2 (1972).

Hasenfeld, Y. *Human Service Organizations*. Englewood Cliffs, N.J.: Prentice Hall, 1983.

Hasenfeld, Y., and A. English. *Human Service Organizations: A Conceptual Overview*. Ann Arbor: University of Michigan Press, 1974.

Hudson, Peter, and Brad McKenzie. "Child Welfare and Native Peoples: The Extension of Colonialism," *The Social Worker*, 49, 2 (1981).

Irving, Allan. "Canadian Fabians: The Work and Thought of Henry Cassidy and Leonard Marsh, 1939-45," *Canadian Journal of Social Work Education*, 7, 1 (1981).

Ismael, Jacqueline S., ed. *The Canadian Welfare State*. Montreal: McGill-Queen's University Press, 1985.

Ismael, Jacqueline S., ed. *The Canadian Welfare State: Evolution and Transitions*. Edmonton: University of Alberta Press, 1987.

James, Gayle. "Commentary on a Decade," *The Social Worker*, 48, 1 (1980).

Johnston, Patrick. *Native Children and the Child Welfare System*. Toronto: James Lorimer, 1983.

Jones, Kathleen, ed. *The Yearbook of Social Policy in Britain, 1971*. London: Routledge and Kegan Paul, 1972.

Kahn, Alfred. *Studies in Social Policy and Planning.* New York: Russell Sage Foundation, 1969.

Kahn, Alfred. *Social Policy and Social Services.* New York: Random House, 1983.

Kahn, Alfred. *Theory and Practice of Social Planning.* New York: Russell Sage Foundation, 1969.

Kaim-Caudle, P.R. *Comparative Social Policy and Social Security: A Ten Country Study.* London: Robertson, 1973.

Katz, Arnold. "Income Maintenance Experiments: Progress Towards a New American National Policy," *Social and Economic Administration,* 7, 2 (1973).

LaMarsh, Judy. *Memoirs of a Bird in a Gilded Cage.* Toronto: McClelland and Stewart, 1968.

Lappin, Ben. *The Community Workers and the Social Work Tradition.* Toronto: University of Toronto School of Social Work, 1970.

Leman, Christopher. *The Collapse of Welfare Reform: Political Institutions, Policy and the Poor in Canada and the United States.* Boston: MIT Press, 1980.

Lemon, Paul. *Deinstitutionalization and the Welfare State.* Rutgers, N.J.: Rutgers University Press, 1982.

Levitt, Kenneth, and Brian Wharf, eds. *The Challenge of Child Welfare.* Vancouver: University of British Columbia Press, 1985.

Likert, R. *The Human Organization.* New York: McGraw Hill, 1967.

Lithwick, N.H. *Urban Canada: Problems and Prospects.* Ottawa: Central Mortgage and Housing Corporation, 1970.

Lubove, Roy. *The Professional Altruist: The Emergence of Social Work as a Career 1880-1930.* Cambridge: Harvard University Press, 1965.

Macpherson, C.B. "The Real World of Democracy," *Massey Lectures, 4th Series.* Toronto: Canadian Broadcasting Corporation, 1965.

Marsh, Leonard. *Report on Social Security for Canada.* Ottawa: King's Printer, 1943.

Marshall, T.H. *Class, Citizenship and Social Development.* Garden City, N.Y.: Anchor Books, 1965.

Marshall, T.H. *The Right to Welfare.* New York: The Free Press, 1980.

Marshall, T.H. *Social Policy.* London: Hutchinson University Library, 1965.

McGregor, Gwyneth. "Personal Exemptions and Deductions," *Canadian Tax Papers.* Toronto: Canadian Tax Foundation, 1962.

Mills, C. Wright. "The Professional Ideology of Social Pathologists," *American Journal of Sociology,* LXIX (1942).

Mishra, Ramesh. *The Welfare State in Crisis.* Brighton: Wheatsheaf Books, 1984.

Mishra, Ramesh. *Society and Social Policy: Theoretical Perspectives on Welfare,* Revised Edition. London: Macmillan, 1981.

Morgan, John. *Welfare and Wisdom.* Toronto: University of Toronto Press, 1966.

Moscovitch, Allan, and Jim Albert. *The Benevolent State.* Toronto: Paramont Press, 1987.

Moscovitch, Allan. *The Welfare State in Canada: A Selected Bibliography (1840-1978)*. Waterloo: Wilfrid Laurier University Press, 1983.

Myrdal, Gunnar. *Beyond the Welfare State*. London: Duckworth, 1958.

National Council of Welfare. *Better Pensions for Homemakers*. Ottawa, 1984.

National Council of Welfare. *Guide to the Guaranteed Income*. Ottawa, 1976.

National Council of Welfare. *The Hidden Welfare System Revisited*. Ottawa, 1979.

National Council of Welfare. *Incomes and Opportunities*. Ottawa, 1973.

National Council of Welfare. *A Pension Primer*. Ottawa, 1984.

National Council of Welfare. *Pension Reform*. Ottawa, 1984.

National Council of Welfare. *Poor Kids*. Ottawa, 1975.

National Council of Welfare. *The Press and the Poor*. Ottawa, 1973.

National Council of Welfare. *Prices and the Poor*. Ottawa, 1974.

National Council of Welfare. *Sixty-Five and Older*. Ottawa, 1984.

National Council of Welfare. *Welfare in Canada: The Tangled Safety Net*. Ottawa, 1987.

National Council of Welfare. *The Working Poor*. Ottawa, 1981.

Neave, Davis. "Housing of Welfare Recipients in Calgary," *Canadian Welfare*, 49, 4 (1973).

Osberg, Lars. *Economic Inequality in Canada*. Toronto: Butterworths, 1981.

Patillo, Roger. *Vancouver Planning and Program Budgeting Systems Project*. Vancouver: United Community Services, 1973.

Peattie, Lisa, and Martin Rein. *Women's Claims*. London: Oxford University Press, 1983.

Pinker, Robert. *The Idea of Welfare*. London: Heinemann, 1979.

Pinker, Robert. *Social Theory and Social Policy*. London: Heinemann, 1971.

Piven, Frances Fox, and Richard Cloward. *Regulating the Poor: The Public Functions of Welfare*. New York: Random House, 1972.

Podoluk, Jennie. *Incomes of Canadians*. Ottawa: Statistics Canada, 1968.

Porter, John. *The Vertical Mosaic*. Toronto: University of Toronto Press, 1965.

Quebec. *Report of the Commission of Inquiry on Health and Social Welfare*. Quebec City: Quebec Official Publisher, 1971.

Rawls, John. *A Theory of Justice*. London: Oxford University Press, 1973.

Rein, Martin. *From Policy to Practice*. New York: M.E. Sharpe, 1982.

Rein, Martin. "Social Policy Analysis as the Interpretation of Beliefs," *Journal of the American Institute of Planners*, xxxvii, 5 (1971).

Rein, Martin. *Social Policy: Issues of Choice and Change*. New York: Random House, 1970.

Rein, Mildred. *Dilemmas of Welfare Policy: Why Work Strategies Haven't Worked*. New York: Praeger, 1982.

Renauld, A. "Income Distribution: Facts and Policies," speech delivered at Empire Club, Toronto, 1973.

Rioux, Marcel. *Quebec in Transition*. Toronto: James Lewis and Samuel, 1971.

Romanyshyn, John. *Social Welfare: Charity to Justice*. New York: Random House, 1971.

Ross, David. "A Critical Look at Present and Future Social Security Policy in Canada," *The Social Worker*, 41, 4 (1973).

Ross, David. *The Canadian Fact Book on Income Distribution*. Ottawa: Canadian Council on Social Development, 1980.

Ross, David. *The Working Poor: Wage Earners and the Failure of Income Security Policy*. Toronto: James Lorimer, 1981.

Runciman, W.G. *Relative Deprivation and Social Justice*. London: Pelican Books, 1972.

Salyzn, Vladimir. "Goals in Indian Affairs," *Canadian Welfare*, 42, 2 (1966).

Schackleton, Dorris. "The Indian as a Newcomer," *Canadian Welfare*, 45, 4 (1969).

Schatz, Harry. *Social Work Administration: A Source Book*. New York: Council on Social Work Education, 1970.

Seebaren, Roop. "Social Services in British Columbia: The Axe Falls," *The Social Worker*, 51, 3 (1983).

Sim, Alex R. "Indian Schools for Indian Children," *Canadian Welfare*, 45, 2 (1969).

Smiley, Donald. *Conditional Grants and Canadian Federalism*. Toronto: Canadian Tax Foundation, 1973.

Smiley, Donald, ed. *The Rowell-Sirois Report*. Toronto: McClelland and Stewart, 1963.

Spicher, Paul. *Stigma and Social Welfare*. New York: C.F. Helm, 1984.

Splane, Richard. *Social Welfare in Ontario, 1791-1898*. Toronto: University of Toronto Press, 1965.

Splane, Richard. "Whatever Happened to the G.A.I.?" *The Social Worker*, 48, 2 (1980).

Stanbury, William. "Poverty Among B.C. Indians Off Reserves," *Canadian Welfare*, 50, 1 (1974).

Stewart, Gail. "Comment: Factories or Families," *Canadian Welfare*, 48, 5 (1972).

Sullivan, Barry, and Georgia Williams. *An Enquiry into the Sexual Abuse of Children by School Board Employees in British Columbia*. Victoria: Queen's Printer, 1986.

Timms, Noel, and D. Watson. *Philosophy in Social Work*. London: Routledge and Kegan Paul, 1978.

Titmuss, Richard M. *Commitment to Welfare*. London: George Allen and Unwin, 1968.

Titmuss, Richard. *The Gift Relationship*. London: George Allen and Unwin, 1968.

Townsend, Peter. *Sociology and Social Policy*. London: Penguin Books, 1975.

Trist, Eric. *The Relationship of Welfare and Development in the Transition to Post-Industrialism*. Ottawa: Canadian Centre for Community Studies, 1967.

Trute, Barry, and Linda Campbell. "The Child and Family Services Research Group," *Canadian Social Work Review*, 5 (1988).

Tucker, David. "Co-ordination in the Social Services Sector: The Facts of Life," *Canadian Journal of Social Work Education*, 8 (1982).

Turner, Joanne and Francis. *Canadian Social Welfare*. Toronto: Collier Macmillan, 1981.

United Kingdom Home Office. *Report of the Committee on Local Authority and Allied Personal Social Services*. London: H.M.S.O., 1968.

United Nations. *Universal Declaration of Human Rights*. New York, 1948.

Vaillancourt, François. *Income Distribution and Economic Security in Canada*. Toronto: University of Toronto Press, 1985.

Vanderbergh, Nancy, and Lynn Cooper. *Feminist Visions for Social Work*. New York: National Association of Social Workers, 1986.

Van Stolk, Mary. *The Battered Child in Canada*. Toronto: McClelland and Stewart, 1972.

Warren, Roland. *The Community in America*. New York: Random House, 1963.

Webb, Adrian. "Social Service Administration: A Typology for Research," *Public Administration* (1971).

Webb, Adrian, and Jack Sieve. "Income Redistribution and the Welfare State," *Occasional Papers on Social Administration No. 41*. London: Bell and Son, 1971.

Westerlund, G., and S. Sjostrand. *Organizational Myths*. New York: Harper Row, 1979.

Wharf, Brian. *Toward First Nations Control of Child Welfare*. Victoria: University of Victoria Press, 1988.

Wharf, Brian. "Towards Leadership in Human Services: The Case for Rural Communities," *The Social Worker*, 53, 1 (1986).

Wilensky, H.L., and C. Lebaux. *Industrial Society and Social Welfare*. New York: Macmillan, 1965.

Willard, J.W. "Canadian Welfare Programs," *Encyclopedia of Social Work*. New York: National Association of Social Workers, 1965.

Wineman, Steven. *The Politics of Human Services: Radical Alternatives to the Welfare State*. Montreal: Black Rose Books, 1984.

Wolfensberger, W. *The Principle of Normalization in Human Services*. Washington: National Institute on Mental Retardation, 1972.

Woodsworth, David. *Social Security and National Policy*. Montreal: McGill-Queen's University Press, 1977.

Woodsworth, David. "Agency Policy and Client Roles," *The Social Worker*, 37, 4 (1969).

Yelaja, Shankar, ed. *Canadian Social Policy*, 2nd Edition. Waterloo: Wilfrid Laurier University Press, 1987.

INDEX